Stella's Way:

10 Lessons on Life and Business to Help You Achieve The American Dream

By Stella Daisa Moga Kennedy

and Dustin S. Klein with Destina Moga

Stella's Way: 10 Lessons on Life and Business to Help You Achieve The American Dream

This book may be ordered through booksellers or by contacting:

Daisa Publishing
1504 Travelers Rd.
Avon, OH 44011

ISBN 978-0-615-41712-7

Photography by Studio South, Westlake, OH

Printed by bookprintingrevolution.com

Author's Note

My life has been an adventure. I've experienced my share of tragedies and triumphs, loves and losses, successes and failures, just like most other people on this planet. But what has made my life unique is the path I've chosen to follow, the challenges I've faced, and more important, the methods I've used to navigate this world.

I lived the first 32 years of my life in Romania, where I was born and raised under Communist rule. My family and I faced oppression, prejudice, and hatred because we refused to fall in line and become good members of the Communist Party.

As a child, I faced unfair treatment from my teachers, peers and other adults because of the choices my parents made. I was an outcast and forced to create my own little world in order to survive.

Later, as an adult, I waged a five-year battle against the Romanian government in pursuit of securing passports so that we could leave the country and move to the United States.

I've experienced the death of a child and nearly lost another. I watched both my parents die, too many years before they should have. I've been divorced and found love anew. And I've cried tears of joy as I welcomed grandchildren into this world as American-born citizens.

For the past 30 years, I have been lucky enough to live in the United States, the greatest country in the world, where by working hard and overcoming every obstacle thrown my way I have become the living embodiment of the American Dream and all it has to offer.

I feel blessed to have survived some of the truly dark days of my life. But each time I survived I emerged stronger and smarter than before. The experiences have taught me many things. I have learned how to be a survivor. I have learned how not to be a victim. And I have learned to recognize what is truly important in life.

The odds were against us in 1979, when we arrived in America. I spoke only a few words of English and had no job waiting for me. In my haste to leave Romania I foolishly waited to learn English even though I had ample time to do so. Had I studied even a little English in Romania I might have been able to avoid some of the language-related problems that held me back during our first year here. But I thought that because I was fluent in French, Hungarian and Romanian, and spoke a little Russian, that it would be enough. I never realized just how difficult learning English would be.

Despite this, we were able to eke out a meager living during our early days in Cleveland, Ohio. I never lost my belief in myself and my ability to succeed. I had a dream, and convinced everyone around me – family members, friends and new acquaintances – to buy into it. Looking back, it's a miracle that so many people sacrificed so much on nothing more than faith. But it shouldn't really be so surprising. One common theme throughout my life is that I've always had the innate ability to attract people to me, make them my champions and get them to back my dreams, no matter how far-fetched.

Two years after arriving in America I founded a business with $1,800 I had saved. Today, because of that leap of faith I am a successful entrepreneur with a net worth of nearly $30 million and stand among the top 1 percent of Americans.

I have property in Ohio and Florida. I have built a chain of daycare centers and private schools that break the mold of traditional childcare by employing curriculum and best practices that have proven successful and revolutionary. The concept is so revolutionary that I believe it could serve as the foundation for the future of early childhood education. Bringing the idea to the mass market is my next goal.

I am the mother of two successful children. One, Dee Dee, followed me into the family business and gave me two wonderful grandchildren, Isabella and Marcus. The other, Alex, is married and pursuing a career in law.

After divorcing my first husband 20 years ago, I enjoy a healthy marriage with a wonderful man, Michael Kennedy, who loves me dearly and treats my children and grandchildren as if they are his own. Michael is truly my life partner and has helped me live life to its fullest.

My family and I live in the most incredible place in the world, a country where anything is possible and where any dream can be accomplished by refusing to give up and recognizing that success is a byproduct of hard work.

People always ask how I did it and what I've learned through this incredible journey. I usually answer with a laugh and a short response, "To do things Stella's Way."

But this isn't meant as a joke. Those who are close to me know what

I mean. They've seen me in action. For everyone else, I need to explain.

Stella's Way is how I've lived my life. It's what I learned growing up in Romania. It's how I survived the oppression of Communism. It's the skill set I used to maintain my optimism when I could have easily given up. It's the way I approached things during my early struggles in America. It's my philosophy on family and friends. And it's how I forged ahead despite the naysayers and in the face of seemingly unconquerable challenges was able to build my business.

This book is the story of my life. Through my experiences I have tried to share the lessons I've learned along the way. There are 10 unique lessons which I've summed up at the end. These lessons have led me around roadblocks, helped me navigate detours, and scale what appeared at the time to be unconquerable mountains. They have even served as beacons of light to look toward during the darkest nights. It is my hope that by sharing my failures and successes, my tragedies and triumphs, my loves and losses that Stella's Way can become your own Way.

When we left Romania, we were searched from head to toe. Members of the Securitate, the Romanian secret police, ushered us into separate rooms to make sure we did not have money, jewelry, addresses or phone numbers among our possessions. They planned to seize anything that could help us survive our first few days in America.

Six of us were emigrating: me; my then-husband, John; our daughter, Dee Dee; my sister, her husband and their son. My parents, Marioara and Ioan, planned to join us a few weeks later, once we had settled in Cleveland.

I was led into a small, cold and lifeless room by two police officers while John stayed in the corridor with Dee Dee. They would undoubtedly undergo the same treatment after the men finished with me.

Inside, the room's walls were barren and the gray paint was peeling. The ceiling lighting was dim but oddly bright enough to feel imposing. A metal table stood in the middle of the room with a single, flimsy folding chair beside it.

"Put your bag on the table and sit down," the smaller of the two men commanded. His voice was rigid and emotionless.

I did as instructed without speaking.

The man was short and fat. His clothes didn't fit him well. The shirt seemed a size too big; the pants a size too small. He leaned over and spoke to me. His breath and body odor smelled like a combination of rotten cabbage and cigarettes.

"What are you hiding?" he said.

I stared into his eyes and tried not to show any fear.

"Nothing," I said. "I only have clothing."

For a few moments, the man stared back at me, unmoving, not speaking, trying to look intimidating. The other man, a taller, thinner version of Cigarette Breath, opened my bag and began riffling through it.

Finally, Cigarette Breath spoke. "We'll see," he scoffed, then stood up straight and moved a few feet back, closer to his partner. His eyes remained fixed on me.

I moved my gaze to the thin man and watched him remove every piece of clothing I had carefully folded and packed into my bag. He pulled them out one piece at a time, and then shook each violently in the air several times before dropping them onto a pile to the left of my bag. After about 10 minutes, the bag was empty and the pile was stacked high. He turned toward me, gave me a momentary glance and said to his partner, "Nothing worth taking."

Cigarette Breath grunted, nodded, and then fixed his gaze back on me. "Stand up," he said.

I did.

"Turn around and take off everything but your bra and underwear."

Reluctantly, I did that as well. By this point I felt nothing. This was just one last, small, messy step before I took my leave from Romania to my new country, my beloved America. I no longer felt violated or restrained. These people, in spite of themselves, were going to let me go. And we had reached this point legally. I no longer had to risk my life or my family's lives. We were Americans now. The last decade and the struggles it held had come to an end. These two bozos represented one of the final drops in the bucket of pain. I was almost cordial as they strip-searched me, as if they were offering me a great gift.

They, of course, didn't know how to react, so they just continued being Communist. As I stood there, I knew I would shed no tears for these simpletons. This was the path they had chosen. I had opted for a different one. And now, the patience and perseverance of my brutal five-year struggle was at its end. I had executed our plan like I knew all along that we were going to leave.

In our weakest and bleakest failures, I looked to God to carry us. We followed through on every lead we found, and in the end we completed our mission. When we found ourselves face-to-face with shocking new developments, we worked through our fears and stayed on track. When a brick wall appeared from nowhere, we went around it or knocked it down. Nothing was going to stop me, and nothing did. Why? Because I refused to allow anything or anyone to get in our way.

After what should have been a humiliating search, the men told me to get dressed and repack my bag. They let me keep my wedding ring but none of the other jewelry I had worn to the airport. They also let me keep a few small, handmade presents that I had brought to give to our sponsor, Aurelia Todoran, an aunt who lived in the United States and was meeting us at the airport in New York City.

When the ordeal was over the men escorted me back to the corridor where John and Dee Dee were waiting.

Cigarette Breath pointed at them and said, "You two, come with me."

I looked around. My sister, her husband and son were nowhere to be seen. I guessed that they were taken to a different area for similar treatment. Turning back, I gave my daughter a reassuring smile. "It will be OK, sweetie," I said. "Just go with daddy and do what the men say."

The four of them disappeared into the room and the door closed behind them.

While I waited for what seemed like hours, I comforted myself by thinking about what lay ahead. Soon we would be in America and this hell would be behind us forever.

It's not a stretch to say that our journey to America was arduous. From our home in Cluj we went by train to Bucharest, and from there to the airport. We flew to Amsterdam and boarded a plane bound for JFK Airport in New York City. After three days on the road and in the sky we finally arrived in America on September 16, 1979. I slept for very little of the trip.

The longer trip, my true journey if you will, began years earlier, when I was a little girl. Back then, I had a dream. In my dream you weren't told what you were supposed to think. No one dictated who you were allowed to talk to, where you could go and what you were allowed to believe. In my dream, I was free. I didn't know what freedom looked like, but I knew it was real. And when you believe something is real, you have the power to make it come true, especially when you put your heart into it.

That is probably the most important lesson I've learned in my life – when you put your heart into it, anything is possible. As a result of being a dreamer and believing anything was possible, I reached America.

We arrived in New York City with two suitcases. That was it, nothing more; two suitcases for three people, John, Dee Dee and me. Beyond that, we carried only the clothes on our back and our memories. The rest, everything else we had owned in Romania, our houses, cars, furniture, china, paintings and family pictures, we left behind.

And everything we left behind was required to match an inventory list that government officials compiled shortly after we applied for passports. On the day we left, we literally handed the keys to our home to a government party member who matched the items on that list with our possessions before letting us leave. Then we rushed off to the train station before anyone higher up in the Party food chain decided to change their minds.

That was the second time in my life that in one day my family went from being wealthy to poor. The first was shortly after World War II ended; a few years after the Communists came to power and began nationalizing the country. They took everything away from the citizens. But I was a child then and couldn't grasp what was happening. This time, I was an adult. I knew full well what was going on. More important, this time the choice was mine.

We left houses and cars behind in Romania

2

In Romania, I drove a white Mercedes and wore white leather gloves. I had French perfume and owned expensive clothing. I had a good job, a husband, and a house that was paid for in full. With all that going for me, you're probably wondering why I would want to leave. I had the proverbial good life.

But that wasn't the point. Material things weren't satisfying when you lived under Communist rule. Despite my family's ability to refrain from joining the Communist Party, work the system and acquire luxuries, the reality was that we were still living in Communist Romania and didn't have many freedoms. We couldn't come and go as we pleased. We couldn't own businesses. We couldn't leave the country. And we had to continue bribing unscrupulous and greedy local Party members in order to keep from being harassed. When you really peeled away the skin from the surface, what we were living wasn't the good life at all.

I believed I had a higher purpose in life. I wanted to travel. I wanted to see the world. I wanted to do more than live the basic life we were living. But I was refused a passport every time I tried to get one.

One of the biggest problems of Communism is that it was a living dichotomy – one theory, one reality. In theory, Communism was a system of social organization where all property was shared and everyone worked together in harmony. Everyone was equal. But in reality, in practice, Communism meant all economic and social activity was controlled by a totalitarian state dominated by a single and self-perpetuating political party. And that control was delegated down to a regional and local level, where people who didn't understand the idea behind Communism were put in charge of enforcing it. The result was a group of dumb, greedy thugs who were out for themselves and enjoyed oppressing, bullying and harassing the rest of us.

In Communist Romania, you weren't allowed to be different. The moment one of these thugs saw you trying to express your individualism or wanting something else beyond what they said you could have, they stepped in and pushed you down. Only heads of the Communist Party were allowed to be different. They lived in villas that had been confiscated from non-Party officials. They drove in government limousines. They acted like spoiled children. But if we had given in and joined the Party, my family would not have had the independent thinking necessary to determine our future lay outside Romania. I would not have identified my higher purpose in life and been able to pursue it with enough vigor to bring my family to this amazing country, America.

My story really begins with my father, Ioan, who was born in Sharon, Pennsylvania, in 1919, during an 11-year period when his parents, Valentin and Ioana Daisa, lived in the United States.

My grandparents had emigrated separately from their respective villages in Romania, both of them in search of a new life and the prospective fortune that came with it. They met, married and started a family. A few years later, they returned to Romania, bringing with them the wealth they'd accumulated in America to help their families back home.

My grandparents' time in America changed their spirits. This country has a way of living, feeling and thinking that no other country on earth has. We know that we are the best, and with great power comes great responsibility. We own our fate. We decide how we are going to react. Americans throughout history have proven they are not victims, nor perpetrators. Rather, we are helpers and survivors. As Americans, we stand for honor, duty and order. Even though the Communists looked and talked like they were organized, behind the puppet curtain was a chaotic mess.

Valentin and Ioana thrived in the United States. They knew how to do business the right way. They knew about banking and finance, about customer service and competition; and they felt the warm light of success. The two of them fell in love and married during what was a beautiful time in their lives. When my grandfather recounted those days through his stories I was able to relive this fairy tale time in my family's history. Through my grandfather's tales I learned about a country where anything was possible. I learned about a way of life that I suddenly wanted – the American way. And I realized that the Communist way of life was so far removed from the right way. I knew this in my heart.

Because my father was born in America he held American citizenship, even though his parents never kept a copy of his birth certificate. That birthright eventually allowed him to emigrate from Romania with us in the late 1970s, a few years after U.S. President Richard Nixon and

Romanian President Nicolae Ceausescu reached an agreement that laid the groundwork for Romanians born in America to apply for and receive passports and leave the country.

What fueled my desire to become an American were those stories that my grandfather spun. I was a child and it all seemed so magical, my grandfather's time in America.

America.

For a young girl living under Communist rule, just the word itself offered visions of a new life with opportunities far greater than anything that could be obtained in Romania. The dreams that were born from my grandfather's stories later sustained me for five long years when I fought the Romanian government and demanded that it honor our numerous requests for passports.

As I mentioned, we didn't leave Romania for material reasons. We had already figured out how to beat the system and managed very well for people who weren't Communists. After the government stripped my family of all their possessions at the onset of Communism, they spent the next several years learning how to play the system and, within a decade, reconstructed a relatively comfortable life.

My parents worked full time, as were the rules of the Party, but they also operated a small business – a vegetable farm where they also raised animals. They woke up at 4 a.m. each morning to tend to their farm. Then they dressed and went to their Party-mandated jobs. They were always tired but they seemed happy. As a result, we had land, houses, cars, artwork, fancy clothes, nice furniture and more. We were well off, and our friends and relatives never could understand why I kept saying I wanted to go to America.

"America is here for you," they would say. "Why risk losing it all just so you can start over?"

Nobody understood. But it was our purpose, our destiny, to go to America. The die was cast by my grandparents, Valentin and Ioana, who had prospered there. To better understand my story is to know theirs.

I never met my grandmother, Ioana. She died in childbirth in 1927 while delivering her fifth child, Aurica, but everyone always told me how much I was like her. She was pretty, strong-willed and determined to succeed. Her parents were poor farmers, and Ioana thought she could immigrate to the United States and create a better life for herself.

As my grandfather told the story, in 1912, when Ioana was 19 years old, she left her home in the village of Vintz, near Sighisoara, and walked more than 420 miles to Vienna, Austria. The journey took her several weeks, and it's unknown whether anyone accompanied her on the trip. She remained in Vienna for a while, cleaning homes, and earned enough money to move on. From Vienna, she made her way to a boat in Hamburg, Germany, that was leaving for the United States.

Once in the U.S., Ioana settled in Sharon, Pennsylvania, then a rural industrial town with steel and iron mills and a growing immigrant population, many of them Romanians, and started a new life.

She married, had a little girl named Marioara, and was widowed within two years. But Ioana was smart and entrepreneurial. She owned a house and began renting out rooms to other Romanian immigrants. She served them food, washed linens and their clothes, cared for their children, and eventually transformed her little home into a full-service boarding house for Romanian immigrants.

Over time, Ioana became successful and bought other property, eventually owning four boarding houses. She met my grandfather, Valentin, in 1916. Soon after, they were married.

My grandfather came to Sharon the same way Ioana had. He was raised in the village of Cetia, near Alba Iulia, in Romania. It was a small, beautiful village in the heart of the Apuseni Mountains, part of the Western Carpathians. It was one of my favorite places on earth. As a child, we would go on vacation there. My grandfather described the village as poor, but it had vineyards, a river and very nice people living in it. There was also a little church in the middle of the village. His family, like others in the village, was very poor. They, like Ioana's family, were farmers.

Valentin wanted to go to America for different reasons than Ioana. He planned to make enough money that he could bring it bring back to Romania and help his family climb out of their social class.

He walked to Vienna from Cetia. From there he traveled to Germany, where he found a job shoveling coal into the engines of a boat. He was 20 years old, good looking, strong, and had a pleasant personality. He was, by all accounts, including his own, an extremely hard worker, and upon his arrival in Sharon in 1912 found a job working in a steel mill.

After marrying Ioana, he earned extra money by making plum brandy in his backyard in a homemade still and selling it to fellow Romanian immigrants. And one year after getting married, Ioana gave birth to my aunt, Anuta. Two years later, in 1919, my father, Ioan, was born.

My grandfather always intended to go back to Romania. My grandmother didn't. But Ioana loved Valentin, and she agreed to make the return trip home. In 1923 they sold everything and returned to Romania with the fortunes they had accumulated. The family resettled in Vintz-

Sighisoara, near my grandmother's ancestral home.

Life was good in 1923. It was an exciting time. At the end of March, Romania adopted the Constitution of Union, which created sovereignty through popular representation, established separation of powers, a rule of law and decentralization of power. My grandparents' return to Romania came just as their homeland was embracing democratic principles and providing rights and freedoms to all citizens, who were recognized as such regardless of ethnicity, language, religion or social class. Women still couldn't vote, but the new constitution gave citizens the right to own property in what was called the "Kingdom of Romania." The constitution also guaranteed freedom of expression, assembly and religion.

Valentin and Ioana bought property and founded the first of many businesses they would go on to own. A year later, in 1924, they had a second son, Valentin. They bought land, a house and started another business. They were very well off and moved to Cluj, Transylvania, in the northern part of the country, where they became bourgeois of the city.

Cluj is a very old university town filled with beautiful, classic architecture in the old style of Eastern Europe. It had wonderful restaurants, great theaters and a philharmonic orchestra that was world-renowned. My parents also kept their home in Vintz-Sighisoara, and travelled back and forth between the two homes.

In 1927, their world came crashing down. Ioana died during a difficult childbirth. The child, Aurica, another daughter, survived. Valentin was left alone to raise five children. In those days, when the mother died, the children were left to fend for themselves. The father usually could not hold a household together unless he remarried. Valentin loved Ioana with all his heart. He was heartbroken by her death; never to recover. He loved his children, so he did whatever it took to keep his family together. He had the means to hire nannies and housekeepers. And that is what he did. He kept his family together against all odds.

Valentin's children were the most important thing in his life. He raised them the best way he knew how. He loved them and taught them to be successful and independent. He showed them that through hard work and dedication life's rewards can be huge. He worked hard and so did they. This trait got passed down from one generation all the way to my own children and grandchildren. His way of being came through all of us. We know this and we are thankful to him for his efforts.

Despite Ioana's premature death at age 33, Valentin persevered. He established restaurants; bought real estate in Vintz, Cetia, Teius, Aiud and Cluj; tended farms; cultivated vineyards; and founded a transportation business.

Valentin moved to Cluj full-time after Ioana's death and all of his children old enough to help joined the family businesses. Together, they made it prosperous.

By age 17, the entrepreneurial bug had bitten my father, Ioan. He sold fish in the cities, worked part-time in the family restaurant and dabbled a bit in different types of commerce. He spent two years in college and then went to work full-time in the family enterprises. My grandfather doted upon him because he saw a lot of himself and Ioana in Ioan.

But in 1942, everything changed again. Romania was drawn into World War II on the side of Germany, and the then-23-year-old Ioan was drafted. He went to war against the Russians as a tank hunter, where he got 2nd degree burns doing his job. Later, my father was captured. He was sent to a Russian prisoner of war camp in Odessa, where he would spend the next few years.

Later, dad, along with two other prisoners were being transported from one POW camp to another when they escaped. They leapt from the back of the truck into a river.

The three soldiers walked more than 545 miles from Russia to Romania. They walked during the night and slept during the day. Dad explained to me that had any of them been spotted by Russian troops they would have been captured and killed. But, he says they reasoned if they hadn't made their escape the Russians would have eventually killed them anyway. So what choice did they have?

When Ioan reached home, he found his father sick and was pressed into immediate service running the family business. By that time, the business had become even more prosperous. Dad ran the restaurant, tended to the land, oversaw the real estate holdings, made sure wine was being produced, and operated the transportation companies. He also found time to foster one of his passions – animals.

As a hobby, my father owned pigeons. He trained them to send messages. I remember times when I was a little girl how in our attic we had pigeons and dad would tie messages to their legs and send them off.

The same year dad returned from the war he met my mother, Marioara. At age 20, she was seven years younger than Ioan, but from a very well off family in Cluj. Her parents, Ana and Iosif Muresan, were farmers. They operated what today would be called an agribusiness because their operations were so expansive and successful.

The Muresans were Romanian old money – Protipentada. My grandfather was considered "new money." Marioara's family was called the

Protoprendob of that area. They owned expansive acreage and Marioara was like a princess. She told me stories about how she would be dropped off at school in a carriage with two beautiful horses pulling it along.

Her mother, Ana, was very good looking. My son, Alex, is said to have her blue eyes. Iosif, my maternal grandfather, was one of the most anti-Hungarian protesters of his time. He fought against the Hungarian empire's occupation of Transylvania. His efforts became his eventual downfall because Hungarian spies poisoned him one day while he was in the hospital, and he died. The tragedy left my grandmother, Ana, alone to raise four children and manage the family business. My mother was eight years old when her father was murdered.

So when my parents met and married in 1946 it was a coming together of new and old Romanian wealth. Mom went to work in Ioan's family business in the restaurant as the manager. It was hard, physical work; much different than what her parents had probably expected for her. But my mother didn't complain. She didn't mind having to work hard to become successful.

I inherited that trait. That has been the make-up of our family throughout its history. Everyone tried very hard to become something special, not to settle for being regular, normal, everyday people. We always wanted to improve and be somebody. That was part of our higher purpose.

Both my grandfather and father were amazing people. If you know nothing else about them, know this. During World War II, they helped transport Jews from Hungary across the border to Romania in order to keep them from being sent to Nazi concentration camps or worse, being killed outright by the Germans.

The two of them drove a large bus over the border and brought Jewish children and old people from Hungary to Romania. I have no idea how many times they did this but it seemed like they would make these trips often. I'm very proud of this. Neither my father nor grandfather had anything to gain through their actions; they only had their own lives to lose.

They did it because both of them knew it was the right thing to do. They saw the evil that was happening in the world and believed that the best they could do was their own little part, and that hopefully, it would make a difference. My father and grandfather were pure of heart. They were simply unable to stand by and watch while others suffered unjustly at the hands of terrible despots. As it turned out, no one ever caught my family doing these things and the war ended without any repercussions for them.

Good deeds are their own rewards. When a person discovers the feeling of giving freely with no compensation or selfish payoff life takes on a totally different path. Your passions in life shift. You search out ways to help others. This feeling in you grows like a hot flame. It becomes the driving force in life from the smallest of choices to the biggest life-altering decisions.

Selflessness is the highest point in spirituality. It puts you in touch with the higher power like nothing else can. As a parent, you pass this passion for helping people to your children and grandchildren. You raise the standards of humanity in yourself and generations to come. When my father and grandfather lent their efforts to help lost and poor people during the war and the change within the government systems in Romania they became heroes for me and the people they helped. I know they were risking their lives for the most noble of causes even though everyone said how wrong they were. I followed their lead and started helping people when I was a child. It made me feel good inside. It made me feel God within my own heart. And the goodness from one generation to the next was passed down to me.

On May 7, 1947, I was born. Stella Ioana Daisa entered the world in the aftermath of World War II, and into a family rich with wealth and happiness. Our family was doing well and, with the effects of the war slowly fading into history, they believed the future was going to be very, very bright. My birth was just one more reason to turn the page and leave the past behind.

My parents reveled in me. I was a happy baby and very pretty. I had thick black hair and light brown eyes. I was active and very demanding. My mother told me she would stay up all night and swing me in a favorite swing that I would refuse to leave. As a toddler, I recited nursery rhymes and was a little star, performing in front of any audience I could find.

I remember how my parents' home was filled with nice furniture, expensive paintings, silver, china, and Persian rugs. I even had expensive baby furniture from Italy. By any measure, my parents were wealthy. They had land, buildings, restaurants, and a nice house. They had dozens of employees, including maids in our house. We were a very well-respected family.

In those first few years, I was treated like royalty. My grandfather used to go to a marketplace near the house almost every day and buy fresh watermelon for me because I loved watermelon. He always said I was his little princess.

Things were changing around us in Romania in the days after the war, and we were naïve enough to think it would never reach us. But when I was about five years old, the Communists were in control of the country and I remember vividly how one day they came and just took everything away. We were left with no money, no furniture, and one room for all of us to live in. Just like that, everything my family had spent their lives working for was gone.

Both sides of my mother and father's family were people who knew what they wanted out of life. We lived in a part of the world that had seen a lot of change in power of government. Romania has a turbulent history. It's been conquered many times. The citizens of our homeland were used to upheaval generation to generation. It is in our genes as Romanians to be suspicious and strong. Our family was no exception.

But history in Romania is cyclical. Just when things start to go well politically and the country as a whole is working towards democracy and an expanding middle class, something happens to throw everything back into chaos. It's kind of living in an area where hurricanes occur. Every time a huge storm hits, people know that there will be a major clean up job afterward. The difference of living in an uncertain political climate is that these storms don't just last a few days or weeks. They last five or six decades. People quickly learn how to function in the new system. They learn who to befriend and who to watch out for. They learn what the limitations are and how to push past them in order to secure a decent way of living. My ancestors knew how to recover from the political storms. After all, the things that nobody can take away from you are your work ethic, your passion for life, and your strength to persevere no matter what the odds are.

When my parents found themselves pillaged once again, they did not give up. They put their heads together and developed a plan. They tried to save what was left of their possessions and start to piece their lives back together. They stayed on as managers for the property they had to give up to the government. Most significantly, they kept their paperwork in perfect order of what they got to keep and what the state would take away. They met with government officials and bargained with them about getting to keep some control over what is going to happen to their properties, even in theory. They knew somehow they were going to get back what they lost. They knew it because they trusted God and trusted themselves.

Valentin Daisa in the United States
(between 1917 and 1923)

Ioan Daisa and Marioara (Maria) Daisa (nee Muresan)
on their wedding day (pictured center)

Maria Daisa as a young woman

Stella's parents, Ioan and Maria Daisa

Stella with two bulls in Cetia (1966)

3

America is a wonderful place. But most people born in America take for granted the fact that they are free. And why shouldn't they? When you're born free it's easy to assume you'll be free forever. That's only natural, and for more than 200 years it's been the case here. You are free and your children will be born into freedom. That is the wonderful thing about America – you can count on your freedom. You can count on opportunity. And even when it's going through rough times, you can always count on America.

Europe has never had the same level of stability. European countries, especially eastern European countries, always seem to be in a state of flux. Old world Europe is very different from the new world of America. Eastern European countries change their governments and their borders more often than we, in America, realize. There are inter-country wars, intra-country wars, coups and disputes that continue for centuries at a time. That's what it was like for Romania at the end of the World War II.

We had fought for both sides during that war – first the Axis, then the Allies. But in each case, we believed we were fighting for our freedom and the freedom of our children. That was our motivation; keeping our country free for our children. No matter where you are in the world, nothing is more important than your children.

When the war ended, we thought it was, well, over. We should have known better. Centuries of fighting should have made us smarter. But how can you give up on hope? When it glimmers, you get caught up in it.

The Soviet Union, however, was very clear in its intentions once we had come over to fight on their side, despite the veil of inclusiveness their government tried to project to the rest of the world. When the Allies split Europe, giving the Soviets almost unrestricted control of everything west of the middle of Germany, the Russians bided their time and slowly implemented change.

Few people saw the rise of the Communist Party coming. Families like ours, people in the villages of Romania, never considered the Russians would insert their own people and add us to their growing sphere of influence.

It was worse in Romania than some of the other soon-to-become Communist Bloc nations. That's because the Soviets held grudges.

Loyal Romanians, people like my father, were a key part of the German invasion of the Soviet Union. Romania's late switch in 1944 under King Michael to the Allies' side did little to change the Soviets' opinion of the Romanian people. They were invaders who had failed and would eventually pay for their arrogance and actions. They killed a lot of Russians, and the Soviets never forgot. In the eyes of the Russian leaders, Romania was a conquered territory. Its people were enemies who had been forced to switch sides. And they would soon learn what happened to anyone who crossed Mother Russia.

The Soviet takeover, and subsequent Communist takeover of Romania, was an aftereffect that in retrospect looked choreographed. As the war wound down, Romanian forces fought under Soviet command. They drove through Northern Transylvania into Hungary and then Czechoslovakia, Austria and Germany. Soviet troops stayed in Romania as an occupying force under the pretext that Romanian authorities could not guarantee the security and stability of Northern Transylvania. You couldn't have asked for an easier invasion without actually invading.

While we were busy trying to get back to life as normal in the villages and cities, and expanding the stretched resources the war had left us with, the Soviets were busy in Bucharest pressuring the post-war Romanian government for inclusion of the formerly illegal Communist Party in the post-war government.

By the end of 1947, the year I was born, King Michael saw what the future was about to bring, abdicated his throne and fled into exile. At the same time, non-Communist political leaders were driven from the government, free thinkers were harassed or killed, and in December of 1947, the Romanian People's Republic was born.

At the time, we were living in luxury. Little did we know that our country's resources were being ravaged by the Soviets under the guise of newly created Soviet-Romanian joint-venture businesses. Gradually, people who disagreed with the government or were considered a future threat to the new government's plans began to disappear. Just as the Communists in Russia eliminated the threats they saw from intellectuals, they systemically began to do the same in Romania. Here, they were people who didn't buy into the new Communist way of things. Because they voiced their displeasure they were taken into custody, where they were executed or died of torture and neglect.

My father and grandfather fell into this group. They were among those that the Party considered dangerous, as was every well-off person. All were threats to the Communist way of thinking. And my family would not – and could not – become Communists. I remember many times when my father and grandfather left the house and went into hiding in order to escape being arrested and executed. It was a horrible time.

I was barely a year old when the Romania my parents knew and that my grandparents had come back from America to live in was nearly gone. In its place stood a Communist country filled with new leaders and new rules. It's hard to imagine what was going through my parents and grandparents heads while this was happening. When I was old enough to talk to them about it they refused to go into detail about all the things they did to manage. They refused to complain and only focused on the future. They made themselves believe they wouldn't be affected. But it isn't hard to put myself in their place and think about what I would have done if one day, the country I knew, loved and fought for just disappeared. It didn't look any different. It didn't feel any different. It didn't smell any different. But it was no longer the same.

Romania's new constitution was a sham. On paper it looked real, but it provided freedom only for people who were members of the Party and "worked" under Party rules. Everyone else who wasn't imprisoned was, in effect, marginalized, and they were threatened until they gave in and joined the Party. For land owners and business owners, a series of beatings, intimidation, arrests, and deportation softened their hard line stances until they acquiesced.

For families like mine, the changes were devastating. The Communists wanted people to pay them to work in the businesses they owned. And they expected those people to pay enormous taxes on top of that. When enough was enough and you reached a point where you couldn't afford to pay the taxes, the Communists would take the business away from you and nationalize it. These were terrible tactics, but showing mercy and being fair wasn't part of their playbook.

On top of these changes, the Communists issued new money and put it into circulation. They regulated the economy and made sure the Romanian money had no value. Then, they would demand money for the taxes. When people didn't have money, they took their possessions instead. This is what happened to us. We had once been among the wealthiest in the region. Now we were poor. And it happened to us, literally, in one day.

For some reason that to this day I still don't understand, they didn't take all of our land right away. But they were working under some semblance of a plan. They were building colectivs, where land from numerous groups of people was combined to create a single farm. That group, plus other groups of people, would then work on the land. Together, they would pay taxes to the government for the right to work on the farm. They would also give the government products from the farm for sale. Within a few short years of my birth, the new collective farming initiatives had reached every village in the country.

My family, like others who weren't immediate converts to the Communist cause, didn't want to voluntarily give away everything they had worked so hard to achieve. But what choice did we really have? The Party leaders were killing people. If we stood up against them, they wouldn't have thought twice before putting bullets in our brains. And the people of Romania were living on false promises that the Americans would come and save them from Communism, just as they had saved Europe from Nazism. We were so naïve to think that would happen. We didn't understand the geopolitical machinations that were occurring during the early days of the Cold War.

What we did understand was that Russia was very big and very powerful. The rise of Communist Russia turned out to be one of the greatest mistakes and disasters humanity has suffered during the past few centuries. When it happened, the Communists were the poor people, not very bright, not the intellectuals. But if you were poor enough – and not very bright – you could come to the Communist Party, become a member and have the illusion of power. It was a very attractive proposition for that type of person.

The governments were very vengeful. They hated rich people. They hated intellectuals. They hated anyone who posed any type of threat to their plans. And they killed many people and put others in concentration camps and jails. Families never heard from their loved ones again.

And while the Communists may have said they wanted everything to be the same for everybody, deep down they were hypocrites. They seized the homes of people they killed or sent to jail and lived in them. They took their cars and drove them around town. In essence, they became the new aristocracy. They robbed people like my family and took all the farm machinery, equipment and anything that was used to work the land. Then they put it all in the middle of the farm and burned it. They did this big production as an example to show people that life was going to be hard now. The people would have to work the land with their hands. For them, the easy days were over.

As a child seeing this, it was so sad and terrible to witness. I remember how there was a lot of confusion at the time. People were talking about Communism and what was happening across the country, and what was happening to all the upper middle class and well-off people in every village, town and city across Romania. So many people were simply killed. It was a miracle that neither my father nor grandfather suffered that fate.

And it wasn't long before secret police started popping up everywhere. They would appear on your doorstep and interrogate you. They'd stop you on the street and begin asking questions. They would make you turn against your neighbor. When someone wouldn't cooperate, they'd torture or kill them. These were very scary times.

What was left of the government just let all of this happen. They didn't care anymore about the people or about the country. Romania's infrastructure began to deteriorate. The roads became terrible, impassable in places. The government invested in nothing substantial to help the country; they only helped themselves. Tension in the air became thick. Fear surrounded us.

In the midst of all of this, my mother refused to give in. I have so much admiration for my mother; she was such a brave, strong-willed woman willing to stand up in the face of all of this danger and say, "No."

The local Communist thugs, secret police mainly, started coming around to our house on a regular basis and telling my mother to sign over the land she'd inherited from her father. They could have just taken it, but they were still trying to put on a show for the rest of the world that the Romanian citizens were going along with the conversion to Communism as a way of life. You couldn't do this if you just took land away from people. Instead, they had to give it to you of their own free will and accord.

They threatened my mother often. To this day I'm not sure why they didn't just kill her and make her an example for others who continued to resist. Later, I learned my mother used to bribe the secret police, who were always corrupt. With them, a little money went a long way.

One day, when I was seven or eight years old, a group of four thugs showed up at our house. They wore gray suits and looked like you would expect the secret police to look like – unhappy and serious. They pounded on the door and yelled for my mother to let them in.

My father and grandfather were away in hiding. They'd left the city the previous day and hadn't yet returned, so it was just my mother, my sister and I.

"Go hide," my mother whispered to the two of us. "And be quiet. They're here to get me to sign the land over to them, and they know I'm alone. No matter what happens, don't come out and don't make a sound."

More than once my mother had told my sister and I how hard her parents and grandparents worked to get this land, and that they would have to kill her before she would give it to them. I suddenly feared this would be that day.

"Do not talk," my mother whispered, then hustled the two of us into a bedroom to hide. "Just breathe."

I have many vivid memories of hiding in small spaces when the secret police suddenly arrived. Normally, we were just scared that they'd come and take either my father or grandfather away. But they weren't here today, and my sister and I were terrified. If anything happened to our mother, what would happen to the two of us?

We settled into hiding spaces and listened as the police pounded on the door.

"Open up now!" one yelled. "If you do not open this door in the next minute, we'll break it down and arrest you."

I wanted to jump up, throw the door open and confront these men. I wanted to scream at them and ask them why they were doing this to us. I wanted to order them to leave us alone and never come back. But I didn't. I just crouched there with my sister, silent, while my mother knelt on the floor next to us.

The pounding on the front door continued. Then it moved to the windows.

"We know you're in there!" one shouted. "All of you are in trouble."

Suddenly, I sneezed. The men heard it and yelled even louder.

"We hear you! We know you're home!" screamed one.

We heard the loud shuffling of feet outside and they moved back to the door. The pounding intensified until it sounded like a thunderstorm outside our door.

Suddenly, the door burst open and the men poured into the house. They found us squatting on the floor inside the bedroom.

"There!" one shouted and pointed at me.

I was so scared that I peed in my pants.

The men rushed into the bedroom, pushed my sister and me aside, and grabbed my mother. They lifted her up and pushed her onto the bed. One of them stepped forward and jabbed a finger in my mother's face.

"So, you thought you could hide from us!" he yelled. "Do you realize the trouble you are all in now?"

My sister and I cried. We tried to stand up and get in front of them, protect our mother, but we were little girls and they reached out their arms and just pushed us back down on the ground and into a corner.

"Don't move!" they shouted, pointing a menacing finger at us. "Don't move!"

"Why are you doing this?" I cried. "Why are you so mean? Just leave us alone."

The man just looked at me and scowled. And then the other man, the one who was standing over my mother, shot the other three a glance and said, "Go look around. See if you can find anything that shouldn't be here."

They nodded and went into the other room, where they began opening drawers, kicking over chairs and throwing furniture around.

"Stop!" my mother cried, but the man leaned nearer to her and shook his head. He stood there just staring at her while his men tore up our house.

A few moments later, the men came back into the bedroom. They were holding some jewelry they had found in one of the drawers. They had malevolence in their eyes and smirks on their faces. They handed the jewelry to the man standing over my mother.

"Keep it," my mother said. "Just leave us alone."

The man looked at the jewelry in his hand for several moments as though he were weighing his options. Then he pulled a folded sheet of paper and a pen from inside his jacket. He unfolded the paper and thrust it in front of my mother.

"Sign this and we'll be on our way," he said in the most pleasant voice he'd used since arriving. It dripped with evil. Even at my age I understood that this man had nothing good in his soul.

My mother didn't even look at the paper. God bless her soul. "No," she said. "I won't sign anything. You'll have to kill me and sign the paper with my dead hand if you want our land."

The man raised his free hand and motioned as if he were going to smack my mother. Then he paused, lowered his hand, looked at the jewelry once more and chuckled.

"What if we just take you away to jail right now?" he said.

He slowly shifted his gaze to my sister and me, then back to my mother.

"What will happen to your sweet little girls if their mother suddenly was gone forever?"

My mother held her ground.

"You won't do that," she said. "I dare you to take me away right now."

The man look at us, grinned, and then turned back to my mother. She stared back, not letting her eyes leave his. The two of them gave no ground for what seemed like hours before the man finally chuckled again and spit on the floor. He looked over again at the two of us cowering in the corner and smiled a crocodile's smile. He jingled the jewelry in his hand and cocked his head.

"Let's go," he said to his men. "There's nothing more to do here."

He leaned in once more close to my mother and said, "But we will be back again soon."

He jingled the jewelry again.

"This is the last time. If you don't sign soon, you will end up in prison or dead. Think about your daughters. Do the right thing."

And then, just like that, he and his men left.

In that moment, through the fear, through the terror, I realized just how much I hated Communism. I also realized how strong a person my mother was and how everything you do is for your children. Watching her stand up to these evil men that burst into our house to threaten her taught me that in life you have to stand up for what is right no matter the consequences.

Afterward, I was scared and had nightmares. But I kept telling my mother, "Don't give them our land."

I will never forget what I saw that day and how my mother's actions made me feel.

5

For several months in the early 1950s, after the Communists took everything away from us, my family lived in a small room. We barely had enough food to eat and clothing to put on our backs. We had no money to buy sugar, and my mom used homemade marmalade in my sister's milk. I remember how my parents, after they were stripped of their possessions, weren't even allowed to have jobs. It was punishment by the Communists for their resistance.

Somewhere during that time, I can't remember exactly when, Party thugs seized most of our land. They never did get my mother to sign those papers. There was no fanfare when it happened. I just remember that one day I noticed we didn't have the land anymore, and nobody ever spoke about it.

School was very hard for me because people knew my father was born in America. I was known as "the American's daughter." America, they taught us, was capitalist America, evil America, and I became a pariah because of my father. My teachers and classmates picked on me. It forced me to work harder than everyone else just to get by in the classroom and survive in an increasingly hostile environment. But instead of breaking me, it made me even more confident in myself that I could handle anything that was thrown my way.

We wore uniforms each day to school that demonstrated our "sameness." The Communists mandated that no one should have any more than anyone else. Nobody was supposed to have more than one home, and if the home's square footage was bigger than the Party felt was appropriate, the rest of the house would be allocated to other Communists. We had friends, many friends, who lived in a house and shared bedrooms with other families and used a common kitchen for everyone.

In school, the teachers told us that God didn't exist. They explained that we should not go to church because there was nothing there for us. The only thing we should believe in, they said, was Communism and its philosophies. We read from Marx and Engels, and nobody else. We were not allowed to read American authors or any book that said anything positive about America. And we were not allowed to own foreign currency, especially U.S. dollars. If we were caught with foreign money, we were treated the same way that people are treated in America when they are caught with illegal drugs – we were sent to jail.

Those Communist teachers hated me. As the daughter of the American, they singled me out for scrutiny every chance they had. Then, at the end of the school day, I would come home and tell my parents about how terrible school was. And every day, my grandfather took me aside.

"Stella," he said. "Do not believe these people. Don't do whatever they tell you to do. Do not believe in Communism. It is evil. We believe in other things than they do."

I would cry and explain all the lies they told me that day.

And my grandfather would look me in the eye and say, "Stella, my princess, you are born to be in America. One day, you will go. It is an amazing country."

Can you imagine how confused that made me?

But my family was great, all of them, not just my parents and grandparents, but also my aunts, Aurica, Anuta; my uncles, Iosif, Traian and Tinu; and my cousins, Daniela, Titi and Voica. Our family was very close and we all stood firm together against Communism.

Slowly, I learned how to cope with all this confusion. I was smart enough to become a chameleon. I worked hard and kept my mouth shut. I learned how to gain my teachers' and peers' acceptance by being a good student, getting involved in lots of extracurricular activities, like drama and sports, and not arguing with anyone. I kept my beliefs to myself and shared my true thoughts with no one outside our home.

At home, I listened to my parents and accepted and believed what they said. I excelled because in my heart I knew that it was only a matter of time before I would prove that the Communists were wrong and that we were right.

It's so amazing how my childhood experiences instilled within me the strength to succeed and the confidence of my convictions. My spirit could just as easily have been pummeled, and I could have grown up into a weak person. Instead, I became as strong as steel. And I saw firsthand and up close how to beat the system.

That is probably why I tried so hard and never gave up when everything looked grim in America. And what a wonderful country America is for providing me with all of the opportunities it has so that I could become as successful as I wanted to be. It's not the money. It's not the possessions. Rather, it's the simple fact that I am allowed to do what I want as long as I try hard enough.

What I've accomplished during my adult life could have probably been predicted by watching my younger self. Being a leader and taking charge of any situation always came easy to me. I led rather than followed. Once, when I was when I was 11, my grandpa took me to Cetia, the village where he was born. After a couple of days on vacation there I got bored. There was nothing for me to do so I found this old barn and cleaned it up and told my grandfather that I was going to put together a play. He said that would be fine, and I began to organize a program that was comprised of a play, songs, and spoken poetry.

I was a ball of energy and began seeking out children to get involved. It didn't take long, a few days, before the situation changed and they began to seek me out. Soon there was a large group of us and we practiced the program for weeks. Here I was, 11 years old, and the producer of this amazing show.

When we felt we were ready, we put together invitations and invited the entire village to come see the program. We actually set a price to come see the show and sold tickets. Keep in mind that this was during Communism and people didn't have much money, so for those people who couldn't pay cash I asked them to pay with eggs or chickens or whatever they had.

Our program became this huge village-wide event. Everybody came to see it. It was amazing. And my grandfather was extremely proud of me for putting it together.

By the time I was in high school, the political situation in Romania had begun to settle down a little because of outside pressure from different countries. It also became easier to live there because the corruption among the secret police and Party members grew to epic proportions. The corruption was out in the open. Communists wanted money from people and they would do things under the table, even if everybody else around knew it was going on.

If you were lucky enough to have some money, any money, you could get whatever you wanted from the Communists who controlled the cities and villages. My parents managed to get some of their property back through bribes. I never learned the actual details but it wasn't hard to figure out. One day, my father told me were moving, and we moved from the one room we lived in to another house, a house that had been built by my mother's parents. Suddenly, we had two rooms, a bathroom, and a kitchen. That was a big step toward regaining the lives we'd lived before the Communists took over Romania. And best of all, we were allowed to keep a small plot of land behind the house.

As a result of the payoffs, my parents were allowed to get jobs. That let us do a little better. They also were allowed to start a vegetable and animal farm on the land and, as time went by, they hired other people to work the farm and help produce vegetables. My parents raised animals and sold the meat on the black market to make extra money. They learned how to successfully work the system and we managed to do well.

Mom worked as an assistant director of a hospital. Dad was a farm worker and became valuable to the company he worked for, being named the equivalent of vice president of sales. He collected animals from surrounding villages for export.

I, not surprisingly, developed into a true type-A personality as a teenager. I was outgoing and outspoken. I refused to be a young Communist and didn't follow the rules. That's not to say that I went out of my way to make trouble, because I didn't. But I did do things like go to church when you weren't supposed to do that.

While the Communists didn't close all the churches, if you were seen in a church they stigmatized you. But I loved to go to church. It was a refuge or sorts for me, support for my confusion. I would go alone and hide from the prying eyes of the secret police. And I would pray. I would pray that one day I would go to America and escape this life. I would ask God to listen and answer my prayers.

My family believed in God. My grandfather had seen the good that faith creates in American people. America is a country built on many different faiths. People can overcome insurmountable odds with God in their hearts. My mother would pray every chance she got. She would kneel in our little house and I would kneel beside her. I felt the strength of her faith and the pure joy on her face when we would pray together. I felt it kneeling there with my mother as a little girl. I got to know God kneeling there with my mother.

I trusted Him and when we worked hard, He would deliver. My mother would say, "God doesn't give you what you want. God gives you what you need. And when he gives you hardships, it is only for you to work harder and serve your purpose here on Earth better. When God takes something dear away from you, he gives you something else in return."

When the Communists came and took away our land and possessions, we became closer to the rest of our family. We rarely fought with each other and we helped one another. It made our extended family bonds strong. This is how my mom viewed God, and that is what she instilled in me as a child. Whenever something happened, I always tried to see the lesson even in the worst moments. When you are taught this simple skill as a child, your mind automatically goes to the positive in any event. It's not what happens to you, it's how you react to it that matters the most.

That's why even now, when I get no for an answer, I do not accept it. I knew I was not allowed to go to church but I was confident enough in myself to know that nothing bad would happen to me, even if I got caught. The harder they tried to stop me from going, the more I wanted to go and the more often I would.

My parents raised me in a place where the rules were made of deceit. The reason America is such a successful place for triumph of the human spirit is because people are fair and logic is seen in every aspect of American life. Not so in a Communist country. The people who came to power under Communism did not earn or deserve their titles or positions. They took them. Whenever something is not earned, you do not know how to treat it or how to hold on to it – you don't appreciate it. You misuse it. Power is like money earned. So for me, the general rules and guidelines in Romanian society were a joke.

Within the walls of my family's home life, we adhered to the same universal traits the rest of the world was built on – honor, duty, integrity, and general well being. I became a true free spirit. The American way was alive and well within my own heart. As a student, I studied hard and followed the rules of hard work and dedication. As a student in a Communist Romanian school, I could not have been anymore defiant. Their silly rules did not make any sense, like reading only Communist propaganda and making sure we screamed our allegiance to the Communist Party. Well, I wasn't going to go for all that. When they talked about manifestos and atheist beliefs, I dreamed and prayed to my sweet dear God to help me find a way to my beloved America. So I guess I walked on the positive side of believing the rules didn't apply to me. I could've been angry at how different my thoughts were from theirs and developed a superiority complex that would have only gotten in my own way.

Instead, I chose what was good for me out of the education system and excelled at those subjects and activities. The ones that did not agree with my spiritual make-up, I left behind with a "No, thank you" attitude. I did not beat anyone over their heads with how wrong and ridiculous their system was. I left it alone. And I always did it with a pure heart.

By my junior high school years, I was left to my own devices and everybody loved me. I turned into a great student and my family was proud of me. In school, I became involved in many things, including sports, where I was successful in gymnastics. I also did well in drama and choir.

Track always fascinated me, but I didn't join the team. I did run, though, and one day, the coach needed a replacement. He asked me to take a sick team member's place. The team was competing in a regional meet and I was asked to run in the 400-meter event. I was fast. And, although I had never run this type of event before, I was sure I'd do well.

My father came to watch the competition. I knew I couldn't let him down. So when the event started I ran as fast as I could and won. Then I fainted. I hadn't trained properly and didn't have the right conditioning because I never practiced with the team, but I finished first. And that's all it was about for me – being first.

The drive to exceed expectations led me to want to better myself in all areas, including education. I heard about a high school that was better than the one I was attending. I begged my mother to let me go. She refused and explained that it was too far for me to go each day by bus. But I wouldn't take no for an answer. I kept insisting. Finally, my mother acquiesced and I got accepted into that school. It was far, as far as my mother had warned me, and I walked many miles to school every morning and then home every afternoon. But it was worth it.

When I arrived at the school I found that the students were all more advanced than I was because the school employed better teachers. Soon I caught up with them and became one of the best students. I joined the drama club and though I wasn't a very good singer managed through my personality to become a soloist, compete nationally and win an important competition. I acted and sang in numerous programs and always was the main character in whatever play we put on.

Things truly turned around for me at this school. It was a fresh start, to say the least. And when my parents went in for parent-teacher conferences, the teachers all raved about how well I did in my academics and how involved I was in the extracurricular activities.

Of course, the teachers tempered all those positives with a handful of complaints, primarily that I didn't follow directions very well. None of those things surprised my parents. But they were of the mind that if I did well in school, the rest of it was OK.

Even today, after all these years, it's still hard for me to follow directions. I continue to believe that the rules simply can't apply to me. Despite that, I'm wise enough now to recognize that when it's something serious I have to follow the rules, such as banking or other areas where right and wrong are a matter of legal or illegal.

I ended up graduating high school with honors. At my graduation, my grandfather, took me aside. "Stella," he said. "You don't belong in this country. Whatever you decide to do, you must make sure that you end up in America."

"I understand," I assured him.

My goal for adulthood was simple: go to a university, do well, then find a way to leave Romania and get to America.

Because my high school grades were so strong, I was accepted into one of the best universities in Romania, Babes-Bolyai University of Cluj-Napoca, in Transylvania. I hoped that would be the beginning of my journey to reach the great United States of America.

Stella at school with a friend (1958)

Stella, dressed in a Communist Party uniform,
speaks into a microphone (1959)

Stella's high school graduation picture (1965)

6

Throughout my high school years and into college, if school and extracurricular activities were my escapes, boys were not my main event. Getting a boyfriend was easy. In high school, my friends and I used to hang around the university football (soccer) players. They used to come by our high school, and all the girls were crazy for them. One of the most successful, Sabelli, took an interest in me and we began dating. I was in 11th grade at the time, which in Romania was a senior in high school.

Here I was, successful academically, successful in extracurricular activities and with a university football player boyfriend. It was like icing on a cake.

When I got to Babes-Bolyai University, I was still involved with Sabelli. But he was a very shallow person. He didn't know much about anything other than sports. One night, his hormones got the best of him and he started a fight with a member of the secret police in a restaurant. Even though he was a big star, because he beat up a member of the Communist Party, they threw him in jail. So there I was, Stella Daisa, the big star, with her boyfriend in jail. That was a big stigma.

They finally let Sabelli out of jail because it was a minor offense. But I didn't care; I broke up with him. I realized that he wasn't the right person for me. And then, during my second year of college, I met John Moga in the corridors of the university.

John wasn't especially good looking. He wasn't very social. He wasn't my type at all. And one day, he just walked up to me and began a conversation.

"Hi," he said. "My name is John."

"I'm Stella."

"I know," he said. "You have a very pretty feminine voice."

Not the greatest pick-up line in the world, mind you, and I was not impressed at all with him. John didn't look attractive or even healthy, for that matter. I said goodbye and walked away, figuring I'd never see this guy again.

But I did. This time, he was wearing a white sweater with spots on it.

"Hi," he said. "Do you remember me? I'm John."

I looked at his dirty sweater and pointed at the spots.

"Why didn't you wash your sweater?" I asked.

"I'm waiting for money from my parents to buy detergent," he said. "They send me money every month."

That wasn't uncommon. In Romania, students didn't work their way through college like they do in America. Even the poor ones just went to school. Their parents sent money whenever they could.

I felt a little sorry for John, and I had plenty of money. "Come with me," I said. "I'll lend you money so you can wash your clothes."

We went to wash John's clothes, and we got to talking. I found him smart and interesting. He was different than anybody else around. John was strange. He wasn't very social. He wasn't my type at all. And I don't know why, I can't explain it even today, but I was attracted to him.

Over the next weeks and months, John and I got serious. We fell in love. Everyone who knew me – and my former famous, good looking and rich university football player boyfriend – was shocked about this choice. Nobody believed I could possibly go out with John, much less fall in love with him.

Adriana Hodosan, a good friend that had gone to high school with me and now was in college with us, used to say, "What's wrong with you? Don't you see he's depressed? He acts like an old man in a young man's body."

But I didn't listen.

For Easter vacation, John took me to Bucharest to his aunt's apartment. She was on vacation. It was there that we made love for the first time.

The experience, itself, wasn't very memorable, except for the fact that it was our first time. But the guilt afterward was overwhelming. I realized that I was still in love with Sabelli, the football player, but I knew he was not good for me because he was a womanizer and very shallow. John and I were never really compatible. Anyone else would have been better for me than John.

He was very unhappy by nature; I'm an optimist, even under the direst of circumstances. I was very active, he wasn't. I liked parties, he didn't. I love life, he didn't. John was constantly under the weather; he was always complaining that something hurt. Every day it was something different, a headache, his heart was racing, his leg hurt. Adriana was right. I was just too blind to see it.

We went back to college after the vacation and our relationship continued to get more serious. When the semester ended, we went to our respective homes and fully expected to pick up our relationship when we returned to school in the fall.

My family loved going on vacation. Every summer, my mother, sister and I would visit my mother's sister, Anuta, in Constanta, near the Black Sea. We loved going to the seashore for our vacation. It was so lovely, so beautiful and so tranquil.

In June 1967, the three of us took a train from Cluj to Constanta. It took three days to get there, and when we arrived, Anuta's house wasn't available. But we were undeterred. We found a little house to rent and settled in for our vacation.

A few days into our trip I started to get very sick. I woke up each morning violently ill, more nauseous than I'd ever been in my life and throwing up non-stop. My mother was very worried. She didn't know what was wrong. But I realized I'd missed my period. I didn't say anything. This had to be morning sickness, I decided. I had to be pregnant.

After about four days of feeling sick, I knew I needed to resolve my problem. I was young and the last thing I needed was to have a child. What I wanted to do was find John, have an abortion and be done with it. But in Romania at the time abortions were illegal. We'd find a way, I was sure. Even then, I realized that having an abortion would not be a good thing and my family would not approve.

But I didn't feel like I had a choice. It had to be done. So I decided to leave my mother and sister without telling them where I was going. I told them that I was going out shopping and instead left a note by the water container on the table.

"Dear Mom," I wrote. "I have to go solve a huge problem in my life. I love you. I'll get in touch. Love, Stella."

Can you imagine? I left my mother there without her knowing what was going on. I was 19 years old, and I just took off.

Partially, it was because my parents were very strict with my sister and me. My curfew was 10 p.m. even after I started college. I never wanted to disappoint my family through any of my actions. I was supposed to be a good girl and end up successful; there was no other outcome expected. So you can imagine how sad and scared I was when I found out I was pregnant. This was a big problem that only I could resolve.

I've always liked trains. They remind me of change – either good or bad. I took a train from Constanta toward John's parents' house in Ditesti-Prahova, where I planned to find John, tell him about the pregnancy and get an abortion.

It was a painful train ride. Ditesti-Prahova was so small you could not find it on a map, and you certainly couldn't get there by train. It was a very remote and poor village in the countryside, filled with gypsies. The landscape was dusty, flat, and plain.

The train took me as far as Ploiesti, where I arrived around 11 p.m. From there, I had to hitchhike.

It was late but I was able to flag down a truck on a country road. I don't know what I was thinking. Looking back, what a stupid girl I was to get in that big truck with a stranger in the middle of the night. I was very concerned, but it was the only way I could think of to get to Ditesti-Prahova, and that was more important than making smart decisions in the middle of the night.

I remember the sounds I heard from inside the truck and the bad smell of the cabin. The smell was so strong that I threw up several times.

The driver was very courteous. He stopped the truck without complaint so I could get out and not get sick inside his cabin. I hardly breathed the entire ride. I would sleep, wake up and look around. I was so scared.

The man never said a word. He didn't ask any questions. God bless him. He was a good guy. He could have just as easily raped me, killed me or robbed me. But he didn't.

When we reached the outskirts of Ditesti-Prahova, he stopped the truck.

"This is the end of the road for me," he said.

"Where are we?"

"Edge of town. You'll need to walk the rest of the way."

"Thank you so much," I said, and then climbed out of the cab.

The man leaned toward the window and waved. "Be safe," he said then drove off, leaving me alone on the side of the road.

It was a warm night, pitch black, with a sky full of stars. There was a small, primitive, country sign that said "Ditesti." I followed the sign's directions down the road toward a small village. I was tired, hungry, pregnant, and scared, but I was determined to solve my problem.

Abortion in Romania was for blue-collar people. It was illegal but people still did it. But I was an aristocrat, a rich girl. I was not supposed to make mistakes and I certainly wasn't supposed to have an abortion. But none of that mattered to me at the time. Abortion was the only answer for my problem.

I brought John's address on a small slip of paper. I walked through the village in search of the street and his house. It was about 1 a.m. when I finally found it.

His entire property was fenced in. There was no doorbell, but a gate. I found a rock and I knocked hard at the gate. I knocked a few times.

After a few minutes, John's father came out.

He looked at me and said, "It's 1 a.m., who are you and what do you want?"

"I'm a friend of John's from college," I told him, not mentioning my name. "Is John home?"

"No. Lelu is not home," he said, using John's nickname. "He is at a party in Cimpina. But he is coming back tomorrow. Come back then."

And that was it. John's father did not invite me in. I was so nervous – my heart was pounding – so I didn't ask. Instead, I turned and left.

I walked slowly down the road, crying softly and thinking about my next move. It was the middle of the night. I was alone. I was cold, I was hungry. And I had nowhere to go. Cimpina was at least two hours away by car so John certainly wasn't coming back tonight. I remembered a grocery store I had passed on my way through the village. There was a bench outside it. I headed to that bench, lay down, and cried myself to sleep.

The next morning, I awoke at the crack of dawn and sat up. I didn't leave the bench, though. I just sat there by myself, thinking and watching people go by. By coincidence, John's mother went to the store to buy bread. I hadn't met her yet, but John had shown me her picture so I knew who she was. She, on the other hand, didn't know who I was or anything that had happened the previous night. But she saw me there by myself, looking sad, and came over.

"Can I help you, sweetie?" she said.

She was a tall, beautiful woman, very classy and kind. John had told me she was a teacher.

"I'm a friend of Lelu's," I told her.

She didn't act surprised. Instead, she sat down next to me and smiled. "Are you Stella?"

I nodded.

"Lelu's mentioned your name. He's spoken about you to me. I'm Maria Moga, his mother. Why don't you come with me to our house? He's with some high school friends in Cimpina. You can wait for him there rather than here, outside, on a bench."

I nodded again. "You're very kind," I said. "OK."

And we got up and walked to John's house together.

John's parents were both very nice people. They were very different than John. I waited for several hours with them until John arrived. I apologized for waking John's father in the middle of the night. He said it was OK and that he felt bad that I had to sleep on a bench all night. Had he known that's who I was, he would have insisted that I came in and spent the night.

A few hours later, John arrived. He was surprised to see me, but very happy.

His parents left the two of us alone.

"I'm here to let you know I'm pregnant," I said. "I want to have an abortion, but I want it to be both our decisions. It's your child, too, and I cannot decide for both of us. I need help, Lelu. I cannot do this by myself."

John shook his head in protest.

"I'm in love with you, Stella," he said. "Let's have this baby together."

We discussed it for a long time before John finally got up and brought his parents into the room so that we could tell them.

"Having a baby is a wonderful thing," his mother said after we delivered the news. "You cannot get rid of it. You two are very young. You will get married and have this baby. It is the right thing to do. You will see. We will have a beautiful wedding for you."

Maria was so kind to me. Her parents never liked John's father, who came from a very poor family, but she married him anyway. Because of that, Maria's parents stopped talking to her. And they refused to give the two of them any money when they got married.

Maria paid for her decision the rest of her life. The two of them struggled. They had seven children and John's father didn't make very much money. Maria struggled to raise the family. But all seven children attended college. If you don't know anything else about how good those people were, that's all you need to know.

I stayed with John and his parents at their house for a few days, then got in touch with my mother and sister and told them where I was and to come get me.

"What's happening?" my mother asked, a mixture of panic and relief in her voice.

"Just come get me and I'll tell you all about it."

And they did.

My mother and sister arrived at John's house the next day to pick me up. I took her into a room where just the two of us could talk.

"Mom, I'm pregnant," I said.

"You're what?"

"Pregnant. John got me pregnant."

"Stella, how could you?" she protested.

"It just happened, mom."

My mother sighed. "So what are you going to do?"

"Marry John."

She closed her eyes, let her head drop and slowly shook it. Then she raised her head and opened her eyes. "OK," she finally said. "I'll support your decision. You need to tell your sister. And then we need to go home so that you can tell your father."

"I need a few days before I can tell dad," I said. "Please?"

She pondered my request for a moment before saying, "OK."

We returned to the other room where I told my sister what was happening. The three of us stayed in Ditesti for a few days before going to the train station and taking a train home to Cluj, where I would have to tell my father.

Unbeknownst to the three of us, while we took the train to Cluj, John's father, brother, and brother-in-law took a car and went to Cluj to meet my father first. In Romania, tradition holds that you must ask a father for his daughter's hand in marriage. Often, it is the father of the prospective groom rather than the prospective groom, himself.

John's family arrived in Cluj before we did. They were waiting outside my house when my father got home from work. He saw them and didn't know who they were. John's father got out of the car and introduced himself. My father knew John's name and asked them in.

Inside, John's father said, "My son, John, wants to marry Stella. We came to ask your permission."

My father wasn't pleased.

"Tell your son that Stella is not to get married because Stella has so much to do. She is not ready to get married."

John's father pled his case.

"My son wants to do this. He's spoken to Stella about it. She wants to as well."

My father nodded and stood there in silence.

Finally, after several moments he said, "If this is what they want, then I'll discuss it with Stella."

Then John's father and his family left. My father didn't know I was pregnant. They didn't tell him. I was appreciative because I wanted to tell my father. You have to understand, I was very popular and successful, everything that a parent could expect from a young girl. I was my father's everything. He loved me from the bottom of his heart. For him to find out what I did from other people would have made him very, very sad.

The next day, I arrived home with my mother and sister. I'll never forget how I took my dad in another room and broke his heart.

"I am pregnant," I said. "Dad, I have to get married."

My mother and father endured a lot of trials and tribulations in their lives. They always recovered. Always. When my father and I sat together in that room and I told him that I was pregnant and that I wanted to marry John, he was so disappointed. He had endured so much emotional pain in his life from his mother dying when he was a little boy to watching his family's fortune disappear, to going into hiding, and being a prisoner of war in Russia. However, all those horrible life experiences were behind him. Somehow, his heart and spirit were untouched by life's circumstances. Besides, those incidents were out of his control.

As I stood before him and uttered the words, his spirit crumbled. He knew the kind of life I would endure with a man like John. He knew even if I didn't. He felt sorry for me. How can someone so beautiful, vivacious, and promising choose so wrong?

He always had his heart tucked away somewhere safe within his spirit where nothing from the outward world could touch it, good or bad. But I was my dad's heart. He loved me with everything he had. He knew that even though life had failed him so many times, that I was somehow immune from that, protected by his steel will and work ethic. Whatever I wanted he did without question. In me the future was bright, pleasant, and right. Somehow because he paid so dearly I wouldn't have to. He made sure of that.

In those few moments in that room a daughter broke her father's heart. The heart that wasn't touched before was vulnerable, and he was sad. Really sad. For a minute, he saw me five years old dancing in the yard, happy and carefree. He knew that the clouds were coming and his dreams for me were fading. He tried to talk me out of it. Both my parents tried. But somehow they couldn't reason with me. So they gave up and supported me unconditionally, as before and as always. He could have scolded me. He didn't. Instead, he just hugged me.

"Are you in love?" he asked.

"I don't know."

I told him what had happened.

"I think it's love, I guess," I said.

"OK," my father said. Then he smiled. "We are going to have a nice wedding for you and we are going to make it happen."

I learned something important in that one moment: a parent's love for a child is unconditional.

Stella and Sabelli (1964)

Stella at age 20 (1967)

My ex-husband, John, was a curse. I only married him because I was pregnant. I never listened to anyone back then – my parents, my relatives or my colleagues from the university. Everyone was shocked when I decided to marry John because here I was, a very good looking, well-off girl marrying a very poor man from the south. It sounds a bit prejudiced, but it's true; people from the north of Romania just didn't marry people from the south.

But that's exactly what I was going to do, marry John. I was pregnant with his child and it was the right thing to do.

We applied for our marriage license on August 4, 1967, in the village of Ditesti where John's family lived, and were married on September 2, 1967, in Cluj. It was during my third year of college, and I designed and made my own wedding dress.

Three days before the wedding, I had second thoughts and wanted to run away. I don't know why I didn't do it. I don't have much of an excuse other than I was pregnant and realized my life would be changed forever. I wasn't very happy with my fate, but I went through with it, and we had an amazing wedding and reception, which was held in one of the most prestigious restaurants in the city.

My father gave us a car and a house as wedding presents. The whole town talked about the Renault 16 he gave me, a wonderful French car that was burgundy, beautiful, and brand new.

John's parents gave us a set of silver spoons and knives. They didn't have much money, but I knew they made an effort to come to the wedding and give us a gift. They were such good people, and I was so appreciative of them.

But I wasn't very excited about my marriage to John. The prospect of having a baby was exciting, though. I was sure it was going to be my salvation, and that it would become the glue for our marriage.

In mid-January, I started having contractions and went into labor. On

January 18, 1968, Ioana Claudia Moga was born. She was a healthy little baby girl and very, very pretty. She had dark hair and big eyes. What an amazing creature she was. I fell in love with her instantly.

Because I had a Caesarian-section, Ioana and I spent a little more than a week in the hospital. A few days before we left, she didn't feel well. She had a slight fever and the doctors were a bit concerned. But they decided that the two of us would be more comfortable at home and discharged us.

It turned out to be a mistake.

We went home, and the next evening Ioana's condition worsened. She began throwing up. Her temperature rose. And she had a terrible fever. We rushed her to the emergency room, and when the doctor drew blood, he discovered what was wrong. Ioana had a staph infection that she must have contracted in the hospital. At that point, everyone became extremely concerned.

Later, we learned that the hospital where Ioana was born wasn't very clean. Nearly 20 babies had died from staph infections they contracted there during a short period of time.

Ioana survived for two months. The staph infection ate her. At the end, she had a big hole in her back because the infection ate her flesh. It was the worst thing you could imagine, and it made me crazy. I can't explain how distraught I was; I was with Ioana in the hospital all day and all night during those two months.

It was hard. I remember the ugly hospital. I remember that everybody tried to save her. I even prayed to God, but nothing helped.

Then near the end, on March 18, 1968, my mother pulled me aside. She was a smart lady and knew Ioana was about to die. She wanted to spare me the terrible pain of watching my daughter die.

"Go home, Stella," she said.

"I can't, mom."

"Go," she said. "Change your clothes, take a shower and then come back. I will stay with Ioana."

My mother knew what was about to happen. She knew that if Ioana died in my arms I'd never recover from the loss. So she did what any good mother would have done, she protected her daughter.

"OK, mom," I finally said. "I'll go."

I left. I went home and showered and changed my clothes and took a break from that terrible hospital and the dank, dark hospital room. It was the last time I saw my daughter alive. As my mother had foreseen, Ioana died. And she died in my mother's arms.

When I returned to the hospital and found out that Ioana was dead,

I quite literally lost my mind. It's hard to recall everything that happened after that. I was very, very depressed for quite a while and they had to keep me in the hospital for a few days. My mother stayed with me to help pull me through that challenging time.

We buried Ioana in a very little casket in the same grave as my grandfather. He was one of the best people the Earth had ever seen, and I wanted my little girl to be with him forever. They made a little hole in the dirt at his grave and put the casket in there with him. Years later, I wanted to bring Ioana's remains from Romania to America, but they couldn't find any bones. She was so, so tiny when she died.

My whole world changed with Ioana's death.

Nothing ever was going to be the same again. Nothing. In the days that followed, I felt so guilty. I wondered if because we had sex before marriage that God was punishing me with bad luck. That was an old Romanian superstition, and I was sure it had happened to me. I should have divorced John right then, after Ioana died, but I didn't. Everybody told me to stick with him, that it was just the grief speaking. So I stayed with John. And together, we went back to finish college.

The first year after her death was a blur. I didn't want to go on. Holding that beautiful angel in my arms was all I wanted to do. I went through all the stages of grief just like every normal human being. I had no idea then why this had to happen. God doesn't make mistakes. We may not understand why horrible things happen to good people.

Once I started to heal emotionally, I began to ask myself the question why my little girl didn't get to stay with me. I waited and waited for the answer. It never came. I was in too much emotional pain to find the answer buried deep within my heart. I know that God was cradling me through every day of my miserable existence. And I let him.

From deep within the strength of my soul, I wanted another baby. How could I even feel this way? I asked myself that question again and again. But somehow that's what was supposed to happen next for me.

I was gentle with myself. It was the darkest year of my life. I learned then one of the biggest lessons of my life – that this too shall pass. I wasn't ready to get back to feeling good about myself and my life. Somehow, staying in a perpetual state of grief kept my daughter alive and close to me in my thoughts.

My parents were very seasoned in dealing with tragedy. This one was their worst moment as well. Just when you think you can handle anything, life in Romania threw us another disaster. I don't know how my mother and father pulled me through, but they did. They watched me fall apart in a million pieces. And they took each piece of my broken heart and put it back together – piece by piece. I knew I was loved. It took a disaster of outrageous proportions to fuse our family together. Our unconditional love and support for each other pulled us through. Every moment from there on felt like a gift and innately we all knew it.

It was a very hard recovery. I was in my last year of college and had to take my final exams. I was so out of it, and so sad, that they had to give me high doses of medication to get through the days. But little by little, day after day, with my high, resilient personality and help from my family, I began to recoup and eventually recovered from the worst moment of my life.

Fate always nudges you forward, even when you don't want to go and you don't agree. My mother always said "You don't get what you want in life. You certainly get what you need. Sometimes what you need is not good. Look inside yourself and align your wishes with what God gave you. Only there you will find some peace."

What I needed was to have another baby. I didn't know how and why at the time, but I got what I needed.

John had done little to console me during this time, and the little voice in the back of my head began saying that our marriage was a mistake. But it was too late to do anything about it and I was stuck. Like many women before and after me who found themselves in a bad marriage, I mistakenly thought that having a child would be the answer to our problem. And so, in the spring of 1969, I became pregnant again.

This time, the pregnancy had no complications. I was able to forget about my troubles with John and, before I knew it, I was a happy, waddling, pregnant woman. Finally, on November 16, 1969, Lavinia Destina Moga was born two weeks late, delivered through a second C-section.

Dee Dee, as we came to call her, was a healthy baby girl who weighed nearly 10 pounds at birth. She had light brown hair, big cheeks, and large, brown eyes.

Dee Dee came to a family that was struck by the death of a child. But this was no ordinary family. Yes, we were all broken hearted. Yes, we were scared to death. However, we were faithful to God's will and we surrendered completely to his decision to take Ioana back. We were stronger than ever in our unconditional loyalty to each other and to our higher purpose in life.

My daughter was born in love. She came as a ray of sunshine. She was the phoenix rising from the ashes of our burned spirits.

Dee Dee was a huge, strong, and healthy baby. We protected her from the moment she was born. Just like I was a new beginning for my mother and father, Dee Dee was my new beginning. We were going to do everything together. She was my soul mate and this one I got to keep. I loved Dee Dee differently than I loved Ioana. She was born under such duress, but somehow she was such a quiet and peaceful baby; totally unaware of all that had gone wrong. She slept well, she ate well, and she grew like a beautiful flower. When I looked at her asleep or in her deep brown eyes I found the peace that I so desperately needed. It gave me hope and passion to begin anew. My daughter's future became my new agenda. Dee Dee was going to grow up in America. I wanted more than ever to get my family out of this country, where there was no logic or peace expected in its future.

There were, however, complications for me from the C-section. Doctors left a piece of gauze in my belly. Hours after Dee Dee was born, I contracted a high fever. When the doctors finally realized what was going on, an infection had set in and I was cut open again so they could remove the gauze. The two surgeries left me weak, with an on-and-off fever, and unable to get out of bed.

When I awoke after the second surgery and got my wits about me, I asked about Dee Dee.

"Where is my daughter?"

"She is in the nursery," a nurse explained.

"Can you bring her to me?"

"No. The doctors said you can't see her until the infection and your fever are gone."

"I'm better," I argued. "And I want to see her now."

The nurse refused and left my room. A few hours later, I decided that the only way I would get to see Dee Dee was if I took matters into my own hands. The nursery was on the other side of the hospital, quite a distance from the post-operation maternity wing. I had a friend who was in the bed next to me. Her name was Rina, and she was much further along in her recovery than I was.

"Rina," I said. "I have to go and see my baby. And you have to help."

Granted, I knew I was not allowed. Rina knew it, too. But she agreed to help me anyway.

"OK, Stella," she acceded, and slowly helped me out of bed and to my feet.

Together, we walked to the other side of the hospital. When the nurses saw me out of bed they were very surprised. One came over and tried to stop us.

"Back to bed with you," she said.

I shook my head. "I'm going to see my baby."

"Later," she said.

"Now," I asserted.

The nurse put a hand on my arm. "Not in your condition, you're not. Let's get you back to bed."

I shook her off. In my weakened condition, the sudden motion hurt, but I wasn't going to let her keep me from Dee Dee.

"No," I finally said, pulling myself up straight and firm. "I'm going to see my daughter, and the only way you're going to stop me is physically strapping me into the bed."

The nurse sighed.

After a moment, she said, "OK. You win. What if we bring her to you instead?"

I nodded. "That would be fine."

And so, like most things in my life, I got my way, but my pain was unbearable.

Rina helped me back to my bed and the nurses brought Dee Dee. She was the healthiest and most beautiful baby I'd ever seen, with a huge head and big eyes. When they set her in my arms, however, the nurses proved themselves right. I was so weak that I fainted.

Over the next few days, I became a little stronger but kept having spells where the fever from the infection came back and slowed me down. I started pumping my breast milk so that I would be able to nurse Dee Dee once the nurses allowed me to. I remember one afternoon I was so dizzy because of a high fever but I kept pumping away. And then I'd faint, come to, and pump again. Looking back, my determination to prove everyone wrong was actually pretty funny.

John didn't visit us in the hospital very often. One of the few times he did come he only came to tell me he was going to Bucharest for some so-called important meeting. Years later, I learned that he left me and his daughter in the hospital so that he could go have an affair. It wouldn't be the last time he would do something like that.

When I finally got better, the doctors let me take Dee Dee home. I was the happiest I'd ever been in my life.

Shortly thereafter, I went back to work. In Romania, when you finish college, you don't find a job yourself; the Communists give you one. John and I had teaching degrees. We were assigned to jobs in a very remote area in Moldova. Neither of us was happy to hear they wanted us to leave Transylvania, and my father was adamantly opposed to it.

"Over my dead body you're going to go," he said. "It doesn't matter what they do to me, you're not going."

John didn't want to fight the assignment, but I did. And I didn't want to argue with my father. So we refused the assignment. It wasn't easy, and we were scared about what they would do to us. As it turned out, the punishment was relatively mild. The Communists sent us to an even more remote village in Transylvania, but at least it was not too far from Cluj.

John was posted at a university; I was posted at a high school. The commute wasn't easy, and it took buses, trucks, walking and nearly every type of transportation to get to that village to go teach each day. My day started at 5 a.m. and I didn't get home until 7 p.m. It was a difficult time in my life, but I was able to make a difference in the lives of the children I was teaching, which was fulfilling. And, more important, it planted the seeds for education that eventually led me to the career and life I'm living today.

Stella and John's wedding party (1967)

Stella and her mother, Maria,
on Stella's wedding day (1967)

A pregnant Stella walks along a
Romanian city street (1969)

Stella (right) with her parents, Ioan
and Maria, and baby Dee Dee (1970)

Stella teaches class in a Romanian school (1974)

A two-year-old Dee Dee
plays with blocks (1972)

Dee Dee (right) wears a traditional
Romanian national costume (1974)

Stella in Romania (1974)

Stella with baby Dee Dee (1969)

Our children are our lives. Everything we do, we do with them in mind. That's the natural order of things no matter what country you live in or what socio-economic status you hold. I've been in this country for more than 30 years and I continue to be amazed by the freedom Americans have and, more often than not, take for granted.

If you are born in this country, you can apply for a passport and it arrives by mail at your door in a few weeks. That's it. No waiting for months or years for an opportunity to plead your case before a faceless government official and then hope that the nameless powers-that-be will approve your request. Your neighbors don't look at you with disdain because you want to leave the country. You just apply for a passport and the government issues one.

Don't take this the wrong way, but I often look around at all the people who are naturally born American citizens and think they should have just a bit more appreciation for the gift God has given them by being born in this country. That isn't meant to sound bitter. I don't blame you for your lack of appreciation or bemoan you for being born in America. But I have found that most Americans simply don't have a comparison to understand how blessed they are. I do, and it's why I am so happy to be here and so happy to have given my children and their children the opportunity to grow up in a country with so much freedom and opportunity.

I understand how fragile freedom is. It cannot be bought; it can only be given. And it can be stripped away in a heartbeat.

Our ability to get passports so that we could immigrate to America came about very slowly. It was spurred by U.S. President Richard Nixon's 1969 visit to Romania. Following that historic trip, and Romanian President Nicolae Ceausescu's subsequent visit to the United States the following year, Nixon asked Ceausescu to let all Romanians born in the United Sates emigrate to the U.S., where they were considered American citizens. Like my father, there were many Romanians whose families had lived in the

U.S. during the early part of the century and returned to Romania before World War II.

Ceausescu agreed, and while it looked good on paper – the agreement was one of the things that led to the 1975 decision by the U.S. Congress to grant Romania Most Favored Nation trade status – in reality, it was extremely hard to go through the process of receiving passports from the Romanian government to leave for America. Promises were one thing; the reality of a Communist bureaucratic government was another.

But with that news in my head I began to form a plan that would lead to our leaving Romania. I would sit and think about my grandfather and how as a little girl he would sit me down and tell me stories about his years in America.

"Stella," he would say at the end of the stories, "you have to leave this country and go to America. You are born for America. It is where you belong. And one day, you will get there."

So it should have come as no surprise to my father when I began pressing him about what Nixon and Ceausescu had discussed.

"How do we get passports?" I asked.

"We apply," my father said.

"So let's go apply."

"We cannot," my father said. "I do not have any papers to prove I am an American citizen. Grandpa never gave me anything."

That was disappointing news, but it didn't deter me. There had to be something to prove dad was born in America. We just needed to figure out what it was and where we could find it.

While we thought about that, our family began talking about going to America. It became an obsession, and John and I discussed it every day. How would we get there? What we would do there? How would it change our daughter's life? We read a lot about America. I learned about Greyhound and how, if you didn't have much money, you would take Greyhound from city to city. And I started thinking about ways to leave Romania, of fleeing the country.

I learned that if you could swim across the Danube River, you would be in Yugoslavia. From Yugoslavia you could go to Italy; and then from Italy to America. I started to exercise and swim. It sounds crazy but that's what I did. I thought it would work. We had a large park nearby, and I used to go swimming to make sure I was strong enough to swim across the Danube. I had no idea how big the Danube was. I had no idea how dangerous the river might be. But I decided that if I trained and was in shape, I could just swim across it to freedom. I might even be able to carry Dee Dee on my back with me.

Another plan I concocted was to steal a foreigner's passport and flee the country with Dee Dee. For that plan to work I would need to come in constant contact with foreigners. There weren't many people that actually came to Romania, but I learned that tourists from Hungary, Turkey and Belgium vacationed at the Black Sea each summer. So I looked into getting a job with a company that gave tours.

I was hired as a tour guide for Belgian tourists. After a while they chose me to be the director of Planete, a Belgian tourist firm. Dee Dee, my mother and I went back to Constanta, where my mother's sister lived, and I began to spend my summers working as a tour guide for Planete.

It was actually a great job. I used to organize field trips for tourists and make sure they had good food and entertainment. I also did a little side commerce on the black market. In order to get us out of the country we would need as much money as possible. If the police would have caught me with foreign currency or the other items I was trafficking, I would have been put in jail. But they didn't because I used to hide foreign money in the garden of one of my friends in Constanta. We could not keep anything in our hotel rooms because the secret police would check our rooms constantly.

So every fall I would return home to Cluj with lots of money and other possessions I'd spent the summer acquiring. In one summer, I would make as much money as I earned during the entire year teaching. That's just how it was. And I had a good time doing it.

For several summers, I worked at the tour company. They loved me. At the seashore I was a star; pretty and smart and very good at my job. I spoke French, so I was able to talk with the Belgian tourists. And I was friendly and chatty, so I made many friends. I enjoyed myself so much that I nearly forgot about my master plan.

Once, one of John's friends came to see me in action and upon his returned said to John, "How do you allow that beautiful wife of yours by herself at the Black Sea? You can't imagine what's she's doing there. Are you crazy?"

John didn't care. He had his own agenda and I was not a large part of it. I didn't care either because I always had Dee Dee, my mother and other members of my family with me.

Because I was so good at my job, they gave me many privileges the other guides didn't receive, and it became my first serious career in business. That is until the day a tourist got sick. I had her passport in my possession because all the passports were given to me as the guide.

She'd been on a tour the previous day but didn't make it the next morning. Suddenly, it hit me. I could take her passport and, posing as this woman, escape.

I pocketed her passport and took the tourists to the airport for their departure. I got in line with them, and just as we were close to the guard checking passports another tour guide saw me and called my name from a distance.

"Stella! Stella!" she yelled. "What are you doing here?"

At that moment I knew the charade was over. If I made a move for the plane, the secret police would stop me and throw me in jail. Instead, I went over to the woman and gave her a hug and nonchalantly told her I had a sick tourist that needed assistance. As it turned out, the tour guide was an informant and I had to answer many questions about being so close to that plane. After I had spun enough misinformation to satisfy them, I was allowed to leave the airport.

That was the last summer I worked as a tour guide. It was 1974, and I came home and told my father we needed to do something.

"If you do not apply to leave the country to get passports to go to America, I'm going to go anyhow and find a way," I told him.

"Don't do anything foolish," he said. "We will find a way."

And as luck would have it, in the fall of 1974 Aurelia Todoran and her sister came to visit us. Her mother and my grandfather, Valentin, were distant cousins who lived in the same village, Cetia. Aurelia was 12 years old in 1932 when her mother brought her and her sister, Cornelia, to live in America. They had done well for themselves in this country and Aurelia became a millionaire. But she was very humble and frugal, and you would have never known she had accumulated that much wealth.

In 1974, things were beginning to change in Romania. The country was in a sort of flux, and while the government wasn't letting people leave very freely it was letting Romanian-born Americans come back into the country and visit. With this as a backdrop, Aurelia and Cornelia decided to visit relatives back in Cetia. We had heard they were in Romania and invited our cousins to come to our home in Cluj.

They arrived and found that we weren't poor, like many of the other people in the city. They were impressed that we had found ways to work within the system and had build for ourselves a good life under Communist rule. They stayed with us for a few days and were surprised when we confided in them that we planned to get passports and leave it behind for a new life in America.

"If you want to come to the United States I will help you," Aurelia promised. "Just let me know what you want me to do."

We were so thankful for the offer, and we nicknamed her Matusa, Romanian for "aunt."

"We will need sponsoring papers," I explained. "The government won't give us passports and the United States won't give us visas unless we prove to them that someone in America will take us in when we arrive there."

"I would be happy to do that for you," Matusa said. And from that day forward, Aurelia Todoran was our guiding angel.

She left with the promise to track down a copy of my father's birth certificate, send it over and sponsor our immigration to America, so hopes were so high. We were so happy. But we waited and waited, and after about three or four months we received a letter saying that she was unable to find my father's name in any records in Sharon, Pennsylvania. They looked in church records, municipal archives, everywhere. It was nowhere to be found. We were crushed.

But Aurelia didn't give up. She went back to Sharon. She was such a smart woman; she had so much common sense. Aurelia took that common sense with her back to Sharon and thought about the situation. What could the problem be? My father's name was Ioan Daisa, so Aurelia asked the clerk to look for variations of his name but for men with the same birth date.

And that was exactly the right approach. On a birth certificate, instead of being spelled Ioan, the name was spelled Ian. And instead of being spelled Daisa, the last name was spelled Baisa. Everything else on the certificate led her to realize it was, indeed, my father. It had the correct birth date. The names of my grandparents matched. It appeared to be typed errors from when they filled out the paperwork.

"This is it," she told the clerk. "But I need you to do something for me."

The clerk looked at her questioningly.

"It's not a lie," she said. "This is my cousin. His named is misspelled. Will you correct it for him?"

And so, for $20, the clerk made Aurelia a correct birth certificate.

Aurelia knew better than to mail it to us in Romania. The Communists would have opened the letter, taken the birth certificate and that would have been the end of our ideas to leave. Instead, she paid someone to travel to Romania and hand-deliver the birth certificate to us.

When the man arrived, he gave us the paperwork and informed us that Aurelia would be waiting for us once we received passports and came to America. She would take us in and help us get acclimated to America. We just needed to find a way to let her know when we would be arriving.

We were shocked by the man's arrival, but ecstatic. You can't imagine the joy and positive energy that flowed through our household when we looked at that birth certificate. The door to America finally was open. What we didn't realize was that our joy would be fleeting, and that receiving the birth certificate was only the beginning, not the end.

My father and I, and the rest of our family, took that golden birth certificate and went to the police and applied for passports. And with that seemingly innocent move, the war on my family began.

John was a professor's assistant in a university. I was a high school teacher at a reputable high school. My parents had their businesses and were well off. My sister was an accountant. My brother-in-law was an engineer, the equivalent of a vice president, at this huge Romanian engineering company. Suddenly, the word spread – all Daisa want to immigrate to America. Within days, all of us were fired from our jobs. Secret police arrived at our homes and inventoried everything we owned.

I remember very clearly how they came to our house. A few men arrived with huge notebooks and walked through writing down every single thing in there – from paintings to china to silver to memorabilia. Everything was recorded. One of the men stood with John and me as the others did this and harassed us.

"Do you know the real America?" he growled at us. "Do you know how hard it will be for you to succeed there as you are succeeding here? You will not be able to keep up with the pace. America will eat you alive."

"It does not matter," I said. "We will succeed. I am used to making my own pace. I'll do that in America."

The man scoffed. "We'll see," he said. "And when you come back defeated, you'll have none of this." He gestured to my house and my possessions. "You'll have nothing. Just remember that. And you'll have brought this on yourself."

And thus began our real struggles, the wait for passports and our battle to survive without jobs. We waited five long years. Imagine five years without jobs. Day after day, week after week, month after month we were harassed by the secret police and scorned by neighbors. But we never wavered from our goal to immigrate to America and provide a better life for ourselves and our children.

9

For the second time in my life, everything my family had worked hard to achieve was stripped away. Surviving without jobs in Communist Romania wasn't easy, but this time we were more prepared. We turned to the black market and became underground merchants. I sold clothes, everything the secret police didn't record in their notebooks. We were committed to getting those passports and leaving for America, no matter what obstacles the Communists put in our way. There were days we didn't know whether this would ever happen, especially since the secret police did everything they could think of to make our lives miserable.

We were followed everywhere we went. The secret police drove black Volgas and would ride a few car lengths behind us everywhere we drove or walked. When we stopped, they would pull up alongside us, roll down the window and try to intimidate us.

"Why do you want to go to America?" men would ask. "It's a mistake."

Then they would roll up the window and drive away.

For five years we lived with this nonsense and stress.

We even had trouble communicating via letter with Aurelia. While we didn't know it at the time, the secret police confiscated every letter we tried to send. We only discovered this after about a year, when Aurelia sent someone to Romania to see us because she hadn't heard from us for so long. We told her emissary that we didn't know if we would be allowed to leave but were keeping our hopes alive and planned to leave as soon as we were able.

Matusa was so amazing. She continued to send people once a year to check in on us. Had she only sent the birth certificate she would have been a Godsend. And even after all these years, it's hard to believe the lengths that she went through to help our family leave Romania.

The path we took to get out was, to say the least, interesting. I used to camp out every morning in front of the building that housed the local general of the secret police where we had applied for our passports. I would wait for him on the steps of that imposing building and just wait for the right opportunity to confront him and talk him into giving our family the passports. My friends used to say I was crazy.

"They are planning to put you in jail," a former high school friend who worked for the secret police told me in confidence one day. "They're just waiting for you to step over the line, Stella, and do something more aggressive than stand there and wait."

"It doesn't matter. I won't stop," I told him. "I'm going to get the general to issue passports."

"They might even kill you, Stella," he said. "If it gets to that point, they'll do it."

"They wouldn't dare."

"Yes," he said. "They would. Please, Stella, I'm telling you this as a favor. Don't come around here anymore. Let it go."

But I wouldn't listen. I would rather have gone to jail or been killed than stay in Romania under Communist rule. I went every day for every week for every month for more than a year.

Ironically, the general's last name was Ioana. I finally confronted him one day when he stepped out of his car and the time seemed right.

"Excuse me, sir," I said, being assertive but cautious enough not to get shot. "Can we talk today about my emigration to America?"

He knew who I was and thought I was crazy.

"I don't have time for you," he said.

Finally, after I'd worked up the nerve to talk to him for many days in a row he invited me into his office and off the street.

"What do you want?" he asked.

"You know what I want. I want our passports issued so we can go to America."

He laughed. "You know I cannot do this," he said. "Not now."

I left disappointed but with my spirit intact. I intended to follow through on this until the government issued us passports.

The merry-go-round of requests and denials continued for another couple years until I ran out of patience and decided to take my case to a higher level. My cousin, Daniela, had already received her passport and was immigrating to America. She told me that I had to go see the big boss, a general in Bucharest who could make the final decisions regarding passports.

I decided to go to Bucharest and find this man. My brother-in-law joined me because neither my father nor my sister would let me go alone. John could not have cared less. He went back to Ditesti and stayed there for several months and waited for me to either get the passports or die trying.

In Bucharest, we spent several days watching the Securitate building. Every day, a motorcade of cars would pull up to the building and a group would emerge from a black Mercedes limousine and escort the same man into the building. We realized this had to be the general we were seeking.

You have to understand what we were up against. It wasn't something simple. These generals, they were so powerful that nobody dared to confront them. For me to even consider what I was about to do was suicide, literally. They could have shot me right there on the street and nobody would have said a word. But it didn't matter; I did what I had to do.

Finally, after several more days of watching him arrive at work, I decided to act.

God gave me the strength to do so. I was representing my entire family and there was really no other choice. When the limousine pulled up that morning, I knew it was time.

As the general stepped out of his limousine I leapt up from my hiding place and ran toward him. His men tried to stop me, but I was so quick that they didn't have time to react. Luckily, they didn't pull their guns and simply shoot me or I'd have fallen on the spot.

The general saw me and raised his hands, stopping his men from any further actions.

"How can I help you, ma'am?" he said.

"I need to talk to you."

"About what?"

"I have a serious problem that only you can solve," I said.

The man looked me up and down then smiled. "I see," he said.

"Look," I said, "Can I just follow you into your office? We can sit down and talk. I am not a threat."

I was shaking, and probably a pale as a ghost. My brother-in-law, still in his hiding place watching, was probably even more scared.

The man stared at me then looked at his men and back at me. "Follow me," he said, then led me into the building.

We strode through a large, imposing corridor that looked like a palace. There was intricate marble and wood work throughout the building. It made me sick to my stomach to realize how these people were living like kings while the rest of us suffered. Neither of us spoke while we walked. When we finally reached the general's office he invited me in, told his police to leave us alone and gestured for me to sit down in one of the large chairs.

"Now," he said. "Tell me who you are, where you're from and what you want from me."

I was still scared but determined to plead my case. "My name is Stella Daisa Moga. I live in Cluj with my family. My father was born in America. We want passports so that we can leave."

The man nodded.

"I could have been killed just trying to see you," I said. "We want to leave to country. President Nixon and our president made a deal. I just want you to deliver on the promise."

The general nodded again. This time he smiled.

"And?" he said. "What if I don't?"

I'm not sure what came over me at that moment. Maybe it was all the risks I'd taken to get to this point. But I held my head up, looked him in the eye and heard myself say, "Well, if you don't, then guess what. I have many connections, both here and the United States.

"I can communicate with all those people, including my relatives in America. I have a sister-in-law who is a doctor for the queen of the Netherlands. [She had emigrated earlier and was a cardiologist for the royal family there.] If you don't let us leave, I'll get outside pressure on you to deliver the promise President Ceausescu made."

For several minutes, neither of us spoke. The air in the room was tense. How naïve I was. That man had the power to have me killed. And then the general started to chuckle.

"You are a courageous woman," he finally said. "You are very smart, too. But I will have to think about this. It's not a decision I will make right now."

I shook my head and said, "No. You do not get to think about this. We were fired when we applied for passports. Every member of my family lost their jobs. We have no means of survival. Look, this is a serious matter. I am not leaving until you give us passports."

The general slapped his hands together. "OK," he said. "It's obvious you will not leave unless I either kill you or give you a passport. Go into the other room and wait a minute while I make a phone call."

I did as he asked but listened very closely to make sure he really picked up the phone.

He called General Ioana in Cluj and for several minutes the two of them spoke.

"If somebody deserves to leave and go to America, it is this woman," I heard the general say. "Yes, I understand they were prominent members of the community and you had to fire them. Yes, I understand why it had to be done."

And then I heard the words I waited five years to hear. "I'm going to authorize you to issue them passports."

I was nearly crying a few minutes later when the general opened the door and invited me back into his office.

"We are giving you approval," he said. "Go back to Cluj. The general there will issue you passports. But you will have to leave Romania immediately."

I hugged the general and quickly left his office and the building.

My family bestowed so much adoration on me as a child. I was the center of their world. They encouraged and supported me in everything I set my mind to do. That gave me an uncanny confidence level. As an adult, I was told that I had charisma. People genuinely took a liking to me. I was pleasant and used my words as tools to inspire everyone I met. These personality traits got me in the general's door that day in Bucharest.

He saw the flicker of my flame and he wanted to help me. I bet he even wondered himself why he was doing so. And yet, he helped. I didn't give him time to think it over. To this day, I know if I would have walked out of his office, I would have never had a second chance to return. When we made that phone call to General Ioana, our fate was sealed. I learned an important lesson – to do whatever needs to be done and to follow through on my goals.

Aunt Aurelia knew about the hardships in Romania. She had seen and heard about the unfairness of the government on its people. She had a good heart. She followed through on her promises to us. She showed me how one person can change the fate of an entire family and the generations to come. She led by example. When I came to America and settled in and became successful, I too wanted to keep my promise to my beloved friends and extended family that we left behind. I wanted Aurelia's gift to us to be paid forward through me. So I helped every person that I could realize their own dreams for coming to America.

When I walked out of the general's building, my brother-in-law saw me appear and rushed up to meet me. I explained what had transpired and he shook his head in disbelief.

"They're going to kill us before we ever get back to Cluj," he said. "They're not going to let us leave Bucharest."

"They will not," I said. "I heard him make the phone call with my own ears. We're going to get our passports and be able to leave."

He looked around. "Then let's get out of here, quickly."

We saw several journalists outside the Securitate and approached them. To this day I don't know what country they were from, but after we spoke with them they said, "Let's get you to the American embassy before anything happens to you."

They helped shuttle us to the U.S. Embassy, where I explained to the guards at the gate that my father was an American citizen, born in Sharon, Pennsylvania, and what I had just done and that we were going to go back to Cluj, where the government was going to issue passports to us. But right now, we were afraid and needed their help.

"We're being followed," I said. "We cannot go to the train station. We need somewhere safe where we can wait and hide for a few days. Can you help us?"

I don't know why, but they must have felt sorry for us and let us in. It was around lunchtime, about noon, and they brought us white bread and chicken salad sandwiches and cans of Pepsi. And we sat there, the two of us, and ate food and drank soda.

After a while, they brought us a translator who spoke with us in Romanian. Again, we explained our situation, and the translator told us that he would help us get back to Cluj. The Americans kept us in the embassy for about 40 hours before quietly taking us to the train station, where they put us on a train to Cluj.

When we arrived back home we told our families what had happened. They couldn't believe it, but my brother-in-law recounted the tale from his perspective. Together, we rejoiced for the first time since the day we had applied for the passports. I remember that we could not talk about it in the house because the house was bugged. We didn't know how many days it would take before General Ioana issued the passports, but we knew we were going to get to leave and began to prepare ourselves for the departure.

It didn't take long. A few days later, the police called and told us our passports had been issued, and to come pick them up. We did, and just like that, the local Communist thugs came with their list. We gave them all our keys and left for America.

Believe it or not, it was as sudden as that. One day, we were Romanians waiting for our opportunity to leave. The next, we were off to America. Our nightmare was over, our life in Romania was behind us and our new life in America was about to begin.

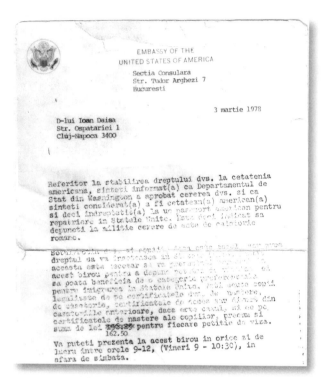

EMBASSY OF THE
UNITED STATES OF AMERICA

Sectia Consulara
Str. Tudor Arghezi 7
Bucuresti

3 martie 1978

D-lui Ioan Daisa
Str. Ospatariei 1
Cluj-Napoca 3400

Referitor la stabilirea dreptului dvs. la cetatenia
americana, sinteti informat(a) ca Departamentul de
Stat din Washington a aprobat cererea dvs. si ca
sinteti considerat(a) a fi cetatean(a) american(a)
si deci indreptatit(a) la un pasaport american pentru
repatriere in Statele Unite. Este deci indicat sa
depuneti la militie cerere de acte de calatorie
romane.

Sotul/sotia dvs. si copiii fara cetatenie vor avea
dreptul sa va insoteasca in si este necesar ca
aceasta este necesar si va prezentati ... la
acest birou pentru a depune pasuri... si ... ca
sa poata beneficia de o categorie preferentiala
pentru intrarea in Statele Unite. Veti aduce conti
legalizate de pe certificatele dvs. de nastere,
de casatorie, certificatele de acces sau divort din
casatoriile anterioare, daca este cazul, si de pe
certificatele de nastere ale copiilor, precum si
suma de lei 196.28 pentru fiecare petitie de viza.
162.50

Va puteti prezenta la acest birou in orice zi de
lucru intre orele 9-12, (Vineri 9 - 10:30), in
afara de simbata.

Document for approval to receive
passports from the government (1978)

Stella's Romanian passport photo (1978)

10

A friend, Mariana, drove us to the train station. We carried nothing but a few suitcases. Mariana couldn't believe we had just given away our houses, cars and other possessions so we could go to America and start all over from scratch. Many people came to the train station to see us off in spite of the fact that all of them would have their names written in the black books that the secret police carried to record information. The police mulled about the building, saying nothing, just watching and writing.

Mariana hugged each of us goodbye, then pulled me aside while the rest of my family said their goodbyes to the others.

"How can you leave all this behind?" she asked.

I smiled. "Mariana," I said. "It's easier than you think."

"But why, Stella?" she pressed. "Why do you have to leave? Why go through all this trouble when you already live like the Americans."

She waved a hand toward my family, who were standing about 20 feet or so away from us and continuing to say their goodbyes.

"All of you," she said. "You and John; your parents; your sister and brother-in-law; what do you really have to gain by doing this?"

I shook my head and tried to explain. "More than you can imagine, Mariana. This isn't about our houses. It's not about our cars. And it's not about all the nice things we own."

"I don't understand, then. What is this about?"

"It's about our freedom, Mariana. We may look like we live like Americans, but we don't. We're not free here." I tilted my head toward two secret police busy watching our group. "Look over there," I said. "Does that look like freedom?"

Mariana stole a glance then looked back at me, disbelief still in her eyes. "So what, Stella?" she said. "If you do what they say, they leave you alone. You bring the trouble on yourself."

"No," I said. "You still don't understand."

She sighed. "But Stella, how can you not even look back and have tears in your eyes?"

I didn't reply. I just smiled at her. And then she laughed, "I think maybe you lost your mind."

I hugged my friend one last time. "Be happy for me, Mariana. I am going to be free in America. We are really going to be free. Watch my parents for me until they leave to join us."

"I'll do that," she said. "You have my word."

Mariana and I joined the others. And that's when I made all of them, our friends and relatives, a promise of my own: When I was settled in America, I would bring them over to join us.

Over the past 20 years, I've kept my word, sponsoring not just Mariana but many other friends and family in their efforts to come live in America. I sent the sponsoring papers they needed and provided the initial room and board when they arrived in America. It's been a blessing to do so, and truly the right thing to do considering how blessed my life has been.

11

When we arrived in New York City, a song was playing over the speakers on the airplane. My English was lacking but I was able to understand the words "Good morning, America, how are you?" in the song. In my broken English I asked a fellow passenger what the rest of the words were. There is no better music than American music.

They tried to explain. As I began to understand, I started to cry. I couldn't explain it at the time, but somehow I felt like I had just come home from a long journey. That song, Arlo Guthrie's "City of New Orleans," was welcoming me home. From that moment on, "City of New Orleans" became my song. To this day, every time I hear it I smile and let the tears roll down my face.

The airport in Romania was a mouse compared with the elephant that was JFK. We were overwhelmed by the airport's size, how organized and clean it was and how polite the customs employees were. Everybody was so nice. They smiled and said, "I'm sorry" if they accidentally brushed up against you or touched you.

Customs and immigration agents welcomed us. They took our pictures and gave us alien cards. We collected our luggage and began to look for Aurelia, who was supposed to be there to meet us in New York, bring us money and take us back to Cleveland with her. We had written her in advance to tell her the time of arrival and thought we'd found a way to get the letter out of Romania.

But when no one was waiting for us in the concourse, we started to get a little concerned.

A few more minutes passed and still no Aurelia.

"What now, Stella?" my sister said with a touch of frustration in her voice.

"Don't worry," I replied. "She'll be here. She'll be here."

"What if she's not?"

"Don't worry," I repeated. "She wouldn't just leave us here. Maybe she's running late."

I spied a bank of chairs across the concourse with enough empty seats for our entire group.

"Follow me," I said, then led the group toward the bank of chairs. "Let's sit down and wait. I'm sure she'll be here in a little while."

We set down our bags, sat, and waited.

Twenty minutes later, my sister's concern became shock and it spread throughout our entire group. Here we were in the middle of that huge airport with no money, exhausted from our travels and with no itinerary. None of us spoke English and we really had no idea what we would do next. It wasn't a good situation. Our naiveté had gotten the better of us. We later learned the secret police had confiscated all our mail to America, not just the final letter. At the time, we didn't know.

For almost an hour we sat in that bank of chairs paralyzed with fear, staring at each other. We were hungry, thirsty, and the children were crying, "We want Pepsi." But we did not have a penny to buy even one drink to share. It was funny that the men in the family didn't take over. Instead, they kept looking to me. For a long while, no one other than the children spoke.

Finally, my brother-in-law asked, "Now what are you going to do, Stella?"

"Don't worry," I said again, trying to reassure him, as well as the entire group. "She'll be here." But as I spoke I could hear the lack of conviction in my voice. I didn't believe what I was saying. Surely Aurelia would have been here by now if she was coming. I began to wonder if, indeed, the secret police had been able to determine the letter we sent was from us and confiscate it in a final insult on our way to freedom.

Dee Dee climbed off my husband's lap and walked over to me. She was crying. Her long brown hair was in need of a good wash and she had this look on her face that reminded me of the poor people wandering the streets of the smaller Romanian villages who had given up all their hope. She held tightly onto her favorite doll and leaned against my legs.

"Mom, I'm scared," she said.

I leaned down, took her in my arms and gave her a little squeeze. "There's nothing to worry about, sweetie," I said. "Everything will be all right; just a little while longer now."

"Where are we going to go, mom? What are we going to eat? Where are we going to sleep?"

I didn't have an answer, and when I looked up I noticed that everyone in the group's attention was on me, waiting to hear what platitudes I spouted next. I looked at their faces, one at a time, and realized I needed to come up with a plan to get out of this mess.

"We'll figure something out," I finally said.

I gazed down at Dee Dee and my eyes fell on her doll. And then I remembered. How stupid I had been.

"Give me your doll for a moment, sweetie," I said.

Dee Dee gave a puzzled look. She looked at her doll, then back to me. "Why, mom?"

"Listen close, sweetie," I said. "Did the bad men at the airport take your doll away from you at all?"

She shook her head. "No, mommy, they didn't."

"Good," I muttered. "Good. Sweetie, let me see your doll, please."

She handed it to me and I began to turn it around in my hands.

"What are you doing?" my husband asked.

"Looking for something."

I found the seam in the doll's leg where it connected to the rest of the body and began to work it back and forth until it popped out.

Days earlier, before we left Romania, I had written the phone number of childhood friends, Nuti and Zoli Zigmond, on a small piece of paper. Dee Dee's doll was made of plastic and the legs came off. I had removed one of the doll's legs, rolled up the piece of paper and hidden it inside the doll's leg.

"Mom!" Dee Dee exclaimed. "You broke it."

I chuckled as I turned the leg over and tapped on the end until I saw a corner of white.

"No, dear," I said. "It's fine."

I took hold of the edge of paper and tugged on it gently until it came all the way out of the doll's leg. I unrolled the paper and took a long look at it to make sure it had what I needed, then snapped the leg back onto the doll and handed it to Dee Dee.

"Thank you, sweetie," I said, then held up the paper and showed it to my sister, brother-in-law and Lelu.

"Here is our next move," I said. "Nuti and Zoli's phone number. We'll call them and ask them for help."

Everyone appeared to be relieved, but we still didn't have any money to make the call.

In 1979, it cost a dime to use the pay phone. "Stay here," I said to no one in particular and stood up. I looked around the concourse until I saw an older lady who looked like she might have been eastern European.

I stepped in front of her, and in Romanian said, "Excuse me. I need some help."

She gave me a questioning look and said something I couldn't understand in what I assumed was English because I didn't recognize the dialect.

I put up a finger and then gestured with both my hands as if I was talking on the phone.

She nodded.

Then I held my palms up, shook my head, touched hips where pockets would have been and shook my head again.

The woman smiled and nodded again. She reached into her purse, pulled out a dime and handed it to me.

I smiled and nodded. Then I looked around, looked back at her and shrugged.

She nodded again and gestured for me to follow her.

The woman led me over to a pay phone and put her hand out. I handed her the dime. She took the receiver off the cradle, put the dime into the pay phone and handed me the receiver. She pointed to the number pad and I nodded. Then I punched in Nuti's phone number, gave the old woman a hug and put the receiver to my ear.

After three rings, Nuti answered the phone. "Hello?" she said in perfect Romanian. When I heard my native tongue on the other end of the phone I almost started crying. Instead I quickly said, "Nuti, it's Stella. I need your help."

I spent about three or four minutes explaining all that had happened over the past few days, including the past couple hours, before Nuti said she would give us money to pay for a taxi to get to her apartment in Queens.

"I'll buy you all plane tickets that will get you to Cleveland," she said.

"God bless you," I said. "So how do we get to your apartment?"

Nuti gave me directions. I found a pencil nub by the phone and wrote them down on the back of the scrap of paper with her phone number. She also explained how to flag down a taxi from the airport curb. I thanked her and told her we'd be there soon.

Then I went back over to where my family was sitting and told them what was happening. They couldn't have been happier.

"I told you not to worry," I said. "Let's go."

We went outside, flagged down a taxi and I handed the driver Nuti's address in Queens. The man said a few things I didn't understand. I nodded as if I did and smiled a big smile. He said something else then looked at me and shook his head.

As we drove I stared out the window. I watched the cars and the people. I looked up at the sky and thought, "The sky is so much closer to us." Whether it was true or not didn't matter. I looked back at the people we passed. Many of them were smiling. This was a contrast with what we had left in Communist Romania. There, people didn't smile. Ever. The whole thing, the spirit, the atmosphere, the people, the sky, the air, it's hard to explain, but I just felt so good that I was here. I didn't care that we didn't have any money. I didn't care that I couldn't speak English. None of it mattered.

We were finally in America. My sweet, sweet home. America. Being surrounded by beautiful scenery was intoxicating. Breathing American air, seeing American people, having our feet on American soil. This is what it feels like to have all your prayers answered. This is what victory feels like. Romania is an old country. The streets are gray. Every shade of gray imaginable. Arriving in America was like someone had turned everything into color. The bright billboards, the yellow taxis, the people all dressed so nicely and wearing bright happy faces. Kindness shined on everything. It looked and felt like heaven on Earth.

I began to cry again. For several minutes I cried tears of happiness; happiness that we had made it and were going to start a new life.

When we finally arrived at Nuti's apartment, she was standing on the curb waiting to meet us. She paid the taxi driver and helped us unload our bags from the trunk of his car.

We exchanged hugs and her husband, Zoli, came outside to join us. The two of them helped us carry our bags upstairs into their home. We were all so happy to see each other.

Sitting together on a couch in the living room of her apartment, Nuti asked, "When do you want to leave?"

"As soon as possible," I said. "We appreciate your help, Nuti, but the last thing we want to do is become a burden for you and Zoli."

Nuti put a hand on my knee and clucked, "Stella, do not think such things."

I smiled and we just looked at each other. It felt so good to see a friendly face so far away from our old home.

"So Aurelia didn't come?" she said. "Are you sure she knew what day and time to be there?"

"We sent her a letter the day we got our passports."

Nuti leaned her head slightly to the side. "So how do you know she got the letter?"

She had a point. I shrugged. "I think maybe the secret police confiscated it."

In the kitchen, Zoli had given the children a snack and some Pepsi. He was sitting with my brother-in-law and Lelu. My sister was in the kitchen, too, but she suddenly appeared at the door to the living room with a drink in her hand.

"Thank you, Nuti," she said, then came over and sat down in a chair across from us.

I shot her a quick glance. "We were just talking about whether Aurelia ever received the letter we sent her," I said. "We'll just have to ask her when we get to Cleveland."

"That doesn't matter now," Nuti said. "Let's focus on getting you all booked on a flight to Cleveland."

She picked up the phone and dialed the airlines. After several more calls she informed us that it was too late to get a flight out of JFK that same day, but she found one that was leaving LaGuardia in the morning that had space available and booked us tickets for the entire family.

"You'll be spending the night with us," she said. "And Zoli and I are glad to have you as guests."

The next morning, they gave us money, put us in a taxi and sent us off to LaGuardia. Our tickets were waiting for us at the ticket counter. Nuti had written down all the information for us in Romanian and a second copy in English with the confirmation numbers for us to hand to the person at the ticket counter.

We expected it to be a bit of a hassle since we didn't speak English, but Nuti's written instructions turned out to work fine and we received our tickets, checked our bags and got on the plane. We arrived in Cleveland at about 2 p.m. on Monday, September 17. Nuti and Zoli had paid for everything and given us enough money to take a taxi from the Cleveland airport to Aurelia's house. We would eventually pay the two of them back later, after we started making money. God bless them and their family. We might never have been able to make that important leg of our journey without their help.

12

We hadn't thought to call Aunt Aurelia from either Nuti's apartment in New York or the airport in Cleveland. It simply hadn't crossed our minds. Despite her no show at JFK a day earlier, we still didn't know she hadn't received our letters. It sounds naïve once again, but despite thinking that perhaps the secret police had intercepted our letter, we weren't sure and still thought we were expected.

Shortly after landing at Cleveland Hopkins Airport in the late afternoon we flagged down a taxi and gave the driver the address for Aurelia's house in Fairview Park, a west side suburb of Cleveland.

Suburban Cleveland was strikingly different from the urban New York City we had just left, and that was yet another world compared to what we were used to in Cluj, Romania. The streets of Cleveland were lined with trees. The properties were large. The lawns were so green and beautiful that it was hard to believe that these were people's homes. It was mid-September and summer was in its final days. Signs of fall were already beginning to show with the myriad colors that accompanied it.

The six of us sat in the taxi in silence and sheer amazement, just looking out the windows and taking in the surroundings. All around, we gazed upon the green grass and beautiful landscaping. I could hardly believe the contrast between this and home. In Romania, there wasn't any greenery around the houses. Just cement. We didn't use lawnmowers to cut lawns; just in the fields. The tranquility and beauty of these residential streets was beyond amazing.

When we finally reached the address in Fairview Park that I'd given the driver our awe continued. The driver must have thought we were a bit batty because we just sat there in his taxi for a few more moments and stared at Aurelia's house.

Until our drive through the suburbs that day we had never seen an American house before. And here we were idling in front of one that belonged to someone in our family. It was truly a shocking sight.

None of us could accept that one lady could live by herself in a house so large. In Romania, a family of 10 lived in one little house, much, much smaller than this one.

We got out of the cab, took our bags, paid the driver, and walked into her yard. We must have looked like quite a sight to the neighbors, the group of us mulling around Aurelia's yard like tourists. The yard was meticulously manicured. We looked inside her garage, which by itself would have been an entire house in Romania, and saw her large car, a powder blue Lincoln Mark IV, parked inside.

The six of us carried our bags to the front stoop and anxiously rang the bell. A moment later, the door opened and there stood Aurelia. She stepped back and sized up the motley collection of people standing on her porch. She stared at us for a moment with this look of surprise on her face. And then, just as quickly as it had appeared, it melted away into a smile.

"Oh, my gosh," she said. "I never thought I'd see you again."

I stepped forward.

"Matusa," I said. "We are finally here."

"But how?" she said.

"They let us leave," I said. "Didn't you get our letters?"

Her smile never left her face but her eyes gave off a puzzled expression. "Letters?" she said. "I never received any letters."

God bless her heart, Matusa was very welcoming. Even though she wasn't expecting us she treated our group as though we were arriving as part of a planned vacation. She hugged and kissed each of us.

"Never mind any of that now," she said. "Let's get you inside and settled."

She looked at the children and then let her gaze sweep over the rest of us. "Who wants something to eat?"

Matusa brought us inside. Her house was the biggest thing we'd even seen up until that point of our lives that didn't belong to the government. It had four bedrooms, a finished basement, and was filled with more furniture than we could have possibly imagined. Everything seemed so huge to us. In Romania, two or three families could have lived in her house.

She directed us to put our bags in one of the bedrooms. We did. Then she led us toward a sitting room, where we spread out.

"So, what can I get you to eat or drink?" she asked. "And then I want to hear all about your journey."

We were tired, hungry and thirsty. Matusa fed us, gave us all something to drink, and we sat and talked. Matusa was so amazing. Think about it. Six of us had suddenly arrived at her door with no advance warning and she was not even bothered by it. She took it all in as though it was the most natural thing.

"You mentioned letters," Matusa finally said after everyone was settled. She sat on a well-crafted wooden chair with a plush cushion. My sister and I sat on a sofa across from her. My brother-in-law and Lelu were in the kitchen. The children were in there with the men, eating something Matusa had whipped up for them. "Tell me about these letters."

"Once the government issued us passports we sent you letters to let you know what was happening," I explained. "We sent the last one after we had booked our flight and knew when we would be arriving in New York City."

Matusa nodded. "I see," she said, then chuckled. "And by now you know I never received any of them."

I sighed. "Yes. We should have figured that out when you weren't at the airport in New York."

"So what do you think happened to all those letters?" my sister said.

"I'm sure the Communists seized them," I interjected. "They probably opened the letters, read them and thought it would be a good joke."

"I doubt it was a joke," Matusa said.

"You're right," I said. "They just wanted us to suffer."

Matusa took a sip of her iced tea and leaned back in her chair. "So Stella, tell me," she said. "Tell me all about what has happened to you since we last saw each other at your house in Cluj."

For the next two hours my sister and I described all that had happened over the past few years. Matusa sat there and just listened. Every once in a while she would interrupt and ask a question, but most of the time she just sat there, nodded, and smiled.

It was five years after we had last seen her in Romania, and here we were sitting in her home in Fairview Park, Ohio, as newly arrived immigrants as though we were old friends catching up.

Hours later, after exhaustion finally got the better of us, Matusa set us up in beds in each of the bedrooms. Sleep came easy.

The next morning, Matusa offered to take us to the grocery store so that she could buy enough food to feed our large group. All of us went.

We were mesmerized the moment we walked into the store and saw aisle after aisle of food. We couldn't believe our senses. It's difficult to explain the amazement we had. In Romania, grocery stores were typically filled with empty shelves. They were gray, very dusty, and usually had only old bread, old salami, old everything. When new merchandise was brought in, the lines were so long that the waits lasted several hours.

Here it was different. People were shopping. They were pushing carts filled with food. The word "shocking" best describes our initial impressions of the grocery store that day. We were quite literally shocked that a place existed that had so much food that people could buy.

The prettiest place in America for me was the grocery store. The American grocery store is the heart of this country. Every person has the luxury of shopping in this Eden. It doesn't matter if you are in the poorer part of town or in a suburb. The grocery store still has the riches this country has to offer. The rows of fresh fruit. The vegetables in every color of the rainbow. The meat section with carefully inspected cuts of meat by the U.S. government. The dairy section with fresh milk, butter, eggs, and every cheese imaginable. The frozen food section with every flavor of ice cream that your sweet tooth craves. The reason that every American is one of the richest people on Earth is because no matter of your socio economic status, you get to feed your family in the best conditions known to man.

Matusa bought us everything we wanted that day, including a whopping 10 pounds of bananas. There was no special thing about bananas that I can remember; we just wanted bananas. Lots of them. They were all eaten in a matter of a few days.

During those first few days, Matusa did everything she could to make us feel comfortable and at home. It couldn't have been easy for her, but she never made it seem like it was a chore. She was truly our angel, and would remain our angel until she died in October 2007.

Family group photo taken in Cleveland, Ohio. This is the first family group photo taken in America (1979)
(Front row: Dee Dee, Stella, John)

Stella, John and Dee Dee enjoy their first taste of ice cream
in America (1979)

Family picnic with sponsor Aurelia Todoran (1981)

13

Our first several days in Cleveland felt like we'd fallen into a time warp. We slept during the day and stayed awake all night. We were barely acclimated to our new surroundings before Matusa declared that we needed to become part of society.

First, she said, "the little one" [Dee Dee] needed to go to school.

"How else will she become an American if she doesn't learn English in an American school?" Matusa said.

She was right. So on the morning of our third day in Cleveland – Thursday, September 20, 1979 – the three of us went to an elementary school in Fairview Park and enrolled Dee Dee.

I remember that first day of school very well.

John and I left Dee Dee with a teacher who looked like a witch. She was very scary looking but so kind to our daughter. She wasn't really a witch at all. And looking back, what an idiot I was to let Dee Dee, only nine years old, go to school without speaking any English. That little girl didn't even know how to tell anyone that she needed to use the bathroom. It wasn't something I'm proud of, but John and I just dropped her off at school and left.

Dee Dee managed. She was self-sufficient like that. And within three months, she was doing so well that a local newspaper wrote an article about this little immigrant girl who came to America and quickly learned English and became one of the best students in her class. We were so proud of her.

The second thing Matusa told us that we needed to do was to apply for welfare so we could bring in some money.

We were back in her home, about an hour after leaving Dee Dee at school.

"What is welfare?" I asked.

"Money from the U.S. government," she explained. "The government here provides money to people who don't have any and need it."

"You mean poor people?"

"Yes."

"But we're not poor. We're just new."

Matusa laughed.

"Do you have money, Stella?"

"No."

"Then you're poor," she said. "Tomorrow, we will go to the welfare department and you'll apply for welfare assistance. They'll give you money until you find jobs."

I was leery, but agreed to go. Something about taking money from the government and doing nothing to earn it didn't seem right. We had just arrived in this country and suddenly the government was going to give us money without us working for it.

The next morning, we woke and dressed elegantly in our best clothes like we were heading to church. The men wore suits and ties. My sister and I dressed up in the nicest clothes we brought.

We were standing in the kitchen when Matusa came downstairs and saw us. She burst out laughing.

"What's all this?" she said.

"We're dressed to meet with the government," I explained.

"You can't go like this. They'll see you dressed so nice and refuse to give you even a penny."

"I don't understand," I said. "Why would how we dress matter to the government?"

"They won't believe you," she said.

"But this is who we are," I said. "If they think we deserve the help, they'll give it to us. Right?"

Matusa waved her arms in defeat.

"Fine. Fine. Fine. Let's go," she said, then led our group to her car and drove us to the welfare department.

We arrived and found one of the saddest looking places I'd ever seen in my life. It was gray and cold and people who looked much needier than we were stood in line with a combination of blank and sad expressions on their faces.

"Let's go," I said. "We shouldn't be here."

"Just get in line," Matusa said. "You need to do this."

We did.

For three hours we stood in line.

Finally, I turned to Matusa and said, "We shouldn't be here. We just got to this country and we haven't done anything yet to deserve any help."

I pointed at different people in the room. "Look at these people. They deserve help. We don't have any right to ask the government to pay us money to be in their country."

I looked at my family. "Let's leave, OK?" I said. "We don't need to do this. If this is what we will have to do to survive in America we might as well just go back to Romania."

"But Stella," my sister said. "What will we do for money?"

"We'll get jobs," I said. "We'll find work and make money and earn our way."

"Is that what you really want, Stella?" Matusa interrupted.

I looked into her eyes, resolute. "Yes."

"Then let's leave," Matusa said. "I'll help you find jobs instead."

And so we left the welfare department office without applying for any help.

Looking back today and knowing what hardships we would endure during the weeks and months that followed that decision, we probably should have stayed in the office long enough to have spoken with someone about our desire to find jobs. I know now that they would have told us we needed to learn English and explained how to apply for free tuition assistance for English as a second language school. But we never learned that was an option.

So picture this: The country was right at the end of the Jimmy Carter era. The economy was terrible. Jobs were in short supply. We spent the next two days seeking employment but couldn't even find a job cleaning bathrooms.

Finally, on Sunday, Matusa took us to her church.

"Someone there will help you find jobs," she explained. "They are good people. They'll help."

Again, we packed into her car and together drove off, this time to Buna Vestire Church, a Romanian church in Rocky River.

Matusa brought us inside and made introductions to the priest and numerous members of the congregation. Everybody was so nice; they accepted us into their congregation immediately. The priest even invited us to lunch at his house. We eventually became members of Buna Vestire, something that continues to this day. When my current husband, Michael, and I were married, our ceremony was held at Buna Vestire.

The inside of the church was so bright and lively that I was shocked by the sight. Romanian churches, as beautiful as they had been on the outside, were very gloomy and so serious on the inside. But here it was different. People were happy. The place was well lit and welcoming. The service was uplifting.

After services, people came up to us and hugged us and shook our hands and told us how happy they were that we were there. It was almost surreal. They gave us food. They gave us pastries. They gave us coffee. They gave us Pepsi. The children were ecstatic.

And then we went to the priest's house for lunch and he was the nicest man we'd met. He asked us to tell him about ourselves. He asked what skills we had and what trades we knew how to do. In turn, each of us explained what we were good at and the priest offered to help all of us find jobs.

We left so optimistic and sure of our decision to forgo welfare and jump right into the job market. Unfortunately, the priest wasn't able to come through immediately, and for several more days we looked for jobs without success.

Finally, after making dozens of phone calls, Matusa spoke with a friend of hers named Clara. Clara worked at Stouffer's Westgate Restaurant in Fairview Park, right on the border of Rocky River and Fairview Park. Clara said they were looking for help in the kitchen and offered to get me a job.

Matusa failed to tell Clara – or the people that hired me – that not only didn't I speak English; I wasn't very good in the kitchen either. In Romania, I had been a princess. Even when we didn't have much, I didn't have to do physical labor. My parents had worked the Communist system to rebuild their lives to the point where we had maids in our house. I never had to cook or clean in the kitchen. So here I was on my first day of work, not knowing what to do and put in charge of baking the breakfast pastries.

I survived the first two days without any major incidents. I put the pastries in the oven, as they showed me, and when they were done took them out and put them on plates. But on the third day, I met a lady who spoke Hungarian. She was also working in the kitchen. I was so elated to meet somebody who spoke a language I knew that I became distracted.

While we spoke to each other I put the pastries in the oven and ended up paying more attention to my conversation with her than the pastries. Suddenly, smoke started pouring out of the oven. By the time I got it opened and pulled out the trays, all the pastries were ruined.

The supervisor saw the black smoke and rushed in.

"What happened?" he yelled.

In broken English I tried to explain it was an accident. But others in the kitchen told him I was too busy talking with my new friend than paying attention to the pastries. He fired me on the spot.

That was a devastating and embarrassing moment. Matusa had finally found me a job and I'd lost it through my own stupidity. I went home with my head hung low and explained to Lelu and Matusa what had happened.

"I'm so sorry," I cried. "I was just so excited to be able to talk to somebody outside the house that I didn't pay attention."

Matusa put a hand on my shoulder and told me to sit down.

"Listen to me carefully," she said. "It's OK. You came here to the best place on Earth. These Americans will let you become whatever you want to become. You made a mistake. It happens. But these are very nice people. They accept immigrants. They understand mistakes. You'll learn from this one and do better next time. Stella, it is up to you how you want to succeed. Do you understand me?"

The Stouffer's restaurant job fiasco was quite a lesson in humility for me. It was so hard to be defeated. I tried so hard, and messed up so badly. In an instant, a blessing turned into a brick wall. When I came home and had to tell my family that I was fired, well, it was really hard. I after all, was the super woman who always defied the odds against me. I felt sorry for myself… briefly.

I wiped the tears from my eyes and felt my confidence return. I got my wits about me and as always started looking at the bigger picture. I changed my mind on how I looked at the outcome. It's not what happens to you that matters, it's how you react to it that determines who you are. So I put the incident behind me and got back onto the proverbial horse. I knew that God ended my career as a baker because he had other things in store for me. My job hunt began again.

"Yes," I said. "I do. And I'll do better next time."

"Good," she said. "I'll take you back to the church and we'll see if the priest has found anything."

He had.

"There is a clothing manufacturer called Joseph and Feiss," he explained. We were sitting in his office at the church with Matusa. "They have a factory on West 53rd where a job is waiting for you. It's hard work but good work."

"Oh thank you, thank you," I said.

"I don't know all the details but it is what they call clothing piece work. You'll be using a sewing machine to put together pieces of clothes. The hiring manager there said they will teach you how to do the work and that if you know how to use a sewing machine you'll do just fine."

I had never done physical work before but knew how to use a sewing machine.

"I can do this," I assured him. "And I'll do a good job at it; I won't let you down. Thank you!"

The job turned out to be much harder than I could have expected. I would spend between eight and 10 hours each day sitting at a sewing machine doing piece work. You weren't allowed to get up and wander around. I'm the type of person who has trouble sitting in one place for extended periods of time, but I managed.

Within two weeks, Matusa helped us find an apartment that the three of us could move into. We were so excited. I had a job. We had our own apartment. We were on our way.

But the day I received my first pay from Joseph and Feiss I experienced another culture shock. The manager came around and handed me an envelope. I quickly opened it and instead of cash found a piece of paper. I didn't know what this was and thought I'd done something wrong and was being written up instead of getting paid.

At the end of my shift I went home and called Matusa.

"I didn't get paid," I cried. "They didn't give me any money. They gave me a slip of paper and I'm in trouble again and I don't know what I'm going to do."

"Calm down, Stella," she said. "What is this piece of paper?"

"It says my name on it and a number – $96," I explained. "But I don't understand anything else on it."

Matusa broke into a laugh.

"This isn't funny," I cried. "What am I going to do, Matusa? I can't get fired from two jobs; I'll never find another. How are we going to eat? How are we going to pay rent?"

"Calm down," she repeated. "Just calm down. Everything is fine. You're not in any trouble."

"I'm not?"

"No. You're not. They gave you a check."

"A what?"

"A check. You have to take it to the bank and give it to a teller. She'll give you money in exchange for the check."

"Well why didn't they just give me the cash instead?"

"Because that's not how it works here."

"Go down to a bank, get in line, and give the teller your check," Matusa said. "She'll know what to do with it and you'll get cash."

"OK," I said. "But what if she doesn't?"

"She will. If you have any problems, just call me and I'll come down and help."

I hung up and for several minutes stared at the check. It seemed a bit too complicated for something as easy as getting paid, but what choice did I have? I took the check and walked to the nearest bank. I got in line and waited. When I reached the teller I handed her the check and smiled my best smile.

She looked at me then looked at the check, then back at me and said, "No."

"No?" I repeated.

"No," she said, and handed me back my check. "You don't have an account here."

I stood there for another moment in shock, wanting to yell and scream and cry. But I didn't do any of those things. Instead, I straightened myself up, walked out of the bank, went home, and called Matusa again.

"They didn't want my check," I said. "The woman just handed it back and said, 'no.'"

"Did you open an account?"

"Did I what?"

"Never mind," Matusa said. "I'm on my way. I'll be there in a little while."

Matusa picked me up and took me back down to the bank, which was also the bank where she had an account. She helped me open an account and vouched for me. They cashed my paycheck and we left.

It was another step toward my Americanization, but the joy was short-lived. Within a few weeks we came to a terrible realization – not only couldn't we afford the apartment we were living in but it also wasn't large enough for my parents to live with us once I brought them over from Romania.

We found a small, run-down house on the West Side of Cleveland, near the railroad tracks, that was within our means. My sister and brother-in-law, who had also found jobs, moved with their son into a small, summer house in Fairview Park that didn't have heat. A few months later, when fall turned to winter, they had only an electric heater to keep them warm. How they ever survived that first winter in that house I'll never know.

The house that John, Dee Dee and I moved into was terrible and in a very poor neighborhood. Cockroaches were everywhere. There was a crack in the wall of one of the upstairs bedrooms that was so large that you could see outside through it. The house was in such poor condition that every time a train went by the house would shake and shiver so violently that we thought it was going to fall apart with us in it. Our neighbors were, for the most part, scary. They were the type of people that we wanted nothing to do with and stayed away from while we lived there.

We barely had enough money for food and rent, so Dee Dee didn't have any toys. One afternoon, the two of us were sitting at our meager kitchen table. She was playing with the doll she'd brought with her from Romania and looked up.

"Mom," she said. "When are we going to arrive in America?"

I was stunned. It was a heart-wrenching question, but I understood what she was talking about. When we were in Romania, we'd seen a TV show called "Dallas." The people all lived in beautiful houses with swimming pools. They wore fancy clothes and drove expensive cars. And here we were, living in squalor in a foreign land.

"Sweetheart," I said, taking Dee Dee's hand in mind. "This is America. We have to see another side of America before we get to see the side of it we saw on TV. We will get there, honey. Just be patient with me."

"OK, mom," she said.

There was no doubt about it. This was a drastic change from our little piece of heaven in Romania. The material possessions and nice house we owned were long gone. This rundown home with cracks in the walls and with a train in the back of the house was our heaven now. Everybody in the family was upset with me because I made them come to America.

But this was our reality now. We were here and couldn't go back. I told everyone that our situation was only temporary. I assured them that if we refused to feel depressed, get down on ourselves or squabble about the situation that we could manage. Day after day, I told John, my sister and brother-in-law that our misery was temporary and that all we had to do was keep working hard and believe in ourselves. It was only a matter of time before our fortunes changed.

Dee Dee and grandfather Ioan Daisa
on Dee Dee's first day of school (1980)

Stella's first apartment (1980)

Stella and Dee Dee at Niagara Falls
during their first American vacation (1980)

Stella: Happy in America (1980)

Stella and her parents in America (1980)

Franklin Elementary
529-4221

Carolyn Ezzo

Education In Action

LAVINIA LEARNS ENGLISH

Lavinia Moga, presently a fifth grade student at Franklin, came to the United States from Romania only one year ago when she was nine. When she arrived in America, Lavinia knew just "yes" and "no" in English. She came to Franklin after short stays in two other schools where she had added little to her English vocabulary.

At Franklin Lavinia made several visits a week to the learning resource center where she was helped by the learning center personnel. She pronounced the names of objects pictured on flash cards, watched filmstrips and listened to tapes about numbers, and read books while listening to tapes of their contents. Whenever Lavinia was corrected she always said, "Yes, yes," and progressed amazingly fast.

In the classroom last year, Peg Cachat, Lavinia's teacher, prepared special assignments for Lavinia throughout the year. Lavinia remembered that her teacher had helped her especially with math and spelling, and she said, "Mrs. Cachat helped me so much. I learned lots of things from her."

It was, however, Lavinia's friends who helped her the most to learn English. She stated that the other children were very friendly and patient as they explained the meanings of any words they thought she might not understand. Lavinia picked up some English from watching television, but she credits her friends with doing a great job of teaching her our language.

Lavinia still speaks Romanian at home, but she believes she reached the point of being able to understand all that was going on around her by the end of school last spring. She now is doing the same school work as the other fifth graders and says, "It's getting easier and easier."

Student Activities

ELECTION

Election! Ballot! Campaign! Vote! Platform! Register! Speeches! President! Candidate! An election year spelling list? Yes! However, this list also tells of the activities which occur in our annual Franklin School Student Council election each Election Day. Prospective officers will campaign, campaign managers will direct poster and platform activities, students will register and vote by secret ballot, and we'll know our winning candidate by 2:30 p.m. on November 4. Student council Advisor, Jean Hines, organizes staff and students in creating an exciting practical learning activity for our future citizens.

SAFETY PATROL

Tina Fitzpatrick, Room 203, attended Safety Patrol Camp this summer to learn her responsibilities as Captain of Franklin's Safety Patrol. She performs her duties in a most conscientious manner and is seen checking her "force" daily. We are very grateful for the services provided by these students: Tina Fitzpatrick, Captain; David Bass, Jimmy Bouzis, Gina Bruno, Tammy Cunningham, DeeDee Doyle, Mike Ferguson, Carolyn Flemming, Laurie Guzay, Ted Kiernozek, Tom Long, Peter Menyhart, Jim Morana, Steve Mrozinski, Bill Neumann, Donna Pastirik, Baird Radford, Brendan Ryan, Jenny Schopf, Jim Shipman, John Skourlis, Korey Stearns, Beth Toth, Beth Watts, Alice Wondrak and Julie Zickes.

Student Achievement

FIRE CAPTAINS

Congratulations to Franklin Honorary Fire Captains Jenny Schopf and Mike Upton for their winning fire prevention essays. Jenny was one of the three Honorary Assistant Fire Chiefs for the city.

News article about Dee Dee learning English

14

I've always been a leader rather than a follower. When I put my mind to it I'm able to get whatever I want. It's always been like that. That is a special trait that's helped me work my way out of many difficult situations. I'm not sure why, but nobody wants to say no to me. They just acquiesce.

When I was five, I was de facto leader of the neighborhood children. Even though I was one of the youngest, I'd organize the group and usually get us into all sorts of trouble. They would listen to me, and I would delegate jobs during playtime – you're the father, you're the brother, you're the mailman. They'd do what I told them. I was the big boss, even as a little girl.

Once, we found a construction site with a large pile of sand. It wasn't your ordinary pile of sand; it was tall and wide, almost as large as a sand dune. The area was abandoned that day; no workers were on the job and no one was guarding the site, so we decided it would be a good place to play.

All of us just stood there staring at the massive pile of sand until I clapped my hands and said, "OK, we are going to determine which of us is the most courageous by climbing to the top of the sand pile and leaping off."

Bursts of "Yes!," "Sounds good!" and "OK" rustled through the group. Of course, I had to go first. It didn't matter that I was so young; I had to be considered the most courageous.

I climbed up onto the edge of the pile and began inching my way toward the top. It wasn't easy, but I climbed and climbed until I reached it. Then I looked down. All the other children were shouting, clapping, laughing, and yelling. They looked like ants from my perch atop the pile.

"Jump, Stella, jump!" they called.

I spread my arms and leapt, floated through the air and then landed with a sickening thud.

My face hit the ground first and I heard the sound of teeth cracking on impact. Then I bounced onto my head, banging it hard against the ground and some of the construction waste that was all around. I felt something warm and wet in my hair then saw a thin stream of blood cross my left eye.

I was a bit woozy but I managed to pull myself to my feet and throw my arms into the air. Triumph! I was the best. I was the most courageous. I'd proven it.

"I think you should go home," one of my friends said. "You don't look so good, Stella."

"I'm fine," I assured her. "Just a few scratches." But I did go home, and when I got there my mother took one look at my battered and bruised body, the puncture wound on my head that was still oozing blood and asked, "What did you do now, Stella?"

"Proved I was the best," I said.

My mother just shook her head in disbelief. "Well, we need to get you to the hospital now."

And she did. The doctors fixed the wounds, stopped the bleeding, and patched me up. I still have a scar on my forehead to this day as a reminder of my bravado in that construction yard and that the next time I should look before I leap.

Another time, on a cold November afternoon, I was at home playing with my cousins, Daniela, Titi and Voica. My mother had gone out with her sister and left the group of us there. I decided that we should have a pool party.

Mind you, we didn't have a pool, but we did have a big container on the farm from which the cows would drink water. So we went into the yard and filled the container and all of us climbed into it and had a party.

My mother and Anuta came home, found us there and weren't very happy. It was, after all, November, a very cold day, and there we all were in the pool without our clothes on. Needless to say, we all got sick. I even got pneumonia and, according to my mother, almost died. But that didn't matter; it was all about me telling everybody what to do. I still do it today, although now I think about consequences.

This trait, being able to take charge and be decisive, has been very useful throughout my life. It's helped me every time I faced adversity or a challenge.

When I was working in the factory at Joseph and Feiss, I wasn't used to the hard factory work. Working hard wasn't the problem; it was staying in my chair for so many hours at a time, day after day, without being able to leave or switch to a different task.

I began to feel ill, but I wasn't sure what was happening. We didn't have enough money for me to go to the doctor, and most likely, I wouldn't have gone even if there was money. Over the course of a few weeks, I began to feel weaker and weaker, I got thinner and thinner, until one day, I fainted at my sewing machine.

The supervisors tried to revive me, but they couldn't and called an ambulance, which rushed me to a hospital. It turned out that I had overworked myself and neglected my personal health. I got better, but it was after that episode that I realized I just couldn't go on living like this. I needed a change. And in order to facilitate change, I needed to learn English.

Passion in life doesn't start when you reach your goals. Passion starts as an idea that sparks a goal. A goal is something that you work towards in spite of your current circumstances. I was not that job in the factory. I was not that rundown apartment by the railroad tracks. I was a woman of substance and great courage. And I knew that for sure. So now what?

America has many standards of living. As an immigrant, I could pick any standard I chose according to the amount of common sense and work ethic. And I knew I had plenty of both. First, I said to myself, "Don't worry. The best part is that you are not stuck in your current lifestyle. This is just a stepping stone to the life you are about to start earning."

And that's what I did. I put the passion back into my spirit and made a plan. Learning English was the very first step and I could not put it off any longer. I began to absorb the language like a sponge. I tried to not only speak English but think in English, too. I asked Dee Dee to only speak to me in English.

I didn't understand a lot in the beginning, she would speak half English and half Romanian. I would eat, breathe, and drink English. It became my number one goal in the long list I made to get my family to the America I wanted, not the run down America that was our current home.

Once I tapped into my strength again, my disposition changed and I began to feel better and act better. Things began to flow again. And, as fate always delivers when you finally climb or go around whatever obstacle gets in your way, new doors opened.

At that time we were living in that run-down house by the railroad tracks. One of our neighbors was a single mother whose name to this day I can't remember. But she had a daughter named Molly, and Molly became an important part of our lives.

Molly was around the same age as Dee Dee. Her mother worked many hours a week to make ends meet that we began to take care of Molly while her mother was at work. I would sit and play with the two girls and listen to them talk. By doing this, Molly helped teach me English.

I read children's books because they were so easy to understand and the pictures were very explicit. Molly sat with me and helped me read. I learned English from Molly and those little books. I could have gone to school for English, returned to the welfare office and enrolled in one of their programs, but I didn't. I chose the hardest way to learn things. That was my style back then. It may not have been the smartest path, but it was, well, Stella's way.

For eight months I worked at the factory, saving money and learning English from Molly, practicing it every chance I had. One of my biggest accomplishments came when I learned that the verb "to get" could replace many other words I was not familiar with. I used it in phrases like "I'm going to get there" or "I got this." That verb became gold as part of my vocabulary.

One day, I was bathing the two girls in the bathtub and they were giggling and talking to each other in English, and without thinking about it, I was participating in the conversation. Suddenly, I realized that I understood what they were talking about. That was a big revelation in my life. I realized I could communicate in English, and it was due, in large part, to that wonderful little girl, Molly.

When I felt I understood English well enough to get a better job than the one at Joseph & Feiss I made an appointment with the Nationality Service Center. I had heard from some of the other immigrants I'd met at Joseph and Feiss that there was a woman named Lucretia Stoica at the NSC, and if you were able to impress her with your personality and skills she would help you get a good job.

I arrived at Ms. Stoica's office. It was very impressive. She welcomed me in and I sat down. She began to speak to me in English.

"Good morning, Stella," she said. "How are your language skills coming?"

I nodded.

"Do you think you're ready to work somewhere where they only speak English?" she asked.

I nodded again.

"Are you capable of communicating with anyone and everyone?"

I nodded and smiled.

Ms. Stoica could have talked to me in any language, but she chose English. I went there with the intent to show her my new English skills, but I had thought we'd spend most of the conversation in Romanian and then

I'd just show her how well I was doing with my English.

She spoke quickly and used many big words I hadn't yet learned. It wasn't very long into the conversation before I started to lose my ability to follow her. After that, I realized I no longer understood anything she was saying.

She suddenly switched to Romanian. "You don't understand me, do you?"

"No," I sheepishly replied.

"I had to speak with you in English only to see how much you understood."

"Apparently, it's not as much as I thought."

She smiled. "Stella, if you want to do well in this country you will need to do better. You have to understand more English than you do before I can find you a better job."

"No," I pled. "I can do this. I'm working very hard on it. If you find me a better job, I'll keep practicing and do better."

"I'm sorry. I can't do that."

But I was adamant. "Please," I said. "I'm not going to leave your office until I see you calling around and trying to find me a job. I can do this. I know I can."

Boy, I knew this lesson well.

Ms. Stoica stared at me. For a few long moments neither of us said a word. As with all the people who helped me before her, she saw the moxie in my spirit. She, too, wanted to help. Finally, she clapped her hands together. "OK," she said. "I will find you a job. But you cannot disappoint me. You have to learn better English. You have to keep working on your language skills. And I'm going to check up on you to make sure you do it."

I was so elated that I nearly leapt from my chair and gave her a big hug.

"I'm going to send you to a department store called Halle's to interview for a sales job," she continued. "You will really have to improve your English in order to do well there. It will not be easy."

"Thank you," I said. "I won't disappoint you. I promise."

And Ms. Stoica called Halle's and set up a job interview for me.

At Halle's, my first interview was with the sales department manager. It was at the downtown Cleveland store, and I was pleasantly surprised by how large it was and how many different things they had for sale.

But the interview was an eye-opener. It didn't take very long before I realized that there was no way I would be able to sell anything in the store because my English skills just weren't good enough. I hated to admit it, but Ms. Stoica was right.

I refused to give up, however, and went back to the Nationality Service Center. Before Ms. Stoica could tell me that she was right and I'd disappointed her, I assured her I could manage.

"If you help find me a different job in the store that doesn't require so many English skills, I can do it," I said.

Ms. Stoica took a liking to me. She told me that once I learned English I would become very successful.

"America was built on fierce spirits like yours, Stella," she said. "I'll see what I can do."

And so Ms. Stoica found an opening in the administrative offices, and sent me back out to Halle's. This time, I prepared differently for the interview. I taught myself a prepared speech in the clearest English I could muster, as well as a stock answer to use when I had trouble understanding the interviewer: "I'll manage, please give me a chance."

That was my phrase.

This interview went much better than the first. The job was better suited for me because I would be in an office, working with the same people every day. And, every time the interviewer asked something I didn't completely understand, I said, "I'll manage, I'll manage. Please give me a chance?"

And she did.

I didn't know it at the time, but the only reason she hired me was that Ms. Stoica told her that I was a very determined woman who would do what it took to get the job done. Looking back, I owe Ms. Stoica a lot for getting me the chance at Halle's.

A very tall African-American woman named Leslie was put in charge of my training. I'll never forget Leslie. She was supposed to train me to work as an auditor of store transactions and teach me how to sort cards by department.

But Leslie spoke very, very fast, and I had trouble understanding what she was saying. At the same time, she barely understood me. This frustrated both of us, and after a few hours, she went to the boss and told her that she felt she was wasting her time because we couldn't understand each other.

They called me into the office together and Leslie explained her frustration. I assured both of them that I would do whatever it took to understand Leslie and learn the job and keep working on my English.

Once again, my determination and personality triumphed. I managed to keep my job, and within two and a half months, I was one of the best employees in that office.

The office was lively and fun. The people meshed well together. My co-workers and I got along. I finally felt like my plan was coming to life. We would laugh and have a good time. They also had a good laugh at my expense. They taught me bad words, though at the time I didn't realize just how bad they were. One day, the company president came by and I was using the "F" word, not knowing what it meant. He heard me and called me into the office and disciplined me like a junior high school student. I learned quickly what words were appropriate and which weren't. And my co-workers got a good giggle like children.

Around the same time, my boss started to take a liking to me. She even invited John and me to a party at her house. She told us it was "casual," but we didn't know what that meant and we dressed up like we were going to a wedding.

When we got there the other guests were dressed in jeans and shirts. They looked at us like we were crazy, but it didn't deter us. We still mingled and met lots of people there, people from all different types of backgrounds. And we began to make American friends. I couldn't have been happier.

Despite the happiness, money was still tight. That's probably an understatement. We didn't have much money at all, and this made it very hard on all of us, especially Dee Dee.

At school, all of her friends had Barbie dolls. She wanted one, too. She wanted one very badly, but I was just making enough to barely get by and I couldn't possibly afford one on our budget. So I had to improvise. One day, I stopped by a garage sale in Lakewood and found Barbie dolls for 50 cents each. That made me so happy. They were used, very used, but I bought them anyway and brought them home.

When Dee Dee went to sleep, I cleaned them as best as I could and made them more presentable. I washed their hair. I made clothes for them. I even made tags that I put on the dolls to make them look like they were new.

The next day was Saturday. When Dee Dee woke up, I gave her the dolls. She was so, so happy, and that meant a lot to me. She probably knew they weren't new but she never said anything about it. Ever.

At that time in our lives, we typically had between $25 and $30 a week for groceries. It was very hard to manage with that kind of money. One week, we had an extra $80 besides the normal $25. I'm not sure why, but we did. I wanted to use the money to do something special for Dee Dee.

"Let's go to the grocery store," I said to her. "Just the two of us. You can get whatever you want today."

The look on her face said it all. For a minute, we were like princesses and the world was ours.

We didn't own a car, so we pulled the large suitcase we'd brought with us from Romania out of the closet, wiped it down and decided we would roll it to the grocery store, fill it with the groceries and pull it home by the wheels. It was big, wide, and clumsy, but we thought we could manage.

The grocery store was about a mile from our house in Lakewood, and we made the journey while pulling the suitcase behind us. Along the way, people stared at us like we were crazy. We didn't care.

When we reached the store we walked up and down every aisle. We bought Kit Kat candy bars. We bought cake. We bought chocolate. We bought fruit and vegetables. We bought three different kinds of ice cream. Dee Dee and I had our first shopping spree, and it was quite liberating for both us. It was one of the most fun things we had done together since we'd arrived in America.

After we paid, the two of us packed everything in our big luggage and left the store. We started lugging it back to the house. About halfway home, one of the wheels broke off. Then, a second later, the bag fell apart and groceries started spilling out onto the street. I tried to stop it but it was just too late. There wasn't much either of us could do but watch it happen. We were so sad.

"What now, mom?" Dee Dee asked.

"Not to worry," I told her.

"But how will we get the groceries home?"

"You stay here, and I'll go back to the store and get some grocery bags. We'll pack up the groceries and take them home."

"But mom," she said. "How will we carry all of it home?"

"We'll make a couple trips," I said. "We'll be fine."

So I walked back to the grocery store and they gave me a handful of grocery bags. I trekked back to Dee Dee and the groceries and packed up the bags. There were too many for one trip, so we started making several trips. By the time we had gotten all the bags home all the ice cream had melted.

It didn't matter. By that point, Dee Dee and I were having too much fun. We laughed and laughed. Our disaster had become funny and we enjoyed it together. Today, it's one of our favorite memories and story that we sit around the table with her children – my grandchildren – telling over and over. Each time, the story seems funnier and we just laugh and laugh and laugh.

Life is a journey not a destination. These moments like our disheveled shopping spree at the grocery store are what make memories in a family. My daughter and I have a strong bond. That day, when I shared that extra cash with her, and we went to the grocery store, well, it's one of those small moments that was silly. It showed us a glimmer of how good things can be with just a little more income and it was enough incentive to me as the adult that life is whatever you make it. The small moments are the magic.

Time went by, and over the next several months I was able to secure jobs at Halle's for my sister and father. That was a very happy time for us. We finally worked at jobs that brought in regular paychecks. We were earning good money now and things were doing well. John even got a job in a furniture store. But he wasn't a very good salesperson and it wasn't suited to his personality. In Romania, he was a university teacher. He didn't need a salesperson's mentality back then. Rather, John was your typical intellectual – lots of knowledge and no common sense. Every day, he would come home and I would ask, "How much did you sell today?"

He would shrug.

"I didn't sell anything today because people came into the store and didn't know what they wanted to buy."

"What do you mean, John?" I would ask.

"Well, if they came in to buy a lamp, I cannot try to sell them a sofa because they don't want a sofa."

"John," I would say. "You are not a very good salesperson. The whole point of sales is to get them to buy something. You're supposed to be pushy."

But that wasn't John. He wasn't that type of person. He used to read the newspaper when customers came in to the store, and they would go to another salesperson, and that person would end up making the sale and the commission. John used to tell me about that, and I got very frustrated with him.

The two of us stayed married for 20 years despite an unhappy marriage. My parents always told me, "Stella, you cannot divorce. You have to work things out. You would be the first one in our family to divorce, so you have to work things out."

So I did. I probably also stayed married to John for so long because I always had a life without him. I had my daughter. I had my parents. And I had lots of friends. I didn't know how miserable I really was.

In August 1980, John finally realized he was never going to make it in sales, so he began searching around for other opportunities that were better suited to his personality and abilities. He really wanted to go back into teaching at a university, but he didn't have a Master's degree, and unlike in Romania, he needed one in order to get a good university teaching job.

After an extensive search, he found an intensive course at a university in Vermont that would allow him to get his Master's degree quickly. And, he found a job at Baldwin-Wallace that he could get once he had the Master's degree. That was very enticing, and very good news for all of us.

But then we found out that the course cost $10,000. We didn't even have an extra $100, much less $10,000, to pay for the course. And we didn't have any way for John to get to Vermont because we didn't own a car.

"I'm not going to go," John said. "We have no money. We have no car."

"You will go," I said. "We will get you a car. And you are going to go to Vermont and you're going to take this course, and we are going to manage our money and find a way to pay for your college and survive here."

So we took the money we had saved and bought this very large, light blue Dodge station wagon. It was as big as a house. We packed John up, gave him all the remaining money we had, and he left for Vermont to enroll in the university and take the course. And there we were, once again, with no money and no car.

We did, however, have one thing positive going for us. We had secure jobs at Halle's. And with those, we figured we'd tighten our belts and find a way to manage. Little did we know that life was about to throw us yet another curveball.

My father, sister and I arrived at Halle's one day and were met with news that the department store was closing.

"Go home," my boss said. "We're going out of business."

I couldn't believe my senses.

"That's not possible," I said. "This is a big store. Lots of people shop here every day. What do you mean you're going out of business?"

"It's true," she said. "We're closing."

"But I need the money," I said. "I have to come to work."

"Go home," she said. "It's over."

And we did.

But the next day, we came back. We were certain it was all a big mistake and that when we got the work that day, the store would be open and we'd be able to work our normal jobs.

We were wrong.

Again, we were told to go home.

"Go file for unemployment," my boss said. "That's the best thing you can do now, Stella, until you find another job."

The whole experience was very, very shocking.

15

Shortly after our arrival in Fairview Park, Aurelia took us to meet a few of her relatives who lived nearby in Westlake, an upscale suburb on the city's west side. The man of the house was a lawyer. He and his family lived in very fancy, very expensive house. When I saw it, I couldn't believe such a thing existed – a big home with all the amenities, even bigger than Matusa's.

Aurelia introduced me to them but I didn't speak English yet and they didn't speak Romanian.

"Tell them how beautiful I think their house is," I asked Aurelia.

She did. The wife said something back to Aurelia, who turned back to me.

"They say thank you, Stella, and also that they hope you do well here in America and someday are able to have your own house."

I smiled. "Tell them it will be one just like this."

Aurelia did, and they smiled as though the sentiment was cute, but I could see on their faces that they didn't take me all that seriously. But I was serious. That's how I thought back then, and still do today.

I was so happy to be in America. It was the culmination of a dream I'd held since I was a child. This country was, and is, a magic place, and our difficult situation did little to diminish either my unbridled optimism or opinion of the country. I didn't care that we lived in a very bad neighborhood. I didn't care that I didn't have money to buy groceries. I didn't care that everyone was mired in misery because we appeared stuck in a rut. None of it mattered. It was still America, and deep down, I knew that this was only temporary. I didn't know how or when, but I was convinced success would come.

That didn't change the fact that after Halle's closed all of us were devastated, even me. How could such a large department store have just shut its doors like that? It was inconceivable. Suddenly, we had no jobs and no income. John was in Vermont. We didn't even have a car. Our family was hurting so we applied for and received unemployment checks, but that didn't last very long and we quickly began looking for new jobs.

My father was the first to find one, selling fruit and vegetables at a stand in the West Side Market. It wasn't as high paying a job as Halle's had been but it did pay in cash. My father was also allowed to bring home fruit and vegetables at the end of the day, so an extra benefit was providing food.

I asked my father to check with the stand owner and see if he needed more workers. He did, and soon I was hired as well.

Unlike my other jobs, this was brutally physical work that began very early in the morning. I would get up at 4 a.m. and go arrange the stand, then work for the entire day. For this, I received between $18 and $20 a day plus free fruit and vegetables. The work was demanding and much of it involved lifting large containers and boxes.

A few weeks later, with John still in Vermont, Dee Dee, my parents and I decided we needed to move out of that terrible house by the railroad tracks and found an apartment building in Lakewood with two apartments that we could afford – one for me and Dee Dee; one for my parents. The apartments were on the fifth floor and the building did not have an elevator, but it was a significant improvement over the house.

Once we moved in we set out to furnish that apartment as nicely as possible. Several friends gave us furniture, we bought a few inexpensive new things and then we found a few items on the street that we salvaged.

Dee Dee and I found a dresser on the street and the two of us dragged it up five flights of stairs. It took us a while, but we finally made it. Together, we washed it and made it look nice. Then we opened it, and a most terrible stench escaped.

It turned out that the drawers were filled with cat urine. The smell was awful. Within a few moments that smell permeated the entire apartment. Dee Dee and I realized our mistake and dragged it back down the stairs to the street. The two of us had a good laugh about that.

We bought a telephone. Getting a telephone was a big accomplishment because in Communist Romania to get a phone installed in your house took many years. If you didn't have the right connections, you might never get a phone. Just being able to order it, and then have someone appear at your apartment and set it up a few days later, well, that was unbelievable.

The apartment building was close to the center of Lakewood. We could walk to the grocery store and the library. Dee Dee started to take piano lessons near our home. We weren't making a lot of money, but things were certainly starting to get better, and we were all much, much happier.

And then I began to wake up feeling sick. At first, I thought it was nothing more than a virus or cold. But when it persisted I began to recognize the feeling as morning sickness. I wasn't sure and we didn't have health insurance to pay for a doctor's visit to confirm my thoughts. One of my friends told me that I could buy a pregnancy test that came in a tube at the pharmacy. And so I did, and learned that I was pregnant in my bathroom, alone, from a little tube. It wasn't the most exciting way to learn I was pregnant.

Despite that, emotions flooded over me – happiness, fear, and panic. I was bringing home about $120 a week from the market, which was barely enough to cover all of our expenses. The additional costs that came with a pregnancy were probably more than we could afford. I found myself at a crossroads, wondering what to do.

A few days after learning I was pregnant, I was chatting on the phone with a friend and bemoaning my condition.

"John doesn't know," I told her. "And I'm not sure I'm going to tell him."

"What are you talking about, Stella?"

"I don't have enough money for this," I said. "I can barely afford to support Dee and me. We have enough money to eat and pay the bills. There isn't much left over after that."

"But Stella," she said, "a baby is a gift from God. You can't ignore that."

"Why would God send me a gift when he hasn't given me enough money to pay for the gift?"

"You can't think like that. You have to see this as a sign."

"It doesn't matter," I said. "I think I'm going to get rid of it."

I had finally voiced what I'd been thinking for days, and hung up the phone feeling a bit guilty after saying it out loud. I knew I would still have to talk to John about the pregnancy before doing anything, but there really wasn't much choice. Was there?

I stood and began pacing around the apartment, weighing my options and pondering the dilemma when I heard the soft sounds of sobbing coming from Dee Dee's room. I poked my head inside and found her sitting on her bed with her head in her hands, crying.

I walked over, sat down beside her and put an arm around her shoulders.

"What's the matter, sweetie?" I asked.

"Mom," she said, "I need a brother or sister."

"What?"

"Mom, you can't leave me in this big place, this big country, with nobody."

"You're not alone, Dee Dee. You have me."

"No, mom," she said. "You can't just get rid of it."

Her words hit me like a cold splash of water. Could she have heard my phone conversation? She must have if she was that upset.

"Honey," I said, "If that's what you need, I'll give you a brother or sister."

And so, because of Dee Dee, I decided to have the baby.

That moment changed my life yet again. I had been thrown a negative and found a way to turn it into a positive. My entire outlook shifted. I would walk along those wonderful streets of Lakewood, full of trees and beautiful homes, singing as I strolled. True enough, I was a happy pregnant lady who looked forward to giving birth to either a son or daughter. The money problems hadn't gone away, but I started to trust again that my positive energy would bring solutions to all my problems.

I tried to pick up some extra hours in the market, but there weren't any to be had. So I decided to clean homes in my off-time, and was able to cobble together an extra $50 per week.

One of the jobs was with a family in Westlake. They were very well-off but seemed dysfunctional. The pair, a husband and wife, owned four cats that wandered all over the house, sat on all the furniture and always seemed to have dirty litter boxes. The house, itself, was always a terrible mess and had the type of appearance that screamed that neither of them cared about it.

The husband worked very hard; his wife didn't work at all. Instead, she exercised, played tennis, went out for facials, got her hair done and, as a result, never had any food in the refrigerator.

I also noticed that they never really talked to each other. They barely acknowledged each other whenever I was around and they were there.

That poor husband used to come home and there wasn't dinner for him on the table. Coming from Romania, I found that very strange. In Romania, it was just a part of life that you had dinner on the table for your husband when he got home. So right or wrong, I decided I didn't like this woman very much.

One day I was cleaning their house and the smell of the cat litter was so strong that I was felt nauseous and my head ached. The husband came home, and he smelled of alcohol and seemed a little drunk and angry.

"Are you finished yet?" he barked at me.

"Almost," I said, thinking he wanted me out of his house. "Just a few more minutes."

"Well, did you make me dinner yet?" he said.

"What do you mean?" I asked, surprised.

"My dinner," he growled. "My wife told me she asked you to put a steak in the oven for me. Well, where is it?"

I stopped working and faced him. With my least confrontational tone I said, "She never mentioned anything about that to me."

And that's when he suddenly lost it. He began cursing and yelling and screaming. "Get out of my house!" he yelled. "You're fired!"

Then, before I could respond he rushed toward me, took me by the arm, and escorted me to the door.

"And don't think you're going to get paid for today either," he yelled once we were outside. Then he shut the door and disappeared.

I stood on the front step for several moments silent, in shock of what had just transpired. Had this really happened? Had he just come in, yelled, demanded dinner, and then threw me out without paying me for all the work I'd done? Sure enough, it had.

So there I was, tired, pregnant, and bewildered. I barely had enough money in my purse to afford a bus ride home. But that's what I did, take the bus, and I cried the entire ride.

Irony, however, has a way with making things right with the world. Three years later, Dee Dee, John and I had recently moved into a nice house in Westlake and were attending a picnic that one of our new neighbors was hosting.

It turned out that our new neighbors were friends with that husband and wife. They were invited to the party as well. I saw them from across the yard and recognized them immediately.

It took them a minute to place my face.

They strode across the yard wearing a pair of puzzled expressions.

"Stella, is that you?" the man asked when he reached me.

I nodded.

"What are you doing here?" he said.

"I own a house in this development," I replied.

"This development?" he said.

I nodded again.

He and his wife stole a sideways glance. "Really?" he said, and then chuckled, "What did you do? Rob a bank?"

I smiled back. "No. I worked hard. Anything is possible in America."

And then without another word I turned and walked away, leaving him and his wife standing there alone.

I wanted so badly to look over my shoulder just to see the shock on their faces at the realization that this poor immigrant who they had abused was now living in the same type of neighborhood that they did. But it was empowering enough to see the initial look on that man's face and think, "You jerk! You threw me out while I was pregnant with no money, and I was able to make it anyhow."

16

The next few months of my first pregnancy in America were uneventful. Even after losing the house cleaning job in Westlake I was able to find other families who needed help. Those jobs, combined with the money I was making at the West Side Market, generated enough money to pay the bills. There was even enough to begin putting aside some savings.

Soon, I'd saved about $500 and decided to buy a car. With all the places I needed to go – West Side Market, people's homes to clean, grocery store – I realized I was spending so much money on bus transportation that it was necessary.

Five hundred dollars really couldn't buy you a very good car, even in the early 1980s, but it didn't matter. I looked in the newspaper and found several that were $1,000 or less. I would call people who were selling their cars and ask if they would come to me in Lakewood to show me the car because I didn't have any way to get to their houses.

Finally, after several rejections, an older man from Garfield Heights agreed to come to me. He showed up at my apartment building in a big, blue Oldsmobile. The man wanted $1,000 for the car. I offered $500 and another $300 in installments. He accepted.

But that car wasn't all it was purported to be. It looked decent on the outside, but the problem was that inside, the electrical system was in bad shape. The seller was retired and, in his spare time, fancied himself a self-taught auto mechanic. He had tried to fix all the internal electrical systems himself. Unfortunately, he wasn't very skilled and patched things together improperly.

I didn't learn how bad it was until later, when strange things began to happen. In the meantime, the car was good enough transportation to get me to my various jobs, including the West Side Market.

There was only one terrible incident that happened during my time at the West Side Market worth mentioning. One evening at about 6 p.m., I was carrying a bag of vegetables to my car after a long day at work. A group of hooligans came up behind me and attacked me, trying to grab my purse and the bag. I fought back.

Imagine it: a pregnant woman with a purse and bag of vegetables kicking and swinging and screaming at two would-be robbers. They probably figured me for an easy mark and then thought I was some crazed lunatic.

What an idiot I was. They probably could have killed me right there, but they didn't. I was able to get into my car, scream some more at them in Romanian and drive away.

A few days later, my luck took a turn for the worse. The bumper fell off the car and the police pulled me over for driving around without it. I explained I didn't have enough money to buy a new one and the police told me that I would need to put a wooden bumper on it or else stop driving the car.

I scrounged around until I found a piece of wood and had a couple of my Romanian friends create a makeshift bumper and attach it to the car. It didn't look very pretty but it did the job. I drove around with that shoddy wooden bumper for a very long time, until I had money to buy another car.

But it was that beat up car that eventually led to a very sad moment for Dee Dee. I'd saved up an extra $5 a week to pay for piano lessons, but Dee Dee also wanted to join Singing Angels, a singing group. We were supposed to be part of a car pool that went to meetings and practices on the east side of Cleveland. When it was my turn to drive, one of the children's parents saw my car with its wooden bumper and decided there was no way she would let me drive the kids in it. I was so embarrassed that I made Dee Dee give up Singing Angels. She didn't understand why I did it and was very sad for quite a while.

That episode made me realize that I needed to find a better job so that I could properly support my daughter and not disappoint her.

After poking around I found that if I went back to school I would be able to secure a job as a secretary or something else that would pay more than the combination of working at the West Side Market and cleaning houses. So I applied for a student loan from the Sawyer College of Business on West 130th Street and Lorain Avenue in Cleveland, was approved, and began taking college courses.

I worked all day; then in the evenings my parents would watch Dee Dee while I went to school. I remember being so tired every night in class while they discussed business principles and math, all in English. Because I was so tired it was difficult to understand. But I found a way to manage.

Then in February, when I was about five months pregnant, I began to feel very uncomfortable and sick again. It was February 12th when I woke up with a high temperature and couldn't figure out what was going on. Because I had little money and no insurance I refused to go to a doctor. But I got worse, and finally, found a Romanian doctor that somebody recommended. He told me I had strep throat and sent me home with instructions of how to take care of it.

That didn't help, and I got worse. I was in excruciating pain. I called John in Vermont and told him to come home. When he arrived, I was about a week shy of being six months pregnant. I told him I couldn't take the pain anymore and asked him to put me in his big, blue station wagon and take me to the hospital.

At Parma Hospital, a nurse took me into a room where they found I had 104 degree temperature. Worse, my water had broken, I was in labor and the combination of everything had created a kidney infection. That's why I was in so much pain.

They called a doctor, who came in and examined me. I was so sick that I had a hard time understanding what was going on around me. But I could see the concern on everyone's faces.

I was concerned, too. But I fought the pain and kept a smile on my face. This was America, the best country on earth for everything, including medicine. And with God's help, I would get better.

But then, through the haze, I overhead one of the nurses say something I'll never forget.

"I think she's going to die on us."

The $500 car with its wooden bumper (1980)

My situation seemed dire. Nurses and doctors scrambled around. Disembodied voices, nurses maybe, asserted I was about to die. But in my stupor it was hard to discern exactly what was happening, much less what they were saying to each other. I was only able to catch a few words here and there, but if my situation matched the way I felt, the doomsayer might be right.

Luckily, the doctors acted quickly and administered a variety of medicines to stabilize my condition. Then they performed an emergency C-section, which saved both the baby and me. At 10:20 p.m. on February 18, 1981, my son, Alex, was born. Several months premature, he weighed only 1 pound, 11 ounces and was about the size of a Barbie doll. He wasn't breathing – we later learned his lungs hadn't yet developed – and once they got a breathing tube in his body the doctors found that he was also extremely sick.

Alex wasn't expected to survive the night. Had we been in a Romanian hospital, the pregnancy would have been deemed a miscarriage and my son would have been tossed away with the garbage. Yet another reason to thank God we were in America. Instead, Alex was placed in an incubator to keep him alive.

A nurse wheeled Alex's incubator into my room and set him next to the bed. I was still woozy from the medication, and the awful reality of the situation failed to register. Instead of seeing a tiny, sick baby that had little chance of seeing the morning dawn, I saw a beautiful baby boy. Here was my son, and at that moment the travails we were going to face over the next several months weren't even a consideration.

Alex defied the odds and survived the night. The next morning he was transferred from Parma Hospital to MetroHealth because John and I had no health insurance. Later, I learned that MetroHealth was the hospital that served the indigent and people who did not have health insurance.

I was a different story. I was too sick for transfer and spent the next four days recovering at Parma. Doctors told me that once my health improved I would be discharged. And it was during this time that I came to realize just how much the mind can, indeed, heal the body. I was so anxious to be reunited with my son that I willed myself toward better health. My baby needed me, and I had to get strong. When the doctors finally decided I was stable enough to be moved, they discharged me and John drove me to Metro to be with Alex.

Upon our arrival, we were escorted into a private room where a doctor asked us to have a seat.

"Before we talk about your son, Mrs. Moga, tell me, how are you feeling?" he said.

"Better," I assured him, wanting to end the small talk and join my son. It had been four long days and we could talk later. "When can I see Alex?"

"Soon," the doctor said. "There are a few things we need to discuss first."

"I want to see my son," I pressed. "Where is he?"

"In a moment," the doctor said, then in a soft but stern voice began to explain what John already knew.

Alex was very tiny and very sick. The hospital staff was doing everything it could, but Alex's chances for survival were not very good. There was no optimistic long-term prognosis.

"I refuse to believe that," I interrupted. "He's just a little small, that's all."

"Mrs. Moga," the doctor said, "please understand that your son was born extremely premature. He is so small that we have been unable to detect lungs using an X-Ray machine. He is on a breathing tube in the incubator, and a machine is providing his body with the oxygen it needs to survive."

"It's not true," I said, pleading and looking to John for support. John offered none.

"Believe me, please, Mrs. Moga," the doctor continued. "For now, your son is being kept alive. But we just don't know for sure whether he's going to make it, or even how long it will take before we will know."

I was stunned, too stunned to cry. I'd already lost one child, and didn't think I could handle the loss of another.

"Please, can I see him?" I asked, this time with a bit less moxie in my voice.

The doctor nodded. "Yes," he said, then motioned for us to stand and led the two of us to another room.

Alex was lying in an incubator similar to the one I'd seen at the other hospital. But unlike at Parma he was connected to several machines whose purposes beyond keeping him alive I had no idea. A small tube was connected to his mouth.

He looked so small, so helpless, and the situation so surreal. I remembered how terrible Ioana looked with the tubes connected to her, and the memories came flooding back. It was just too much. I fainted.

Later, after I regained consciousness, I resigned myself to one thing: being strong enough for Alex to keep my composure and help him fight for his survival.

From that point forward, I spent nearly every waking hour of every day at Alex's side. I spoke to him, mostly in Romanian, touched him gently and, when I could get away with it, gave him little massages.

I reluctantly accepted the situation for what it was but never allowed myself to think, even for a moment, that Alex would die. I forced myself to remain hopeful, even when nothing I saw with my own eyes told me I should be.

"What can we expect once Alex gets older?" I asked his doctor one day. "Will we need any machines at our home?"

"I don't know," the doctor said. "But if your son lives, expect him to be blind and possibly retarded."

"Blind?"

"Yes."

It was a common belief at that time that premature babies who needed 100 percent oxygen pumped into their incubators would have their eye sight damaged by the concentrated flow of pure oxygen. A lack of normal mental development was also almost certain because of the severity of Alex's prematurity.

"But isn't there any chance he'll be normal?" I countered. "Can't he just get better?"

"That's not likely. Your son's chances for a normal life are about 1 percent."

As the days turned into weeks, Alex continued his struggle for survival. Complications were a regular occurrence. Sometimes, he would just stop breathing and turn blue. Equipment in the room would begin beeping wildly and medical staff would rush in yelling, "Code blue!" They would huddle around and work on him until he started breathing again.

This macabre scene probably happened at least once a day, and every time, my heart would drop as I was sure it was the end.

After about a month and a half of this, Alex's doctor sent John and me to meet with a surgeon.

"There are problems," the surgeon explained.

"What kind of problems?" I asked.

"Your son's condition isn't improving," the doctor began. "He is starting to develop complications with several of his organs. There is also blood in his stool. Your son is still too small for us to definitively determine the source, but we think there is something wrong with his heart."

I shuddered. "His heart?"

"Yes," the surgeon said. "From what we can tell, it's the most likely cause of the problem."

"What are you going to do?" I asked, my voice shaking.

The doctor focused his gaze on me and said in even, measured tones, "We need your permission for an operation."

"What kind of operation?"

"As I said, we think his heart isn't functioning the way it should be at this stage. His blood isn't oxygenating properly. So in order to see if the situation will improve, I believe open heart surgery is the best option."

I gasped.

"Open heart surgery? There's nothing else you can do other than cutting my son open?"

"Mrs. Moga, I recognize that this isn't an easy decision. And to be perfectly honest, even if we do perform the surgery there is no guarantee this is going to work. But without it, I believe your son's condition is going to worsen."

He paused, then said, "Look, if you and your husband need a little time to talk before making a decision, I understand."

"How much time do we have to decide?" I asked.

"We'd like to perform the surgery as soon as possible. Can you give me an answer later today?"

I looked at John. He and I had been discussing Alex's condition over the past several weeks, and John had read in a book that human bodies, especially those of babies, have the ability to recover from injury and illness. The body, he read, fights against all odds.

John shook his head.

I nodded in return.

"We don't need time to discuss it," John told the surgeon. "We do not want our son to have this surgery."

The doctor looked at the two of us stunned. "You're sure?" he asked.

"Yes," John said. It was the first time in my life I just kept my mouth shut and accepted John's decision.

The doctor shook his head, stood, looked at us once again then left the room without even saying goodbye.

Over the next few days, Alex's condition did get worse. The doctor who was taking care of him on a regular basis finally told us that we should prepare for him to pass away within the next couple of days. I remember praying so, so hard

On the evening of March 20, 1981, I remember it was about 7 p.m., I went home to take a shower and change clothes. I was so sad. My family was already consoling me. All of us expected Alex to die. It was just like what had happened with Ioana all over again.

While I was sitting by myself in the bedroom, our telephone rang. Dee Dee answered it and I heard her talking in Romanian on the line. A moment later, she leaned into the bedroom and said, "Mom, you have a phone call."

"Tell whoever it is I don't want to talk," I said.

Dee Dee left the room and told the caller I was unavailable.

A few moments later, the phone rang again.

This time, I got up and angrily picked it up myself.

"How can I help you?" I barked in Romanian.

"Hello, Stella," a male voice said softly. "This is Lie, a friend from Romania. Do you remember me?"

Lie had immigrated to America a few years before we had. He lived in Chicago. He had been a professor of biology in Romania and he was a scientist.

"I remember you, Lie," I said. "But this is not a good time. I cannot talk."

"Wait," Lie said. "Don't hang up, Stella. That's why I am calling. I know you have a big problem right now in your family. I know what is happening with your baby."

That stopped me from hanging up the phone.

"How did you know I had a baby?" I asked. "Who told you?"

"No one," Lie said. "Just listen to me carefully, Stella. I know you are not going to believe what I am about to tell you, but I had a vision about you and your baby."

"What?" I said. "You're crazy."

"Stella, listen," he said. "I saw your baby in my vision. Jesus was with him and put oil on his back. Your son is going to get better. Don't let anyone tell you otherwise."

"Lie, you are crazy," I said again. "You are a scientist. How can you talk like this?"

"Look," he said. "I am a scientist. But I can't argue with what I saw.

Your baby will get better. I saw him several times – once at six months; and again at two years old. He was blond with blue eyes, and perfectly healthy."

I started sobbing.

"Blond and blue eyes?" I said. "Lie, John and I are brunettes with brown eyes? What do you mean blue eyes?"

"Stella, I know you don't listen to anybody," Lie said. "But listen to me now. I want you and your family to pray very, very hard tonight. And a miracle will happen with your baby before midnight."

It didn't seem real, but I kept listening to Lie.

"You also have to become born-again Christians," he said. "And you have to start going to church on a regular basis and believe in God. And, you have to make sure you are going to make a difference in this life with something you are going to do. I do not know what, but you must make a difference."

"OK," was all I could muster before hanging up the phone.

After I got off the phone with Lie, I went over to the bathroom mirror and stayed there for a few minutes just staring at myself. My thoughts had stood still. And at that very moment, God came and gently said in my own voice. "Stella you are going to be okay. I promise. Nothing is going to happen to your little boy. You must have blind faith in me know. This faith will carry you through."

Dee Dee came to me and asked me what was going on. I looked at her and spoke these words. "I think your brother has blue eyes. How funny is that? Lie said we have to pray. We are preparing for a miracle."

I grabbed Dee Dee's shoulders and knelt before her.

"Honey, my sweet little girl. Mama's angel. Tonight, you must pray with the purest heart. We must pray like we've never prayed before. Let your words be as pure as angels. Tonight, we are going to be asking God for his mercy and let your brother stay with us. Please, Dee Dee, give everything you have."

The pleading with my daughter came so deep from within my heart. We walked into the bedroom and kneeled by the bed. I started to whisper my prayers and Dee Dee chimed in with hers. That night, I went to a place in my mind and spirit so pure and so true. I felt complete surrender through my faith. I felt the strength of a thousand angels. I knew I believed that my fate was rewritten. And when I ended my prayer there was one last thing I needed to say. At that moment, I promised God that I would spend my life taking care of American children and give them the best care possible. Looking back, those words came from somewhere in the future.

I wasn't even working as a teacher at the time. The promise did not make any sense; but it felt like a covenant between a mere mortal woman and her sweet beloved Maker. I stood up. It was time to go to the hospital.

When we arrived, the doctors were blunt – Alex would die at any moment.

But then, at 11:05 p.m., with the group of us standing and sitting around Alex's incubator, a miracle happened. The doctors removed the tubes that were taped to Alex's face, and he started to breathe on his own. The machines that monitored his condition started beeping.

His chest was moving up and down, very quickly, as though suddenly the light had been flicked on. Everybody was shocked. They called Alex's doctor, who came in, checked the machines and checked Alex, and just shook his head.

"I can't explain it," he said. "But your son is breathing on his own."

That evening, I reconfirmed my promise to God that I would do something for helping my baby and children in general. I didn't know what it would be, but I knew it had something to do with helping other children. That moment set me on the path I've taken. And it's been an amazing privilege to make a difference in so many children's lives through my schools.

From that day forward, Alex began to get stronger and his condition improved. There were still times when they needed to connect breathing tubes to him to provide additional oxygen, but for the most part, he was breathing on his own. The doctor's never were able to explain how he suddenly took a turn for the better.

And crazy me, even before Alex improved I had had decided to keep my breast milk. From the day I arrived at MetroHealth I asked for a pump. The nurses just looked at me with pity and gave me one to use. Every three hours, every day, I pumped my breast milk, and every day I would throw it away in the sink. Sometimes, I would cry as I did it. Other times, I would smile.

Finally, one day I got up the courage to ask Alex's doctor if I could give him breast milk.

"Absolutely not," he said. "He is not ready."

Undeterred, I went to a drug store and bought an eye dropper. I boiled it in water on the stove at my apartment and made sure it was very clean. Then, I pumped my milk and filled the dropper with just a tiny bit and hid it in my purse. When I got back to the hospital, I removed the dropper and, when no one was looking, put it in Alex's mouth and gave him a single drop.

The next time, I gave him two, then three, four and more. A few days later, a couple nurses caught me in the act and wrote me up. I received a letter from the hospital that stated if I did not follow directions I would not be allowed to come and see my baby.

Again, I was undeterred. I kept giving Alex little droppers filled with breast milk every chance I got. And when he was about three and a half months old, the doctors finally said I could feed him breast milk. By then, Alex was used to it, so there was little problem for him. Having Alex in my arms, breastfeeding him, was one of the greatest moments in my life.

I also decided that I wanted to give Alex baths. In Romania, they say breast milk and baths every day make the baby grow up healthy. But how Alex lived in that incubator, connected to IVs, didn't make it possible. So I bought a small pot, which I disinfected and cleaned, and I put a little water in it and some baby shampoo, and when the nurses went on break, I took Alex out of the incubator and put him in the little pot and gave him a little bath. Then, before they returned, I put him back. When the nurses finally caught me, they were shocked, but didn't stop me. They even let me hold him in my arms from time to time. Looking back, giving Alex baths in the little pot were more wonderful times during a very difficult period.

As the months wore on, I became so familiar with the goings-on at the nursery that I would offer assistance to other parents who were there with premature babies. I encouraged them. I helped the nurses with their daily tasks. And I became part of the fixture there.

But that didn't quell the excitement and relief I felt when, after four months, the doctor told us we could finally take Alex home.

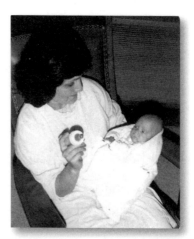

Stella with baby Alex in the hospital
after he was removed from the incubator (1982)

118

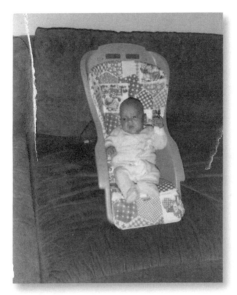

Alex Moga (1982)

Alex with Maria Daisa (1982)

A cry of joy, a cry of pain

Parents, doctors face dilemma in premature or defective births

By Elizabeth Price

An infant's first cry is joyful to most parents, the wide-open beginning of a healthy new life.

But not always. Extreme prematurity, major birth defects or serious illness present some parents with wrenching decisions within hours of birth.

How aggressively should a newborn infant's disease or deformity be treated? How far should doctors go to keep alive a barely viable premature infant? Is there a time to stop treating such children, to let them die?

These questions are not new. But the answers are more complex now, because doctors can do much more to preserve life and to treat defects and disease in newborns than was possible even 10 years ago.

A Danville, Ill., couple recently was charged with attempted murder and child neglect. They had asked that their newborn Siamese twins not be given medical treatment. (A judge dismissed the charges July 17.)

Greater Cleveland parents and doctors wrestle with equally tragic cases. The questions they ask usually center on medical treatment of a newborn. But behind the medical questions loom moral and ethical ones, which can be far more troubling.

When Dr. Hugh B. Anderson began delivering babies more than 30 years ago, there was only one way to deal with a baby diagnosed as hydrocephalic (water on the brain). Puncture its head and drain the fluid so it could be delivered.

"When you did this, most of the time, you committed the fetus to death because there was no way you could drain the head ... without killing the infant. But this was the only choice you had," said Anderson, now director of the department of obstetrics and gynecology at Fairview General Hospital.

Years passed, and progress was made in treating hydrocephalic infants. Delivery by Caesarean section became common, making possible the birth of an infant with an enlarged head, and tubes called shunts were placed inside the head to drain the fluid and prevent brain damage.

One day, Anderson recalled, "a young girl comes into the office, an attractive girl with a minor gynecological problem. So I take her (medical) history."

He was amazed to learn that she had been a hydrocephalic infant who had one of the first shunts.

She also was a college graduate, Phi Beta Kappa.

"And here I am sitting talking to ... a very attractive, intelligent person," said Anderson. "So you sit and look at her, and you think of all the others that you had to destroy because you had no other way of getting them delivered. This is where we've been."

Medical progress has provided options, Anderson noted, and "As soon as we have options coming into the picture, then somebody has to make decisions ... And it isn't all scientific because now you get the moral issues involved. And how an individual faces these is as different as people are."

Very premature infants, born after only 24 to 26 weeks' gestation and weighing under 1.5 pounds, pose one of the most common dilemmas with newborns.

Until the development of neonatal (newborn) intensive care units (NICUs) in the early 1970s, these babies rarely lived. Today a growing percentage survives. Some undergo major surgery, and exist on respirators for weeks.

Some leave the hospital in good health; others leave with lung damage or other chronic problems. Many still die, even after medical heroics.

When these fragile infants arrive in intensive care units of Cleveland area hospitals, it always comes to the decision: Is the baby old enough to live? And how far should you go?" said Dr. Katherine King, director of Cleveland Metropolitan General Hospital's NICU.

"It's the type of situation where a lot of times, you don't want to do anything to make the decision. The baby will make the decision for you. But there are times when it's very difficult ... How small it too small, and how small should you make any effort at all? That's very tough."

Alexander Moga weighed less than two pounds when he was born last February, after 26 weeks' gestation. He was so small that his father's wedding ring could slide up and down his arm.

At Metro's NICU, Alexander was placed on a respirator because his lungs were too immature to breathe alone.

Doctors diagnosed an abnormality in a heart duct, and asked his parents, John and Stella Moga, to consent to surgery. Without an operation, they said, Alexander might die, or develop blindness or lung disease from being on the respirator too long. There also was a chance he would not survive surgery.

Continued on Page 15

News article about Alex's birth

Medical advances are enabling doctors to save more and more babies born very prematurely or with serious defects. At the same time, they are posing a dilemma for parents and doctors about what degree of treatment should be undertaken to preserve and sustain such lives.

Page 1-C

News article about Alex's birth

18

I changed after Alex was born. I was different, and noticeably so. While I had always been grateful for our escape from Romania and the opportunity America provided us – even if we hadn't yet been able to realize it – this was something new, a different feeling, a new sense of appreciation. I began to appreciate many things I hadn't before: God, life, America, and Americans as people.

Today, nearly 30 years later, I understand the change – the experience made me a better person. It taught me how to better respond to other people's needs. It provided me with the ability to empathize with the difficulties people face every day. And it showed me how important it was to work hard to try to make the lives of others better. All of these are lessons I've tried hard to apply to my life.

I came to recognize that God helped us with Alex. And because of that, he became a constant reference and presence in our lives. I had turned to God for refuge as a Romanian youth, but now I turned to him for hope. My view of life was different. The doctors and nurses worked so hard to preserve Alex's life and ease the pain of those four long months in hospital. No one in Romania would have done so much for someone so little. The American system as a whole assumed a new look in my eyes. No longer was it just a land of opportunity. Instead, it also offered a sense of protection. I felt protected by the American system and I realized how insecure I had felt under the Romanian system of life.

All of these things began swirling through my head after Alex's birth, even though it took years for their meaning to crystallize. So when the doctors finally told John and me that we would soon be able to bring Alex home, I knew that our very lives needed change as well. The fifth floor Lakewood apartment we lived in was no longer suitable for a premature baby. No, the doctors said we needed a clean environment. This time, I was going to listen to them. And thus, we began our search for a better place to live.

An acquaintance told me about a condominium for sale in North Olmsted by a woman who was moving to Arizona. Her asking price was $42,000, which was an astronomical amount for us because we had low-paying jobs, no money for a down payment and knew that no bank in their right mind would give us a mortgage. But we had learned that the owner was in a hurry to sell. She needed to move immediately and would probably accept any good offer. I saw an opportunity and went by myself to meet with her.

When I arrived at the condominium complex, I was taken aback by how different it was from our apartment building. There was a pool and a party room and the place was neat and clean. The woman invited me into her condo and gave me a tour. There were three large bedrooms and an expansive living room. New carpet had been recently laid, and the entire place possessed that fresh, new carpet smell.

Afterward, the woman asked me to sit and we began to talk. In my best broken English I told her about me and my family, how we had come to the United States in 1979 and that we had just had a premature baby. Then I explained our financial situation.

"We do not have money for a down payment," I said. "But I very much want to buy your condo."

The woman nodded. "You seem like a nice woman. What can you afford?"

"$480 a month," I said.

We spoke for another 10 minutes or so before she agreed to have a land contract drafted. Either I was a very persuasive saleswoman or she really was in a hurry to sell, because with no money down, no bank to back a loan, and after only two short years in America, I found myself the owner of a very nice condominium.

Our financial situation being what it was, we didn't have money for either new baby clothes or a new crib for Alex. But good luck smiled upon us again, just as it had shortly after our arrival in Fairview Park, when we happened upon the giving hearts of another church and its congregants. As new North Olmsted residents, we wanted to join a church in the community and went to the Columbia Road Baptist Church where we became born-again Christians. When members of our new congregation heard about our plight, many came to our aid. They gave us a crib, clothing, baby bottles, everything we could have imagined and more than we needed. The congregants gave from the bottom of their hearts, and they were wonderful people.

Finally, we brought Alex home. Despite the new condo and wonderful furniture, there remained another big problem that wasn't as simple to resolve. Alex's condition was better, but he still needed constant monitoring because he would still stop breathing momentarily. The doctors explained that it could take another three or four weeks before he cleared that final hurdle. Unfortunately, we couldn't afford the monitor they wanted to attach to his heart and wrist because we had no insurance.

We devised a system where my parents, husband or I would watch Alex non-stop, 24 hours a day, seven days a week in shifts. For three weeks, one of us was always awake by Alex's side until the doctors said he was in the clear. During that time, I didn't work and earned money by babysitting a brother and sister, Amy and Andy Thomas. It wasn't until after Alex was on the road to recovery that I even thought about trying to find another full-time job.

Alex's premature birth created other, more serious and potentially longer lasting complications. The biggest was whether or not he was blind. In the hospital, tests the doctors had administered came back inconclusive because Alex was so small and underdeveloped. It wasn't until he was 5 ½ months old that we were able to make an appointment with an ophthalmologist at Metro Hospital for a more conclusive set of tests. Imagine the fear we faced wondering whether our baby was blind. I didn't care what the test said though because my baby was alive. To me, that was the most important thing, and it made it a bit easier to face the other challenges we tackled on a daily basis.

At the ophthalmologist's office, I wasn't allowed to go inside with Alex and the doctors. For 45 minutes I just sat in the waiting room as no one came out to give me a progress report or any information at all. Those were some of the longest minutes in my life. As I sat waiting, every potential scenario raced through my head: he would be blind in one eye; he would be blind in both eyes; he would have partial sight in both eyes. And by the time the doctor came out carrying my son with a nurse at his side, I had prepared myself for whatever terrible fate awaited us.

But when I saw the smile on the nurse's face, a real smile, I suddenly knew that something good was about to happen.

"This is one of the biggest surprises of my career," the doctor said, handing me my son. "I expected to have at least a little problem with his eyes, if not some level of blindness, but he is perfect. There's nothing wrong with his eyes."

"Nothing?" I repeated in disbelief. "Nothing at all?"

"No," the doctor said. "I can't explain it, but he's perfect. This truly is a wonderful surprise. Enjoy your son." And then he spun on his heels and disappeared back into the office, with the nurse following along behind him.

It was the second miracle of Alex's life, and as I took him home to tell everyone the unbelievably great news I vowed to take care of him the best I could.

As I was pumping for milk, day in and day out, I would reference the night Lie called. I knew that my son was going to be alright. And I began to wonder what that promise I made to God was all about.

Things went well for several weeks until one day we received a letter in the mail from the hospital. I opened it and found a bill for $180,000. I showed it to John.

"Is this real?" he asked.

"No. It's a misprint," I said, then laughed and threw it away.

A few weeks later, another letter from the hospital arrived. I opened it and again found a bill for $180,000. This time, it included a note that said we needed to make an appointment with the hospital to discuss payment.

"This doesn't sound like a misprint," John said. "What are we going to do, Stella? We can't afford that kind of bill."

"It's got to be a misprint," I assured him.

But when the phone calls began shortly after that, I realized something just wasn't right. We were told that the bill was, in fact, real and that because we didn't have any health insurance we were responsible for the full amount.

I stormed into hospital and met with a social worker. I could barely contain myself.

"This can't be a real bill," I said in a voice somewhere just short of screaming. "We don't have money to pay this type of bill."

"I assure you, ma'am, this is real," the lady said. "We need to discuss how you plan to pay off this amount."

I sat there in disbelief for several minutes before finally saying, "I can pay you $5 per month."

The woman scoffed.

"You're kidding?" she said.

"No, I'm serious. That's all we can afford to pay. I don't have a job."

"Well," she said. "It doesn't matter how you come up with the money, you're going to have to do better than $5 a month. You're going to have to find a way to pay the entire amount."

I left her office devastated. If I would have accepted welfare, I would have been in the clear. But I didn't. And now I wondered how I would pay off an $180,000 bill with no job and no money. Today, that equates to nearly $700,000. Getting that paid off wasn't possible, and I couldn't see any way out of the situation. But I wasn't about to give up just like that, so I began talking to as many people as I could whom I thought might be able to lead me in the right direction for help.

Two things kept coming up in conversation – politicians and foundations. I made an appointment with Senator Howard Metzenbaum and intended to ask for help.

On the day of the appointment, I was nervous. But I had rehearsed my speech over and over until I felt comfortable enough to plead my case and ask for him to help our family out. He was very courteous and listened intently to my story.

The skills that I learned dealing with the Communist Party officials were about to be put to good use once again. The life lessons I learned then came back to me like an old friend. I knew how to approach the senator. I rehearsed the speech several times. I wrote down what I was going to say and what I needed him to do before I even left the office. Our entire future depended on his decision. Once again, my own devices were the deciding outcome of our fate.

"If the first immigrants in this country had to pay this kind of bill," I said, "this country wouldn't exist."

The Senator nodded.

"And how can they expect poor people like us, without health insurance, to pay this kind of bill?" I asked him. "We would be paying it for the rest of our lives and for the rest of Alex's life. Even then, we would never be able to pay it off."

"Yes," he said. "It is a lot of money."

I finished my speech and looked at him. "So," I said, "can you help us?"

The Senator smiled. "I might," he said. "Let me make a few phone calls and get back to you."

"No," I said. "I need you to make phone calls now, not later."

And as soon as I said it, I realized I might just have doomed my case.

But instead of being offended by the moxie of this poor immigrant who sat across from him, Senator Metzenbaum smiled again. "OK," he said, then picked up his phone and asked his secretary to bring him the phone numbers for several foundations. Like Ms. Stoica and the general in Bucharest, he saw the flicker of the flame inside me.

"Mrs. Moga," he said. "Let's see if we can get you some help today."

A few minutes later the Senator's secretary came into his office with a few sheets of paper and handed them to him. He picked up the phone and began making phone calls, explaining my situation in great detail during each call.

Finally, one was interested in reviewing my case and the Senator explained to me that there was something called the Hill-Burton program, which might just be able to help. He had his secretary take all the information from me surrounding Alex's birth, the complications and our family's financial situation. He assured me that we would be taken care of and, thanking him profusely, I left feeling as though something good was going to happen.

Sure enough, about a month later, we received a letter in the mail saying that our bill was being paid in full and that we would not be responsible for paying any of the $180,000. We didn't believe it was true. I called both the foundation and Senator Metzenbaum. Both confirmed what the letter had said. Our bill had been paid. At that moment, I could not explain in words how grateful I felt. All I could say to everyone was, "This is my country, and I love it."

Years later I learned that it was an act of Congress that had been responsible for our financial salvation. Congress had passed the Hill-Burton Act in 1946. It was designed to promote hospital modernization through government construction grants for non-profit hospitals. In exchange for these grants, Hill-Burton required non-profit hospitals to provide charity or discounted care to people who could not afford it. The act was amended in 1975 and became Title XVI of the Public Health Service Act. And in 1997, the program stopped providing new funds to hospitals but kept regulations in place for about 300 health care facilities that today are still obligated to provide free or reduced-cost care to people at or below the poverty line.

19

Alex was finally out of the woods. He grew and grew. He did end up having blue eyes. There wasn't one day passed that we didn't think about the day kneeling deep in prayer and the promise I made to God. My new job search was to find a position in education. I wanted to be true to my word to God and I couldn't wait to get started.

The respite on paying Alex's hospital bill did little to ease our overall financial situation, and by the time he was eight months old we still needed money. I began looking for a job, and learned about Bay Village Montessori School, which had recently moved to Bay Village and was seeking a French teacher. I spoke fluent French, had an education degree and decided it was worth applying. I went to Goodwill and bought a very nice jacket, put myself together and looked very presentable, then went for an interview.

I got the job.

How happy I was to be back working in education, doing something I could truly be proud of, helping children. While I worked, my parents watched Alex. We also asked a Romanian neighbor to help. It was so exciting each day, preparing for classes and those children. In no time, they started to speak French. They went home singing French songs, speaking French words, and the parents were so ecstatic about the progress.

I saw the potential of advertising the French program on television and suggested it to the principal. He called one of the local TV stations and they did a story on us. Within a few months, we had garnered a lot of attention for the French program and enrollment was up because of it.

That was a very happy time for me. Unfortunately, it coincided with a sad experience, but one that later was something I looked back upon and laughed about. While I was working as a French teacher, I used to drive that old car with the wooden bumper and park it with all the other teachers in the parking lot. One day, the principal came to me and said, "Stella, we like you. You're doing amazing things with the French program, but you need to park your car in the back."

"Why?" I asked. "Is it an eyesore for everybody here?"

"No, no, no," the principal lied. "We just need more parking spaces in the front because your program has taken off so well."

I laughed nervously. "You don't need to lie to me," I said. "The reason you are making me park in the back is that it's not a good image for the school. And that's OK. I'm going to park in the back because I need this job."

Several years later, in 1986, after I'd founded my own business and was doing well, I bought an expensive Porsche 928 s4 that was the latest and greatest car around. One day, I got in my Porsche and drove over to the Montessori school to show off. When I got there, they couldn't believe it. Here I was, that woman who drove the beat-up car with the wood bumper, driving this expensive sports car.

But in 1981, who could have known what the future was going to bring. I had bills to pay, parents who needed to go back to work to help cover our costs, and a son who needed me to find somewhere I could drop him off during the day. I began looking for a daycare center that we could afford.

I was appalled by our options. The ones I found were dirty. They didn't have enough toys for the children. One, located in an old house in a suburb of Cleveland and spread across three floors, put the fear of God into me. During the tour I became concerned about how children from the third floor would get out in case there was a fire. And during lunchtime, they gave the children Saltine crackers and clear chicken soup to eat. There were no vegetables and no noodles. I couldn't believe what I saw. How could American children get so little in daycare?

I came home very disgusted and pessimistic about what I could find for Alex.

Finally, I found a school in Rocky River. It was dirty and smelly. They had hamsters and guinea pigs in the school and the smell of animal urine permeated throughout the rooms. But I didn't have much of a choice. There weren't too many better options out there that I could afford. So I left Alex there. They let him cry all day. And when I came to pick him up, he was all stressed out. His face was wet. He was so, so sad. He was crying and had obviously been crying all day.

"Why didn't you call me?" I asked.

"It wouldn't have mattered," the teacher told me.

I was furious. I took Alex home and told everyone in my family that I could do it better, that I was going to open my own school. Everyone said,

"How?" and looked at me like I was crazy. I decided to contact a woman named Elizabeth Nemet.

She owned Sunshine Nursery Daycare Center on Lake Avenue in Cleveland. Before I had gotten pregnant with Alex I had volunteered for Elizabeth. She was a Hungarian immigrant, and because I spoke Hungarian I had been able to communicate with her.

Elizabeth was a wonderful person, but she didn't have any common or business sense. I remember how I went for an interview. I got in her office and she had cash and paperwork all over her desk. She was very disorganized and her employees really ran the school. I had already seen enough American business experiences to know something was wrong with how she ran the organization. But Elizabeth did a very good job with the children. She fed them right. She taught them right. She also had good teachers there who were very dedicated to the children. So I knew she had a very solid base to her operations.

Volunteering for Elizabeth taught me a few things. She was a real good person and liked me a lot. She saw my potential, more than I saw in myself, and even back then she confided in me. She even started to pay me for helping her in the school.

"We are going to open schools together," she said. "I don't know when, Stella, but it's going to happen."

It was a good dream, I thought, but an impossible one.

I lost contact with Elizabeth shortly after I got pregnant with Alex. Now, upset about my experience with Alex's daycare center, I again sought her out.

"It's great to see you, Stella," she said when I sat down in her office. It was just as disorganized as I had remembered it. "To what do I owe this pleasure?"

"I think I am going to take you up on your offer," I said. "I want to be your partner and open daycare centers."

For the next hour or so I brought Elizabeth up to speed on my life. I told her about my son's birth, the complications, my job at the Bay Village Montessori School and, most recently, my unpleasant experience with Alex's daycare center. When I was done, Elizabeth beamed. "Well then," she said. "Let's do it."

The first step, she said, was for me to find spaces to open new schools. I was tasked with finding the first location. Elizabeth would then vet it and see if it was a good place. Well enough, I found a place in Westlake on Center Ridge Road in a Masonic Temple, and I talked to the people. Elizabeth came and we decided the space was good enough to start a new school in Westlake.

"It's time then to discuss our business partnership," Elizabeth told me. "You don't have any money, but I do. So here's my proposal – you run the school and I will give you 30 percent of the profits."

I was so excited. Elizabeth had her attorney draw up a partnership agreement. The deal was actually better than first imagined – Elizabeth would own 59 percent of the business; I would own 41 percent. She wrote me a check for $10,000, in my name, and gave it to me to start buying materials and put a down payment on the space and get the ball rolling for the new location. Finally, things were about to change.

When Mrs. Nemet was so eager to partner with me in the daycare business, I was ecstatic. I took the check for $10,000 home and for three days just carried it around with me. I didn't cash it. Something just didn't feel right. I went to talk to my dad. The best advice I ever received was from my father.

Together, we just looked at the check. $10,000. It was the most money I had seen since we'd arrived in the United States and it represented a new chapter in our lives.

"Dad," I said, "what should I do?"

My father took my hand. "Stella, what do you want to do?"

"I know myself," I said. "I do not know if I can work for Elizabeth. She is a good person but everything I can't stand – disorganized, uncertain, and moody. If I do this, I'll be working with her for the rest of my life."

"Stella," my father said, "Then don't do it. You will be her slave. You won't be her partner. You'll work for her and she'll dictate everything for you. You are not cut out for that type of situation. Stella, you cannot have a boss, and you are not going to be happy with the arrangements. If you really want to open a business, you have to do it yourself. God will show you the way."

I stood and gave my father a kiss on his forehead. "You're right, dad. Thank you."

He was right. I am not a partner kind of person. I am a leader. Even in my inexperience as a future entrepreneur, I had an idea of how hard it was going to be for me to untangle my business from Mrs. Nemet, especially from a legal standpoint. All of the hard work and innovation I was about to put forth was certainly not going to be for that lady. It was going to be for my family, especially for my two beautiful children.

The next morning, I showed up at Elizabeth's office and handed her the check.

"What's this?" she asked, confused.

"The money back," I said. "I just can't do this, Elizabeth."

"Why, Stella? Isn't this what you wanted?"

"Not like this," I said. "I want to open my own school. And one day, I'm going to do that."

Elizabeth's face suddenly changed. The confusion turned into disdain.

"What do you mean you are going to open your own school?" she said, bitterness in her voice. "You don't speak English. You don't have any money. Where do you think this is? This is America. To open a business is very hard."

"I know," I said. "I am going to learn like you did. When you opened your schools you had help. And just like you, I am going to do a very good job."

Then I turned and left her office.

Only common sense saved me from tangling with that woman. I had some very strong innovative ideas on how to run a business successfully and to nurture and provide for the children left in my care. None of it had to do with disorganization and lack of respect from employees. Mrs. Nemet had good intentions, but not much common sense.

Now I had to put my ideas into action. I knew that as soon as my plans came to life, the business would do fine under my nurturing way. The question now was how was I going to get there? As always, with one idea grows a plan. When you are ready to work your hardest, God will provide the opportunities. Doors opened and my plan began to take shape one tiny piece at a time. I spent the next several months developing a plan to open my own daycare center. In the interim, the tension between John and I worsened. Our relationship continued to deteriorate and we grew further apart.

One night, in May 1982, when Alex was about 15 months old and had the blue eyes and blond hair just like Lie predicted, while I was sitting on the couch thinking about how I was going to open the daycare center, John walked into the house with the smell of liquor so strong on his breath that I could smell it from across the room.

"What are you doing?" he barked.

"Working on my plan," I explained.

He muttered something unintelligible under his breath before saying, "I hate you."

"What?"

"You heard me," he said. "I hate you because you didn't have patience long enough to keep our baby in your belly long enough to have a healthy baby. The infection you had was your fault. Look at us now."

We argued for a while before John stormed out of the room for the night. I'll never forget that moment. That moment made me realize who this person was in my life and I had to do something to get away from him.

20

I had a friend named Piana, another Romanian immigrant whom I met when I lived in the North Olmsted condominium. She lived in an adjacent condo and was studying to become a psychiatrist. She was a true character and together we had a lot of fun. Piana's husband had been a member of the Romanian gymnastics team and they had immigrated to America. They had two beautiful daughters and were a very happy family.

One day, shortly after we moved in and became friends I said to her, "Let's go see the real America" and we went out to visit some of the new subdivisions that were cropping up around North Olmsted and Westlake. We found a development that was being built by Latina & Latina Builders and went through the model home. It was so beautiful that neither of us could believe our senses.

As we walked out, I turned to Piana. "Give me two years," I said. "I'll have a home like this."

Piana laughed.

I did eventually have a home like that, three actually. But you wouldn't have known it back then, especially when I finally decided it was time to launch my own daycare center.

Unfortunately, I didn't know where to look. And even if I had, I didn't have enough money for a down payment on a lease. I had a total of $1,800. That was it. And it wasn't even in the bank. The only reason I had that was because I had started to sell Mary Kay cosmetics as a consultant and because I spoke Hungarian, Romanian and French I was able to sell enough cosmetics to immigrants to save up a little bit of cash. But I was undeterred, and thought, "Who better to find a solution than the mayor of North Olmsted, Robert Swietyniowski?" So I went down to the mayor's office without an appointment and presented myself to his secretary.

"Can I help you," she asked, looking me up and down. My hair was dyed black and I had a very bad perm. I could see the questioning attitude in her eyes.

"Yes, you can," I said. "I have a personal problem that only the mayor can help me with."

"Excuse me?" the woman scoffed. "Who are you again? What did you say your name was?"

"Stella Moga," I said. "It's very important."

The secretary gave me a second once-over then said, "Look, Ms. Moga, you need an appointment to see the mayor, and it's obvious you don't have one."

I remained adamant. "What is he doing right now?" I asked. "Can I see him for just a minute?"

Finally, she sighed stood up and disappeared into the mayor's office. I'm sure she was telling him, "Mr. Mayor, look, there's a crazy woman in the waiting room who says she has a personal problem with you. Can you see her for a minute?"

But apparently, she must have been a bit more tactful because a moment later, the mayor appeared at his door and invited me in.

Once inside, I made myself at home. "Mr. Mayor," I started, "I want to start a daycare center in your city."

His jaw nearly dropped. He must have been expecting anything but that. "And, what do you want from me that is so important you had to meet with me this very minute?"

"Well, you're the mayor. You know how to get things done. I need to find a space to open one."

The major chuckled a bit then said, "I'm not a real estate agent. I'm busy, ma'am, and I'm not sure I can do anything to help you out." Then he gave me a "you can show yourself out" smile, looked down at some paperwork on his desk and went back to work.

I stood to leave and, slightly dejected, began to walk toward the door. Before I got there though, the mayor cleared his throat and said, "You know what. Let me talk with Pastor Torb from Congregational Church in North Olmsted at the corner of Barton and Lorain. He might be able to help."

I turned, beaming, and said, "Bless you" then walked back to the chair and sat back down. The mayor picked up his phone, dialed a phone number and when the pastor answered explained the situation. After a few moments the mayor hung up and looked at me with a broad smile on his face.

"It is your lucky day, Ms. Moga," he said. "Pastor Torb has a little room in the basement of his church where you just might be able to start your preschool."

I nearly leapt up and hugged the mayor right there. He gave me directions on how to get there and told me that Pastor Torb would be waiting there for me to arrive. And sure enough, he was.

It must have been the weight the call from the mayor held because the pastor treated me like royalty. He invited me into the church and we began to talk. I told him how I had come to America from Romania and that I had done gymnastics when I was younger and I had experience with daycare and that I wanted to open a daycare center where I could make a difference for the children and take good care of them.

The pastor did a good job listening and showed me the room in the basement. There was a mild odor down there that belied the fact that no one had probably been down there in quite a while. The carpet was dirty and smelled a bit musty but you know what, I saw the potential.

The basement had windows, and natural light was coming in. Also, there was equipment – tables and chairs – in the room, and those were things I would have never had enough money to buy on my own.

I offered the priest $500 a month for the space, which he accepted. How in the world I was going to pay $500 a month when I didn't really have $5 to pay was the big question. He must have admired my passion and believed I would make the center work. Whatever he thought, it didn't matter. I had my space and, if I didn't spend too much of the $1,800 on supplies, at least two months worth of rent. So I went home thinking about how I was going to arrange my soon-to-be daycare center.

Next, I needed toys, so I went to garage sales and bought lots and lots of little toys and cleaned them up until they were shiny and nice. Then I took them to the little room in the basement of the church and began cleaning up that space until it was spotless.

While this was happening, I volunteered at a daycare center to get another firsthand look at the business. Several of the teachers and I became friends, and a few of them gave me some materials to put on the walls of the room – alphabet letters, numbers, shapes and colors; things I didn't have enough money to buy. I complemented those with alphabet and number blocks that I made from scratch. I wrote the alphabet and numbers on the blocks in marker by hand. I didn't have a good way of sanding them and when they finally got used, a couple of the children got splinters in their fingers because I hadn't sanded them enough. But with all those materials in place, the daycare center was ready to open. All it needed was a name... and children.

21

"Once upon a time there was a dear little girl who was loved by everyone who looked at her, but most of all by her grandmother, and there was nothing that she would not have given to the child. Once she gave her a little cap of red velvet, which suited her so well that she would never wear anything else. So she was always called Little Red Riding Hood."

"Little Red Riding Hood," by the Brothers Grimm

I remember reading that famous fairy tale when I was a little girl. In the years since, my life has been filled with so many trials and challenges that I've identified with Little Red, feeling I was the little girl going through all the dangers to get to my grandmother's house. So it was only natural when it came time to name my daycare center that I turned to the story that left the greatest imprint on my life. I married the idea with my love of the French language and landed on Le Chaperon Rouge.

"What do you think, Dee Dee?" I asked.

"I like it, mom."

We were sitting in the kitchen of our condominium putting the finishing touches on a sign that we were going to hang on the street corner of Lorain and Barton roads. It said "Le Chaperon Rouge Daycare Center" and I couldn't have been prouder. John and I had made the sign by hand in the back of our condo with hand-written letters. It was very primitive and not very presentable, but it did the job.

Evening had come, and we still had hours of work ahead of us. A neighbor came by and saw us working on the sign.

"What are you doing?" she asked.

"We are opening a school."

The neighbor shook her head. "I think you are crazy," she said, knowing that we didn't have any money.

But we weren't letting that stand in our way. Dee Dee came into the room and looked at our sign.

"It still needs something, mom," she said.

"Like what?"

"A picture or a photo or something."

I held up the sign and stared at it. It was simple – just words – but it did what we needed.

"It says what we need it to say," I said. "It tells the world who we are. We can always add a photo or picture later. Let's start working on the flyers."

For the next three hours, as well as the next several evenings, Dee Dee and I made nearly 500 flyers by hand. We didn't have enough money to get them professionally printed so we scrawled "Le Chaperon Rouge Daycare Center starting September 1 from 6:30 to 6:30 and providing French, gymnastics, meals" on each one, along with our address and an announcement that we would be having an open house every day for one month, from 8 a.m. to 6 p.m., starting on August 1st.

When we were finished with the flyers, Dee Dee and I went all through the neighborhood near the church to distribute them. For several days in late July we walked from house to house, and all through the parking lot at the mall, where we put the flyers on car windshields. People looked at the two of us like we were crazy, but we continued to pass out flyers until they were all gone.

Finally, after days of walking, Dee Dee told me that her feet were sore. I took off her tennis shoes, which I had bought at Goodwill and were not the correct size. Underneath, her feet were bleeding.

"Oh my God, why didn't you say anything, Dee Dee?"

"I didn't want you to make me stop, mom," she said, holding back the tears.

"Oh, sweetie," I said, and left it at that. Luckily, we had finished that job. What needed to be tackled next I could do on my own. The next several evenings I left Dee Dee at home with John and my parents and went to the church by myself. I cleaned the rooms. I cleaned the walls. I cleaned the floors. And when I was done, I had turned that little room in the church basement into a daycare center.

August 1st arrived, and I was ready to start the open house and sign up students. I was going to charge $42 a week. The Gerber daycare center down the street was charging $92. I figured I would get many parents to sign up their children.

Nobody told me that most open houses are supposed to last only a day or two; ours was a month. So every single day, from 8 a.m. to 6 p.m., I went to that open house and waited for parents to bring their children, visit the daycare center and sign them up. And every day but one, nobody came. By the end of August, I had one student.

So on September 2, 1982, Le Chaperon Rouge opened in the basement of the North Olmsted Congregational Church with one child, a little boy named Jeremy. His mother was a nurse at Fairview Hospital and she asked if I would open the school at 5 a.m. so that she could go to work early in the morning. I did.

It would have been easy to have gotten discouraged by the early failure, but Aunt Aurelia had come to the open house on the last day and given me some words of hope.

"Stella," she said, "Don't worry. From this one child, you'll get more. Just keep believing and it will happen."

I did, and within a few days, I was up to three children.

But then we hit a setback. John lost his job at Baldwin-Wallace because enrollment was down and they didn't need him, so he came to the center to help out. In all fairness to John, he loved cars and used to repair them. He made some money on the side during the early years so that we had supplemental income while the daycare center wasn't yet making money. Also, I was selling Mary Kay cosmetics. I became a leader and had about five recruiters working for me. I needed three more to become a director. I liked the work but my calling was to do something for the children so I focused on making the school a success.

The state came in to give final inspection a few days after we opened. I didn't realize I couldn't open before they signed off their approval, and the woman who came from the state board said she was going to have to shut me down.

I cried and explained that I didn't know and the children were there already and I would do whatever they needed me to in order to stay open. One problem was that I didn't have cots for the children. Instead, I had cushions from the sofas in my home. I used to take them in the morning and ask the children to lie down on the cushions and then take them back home in the evening.

When the inspector saw this, she told me that unless I bought cots there wasn't much she could do to let me stay open. She showed me where I could buy cots, which I managed to do, and the state inspectors signed off on the daycare center license and let me remain open.

As the weeks turned into months, we began to enroll new students. By November, I had nine students and a part-time teacher working two hours each day to speak English with the children. My English still wasn't great, so it was a better opportunity for the children with her around. We also started to make good food for the children to eat. We made chicken soup from scratch, we made good pies and we served fresh, healthy vegetables. Word began to spread about this little daycare center in the basement of a church where the children ate well and enjoyed themselves, and the phone began to ring.

I was hesitant to start a conversation with any callers because my English was passable, but that was it. So I used to have a speech: "We are doing this and this and this, and we are offering services for this and this." For a long time, people thought it was a recorded message.

One day, this lady called and realized it was a real person. She came storming in and said, "How dare you start a school and not speak English." But she came back a few months later because she heard what good things we were doing and enrolled her two beautiful girls in our school. Her name was Campagne; she came from Gerber School.

By mid-November, the bills were piling up and there wasn't any relief in sight. One of them quickly became a problem. An original requirement to opening the school was putting up a fence to surround the playground so that the children couldn't just wander off.

I had offered the fence company's owner, John, $800 to do the job, and he accepted it. The only problem was I didn't really have $800 to pay him. I gave him $100 as a down payment and was supposed to pay the balance upon completion. When he arrived looking for the rest of the money, I didn't have it.

"I can pay you $50 or $100 a month," I offered.

"That's not going to cut it," John said. "Either you come up with the full $700 or I'll have to remove the fence."

I didn't believe that he would really do that, so I waited for John to return and reluctantly pick up his first payment of $100. Instead, he arrived with a few men and a little tractor.

I met John at the door and handed him an envelope with $100 cash in it.

"Here's your first payment," I said, then gestured to the tractor. "What are you going to do with that?"

"Take down my fence," he said, "unless, of course, you have $700 more inside the building for me."

I didn't.

I looked at the serious look on John's face then at his men, and finally, at the tractor. Then I looked back at my fence and the reality of the situation hit me hard. I sprinted out the door and ran in front of the tractor. I had to keep them from demolishing my fence. If they knocked it down, I would have to close the school.

"$100 is month is all I can afford!" I screamed; my arms splayed in front of the tractor, protecting my fence with my life. "It's all I can afford!"

It must have been a bizarre scene. The owner watched me standing there, a crazed look on my face, then spat on the ground and gestured for the tractor driver to back down.

"She's crazy," he said. "Leave her alone. She'll pay us eventually."

And I did; $100 at a time for seven straight months.

It was a Thursday morning late in the year when I realized I hadn't enrolled any more students yet, the bills were continuing to pile up and that this notion that I could succeed as a daycare center owner was crazy. I just couldn't go on any longer.

It had nothing to do with determination, because I still had plenty. No, this was all about money. It had become obvious earlier that morning that a lack of money was going to end things prematurely when I didn't have any toilet paper for the children to use. I had gone home and brought back half a roll, which was all we had at our home. Sitting there staring at the bills, thinking about having no toilet paper, I wanted to close the school right then. Instead, I went upstairs into the church, sat down in a pew and began to cry and asked God for help.

"Please God, let me do this," I prayed. "I'll do the very best I know for the children."

I sat in the church for a long time praying.

The next morning, on Friday, three new parents came in with their children. They paid the registration fee and one full week's tuition in cash. Suddenly, I had enough money to continue to the following week. And, little did I know that fortune was about to smile on me in other ways. A school nearby had closed earlier the same week and many parents found themselves with nowhere to place their children. And they learned about my little Le Chaperon Rouge school in the basement of a church.

The next week, more children enrolled. I asked one of the parents if they knew why there were suddenly so many children looking for a daycare center.

She told me and my entire outlook changed. Here was my opportunity. I went down to the other center and found the owner. He told me about his own troubles and how he had closed. He also gave me the contact information for a couple of the teachers he had let go. I looked around at all the equipment he had in the center and asked him how much he wanted for it.

"$8,000," he said.

"I'll give you $1,000 as a down payment," I countered. "And then another $2,000 in two months."

I expected him to haggle with me, but instead he merely shrugged and muttered, "Fine."

So for $3,000 I bought every piece of equipment he had in his closed daycare center. I ended up enrolling most of his former clients and hired a few of his teachers. Within less than two weeks, Le Chaperon Rouge had gone from the brink of closure to a suddenly burgeoning business on its way up. Things couldn't have started looking much better than that.

Or so I thought.

One evening, right around Thanksgiving, while I was still basking in the sudden change of fortune, I was at the school with about 10 children. It was close to 5 p.m. and I heard the crying voice of a baby. We didn't have any babies in the center because we weren't licensed to care for them; the basement center didn't have enough exits to pass the state inspection.

I went upstairs and followed the sound. It was coming from right outside the main door. I opened it and saw a small African-American baby lying there, wrapped loosely in a blanket, bawling its little eyes out. It was cold outside; the Cleveland winter was just starting to brew. It was shocking to see this small child there, all alone, so I took the baby up in my arms and held him close. He was so cold but I could feel his heartbeat. And I took him inside, warmed up a wash cloth and put it on his little hands. Once he started to warm, I called the police.

They arrived quickly, several cars. And they also must have called the TV stations because news vans arrived with crews and they started filming. Every channel on the evening news said that a baby was left in a daycare center in North Olmsted called Le Chaperon Rouge. The baby was taken to the Metzenbaum Child Center in Cleveland, where police looked for its mother.

In that singular moment, I received instant advertising that I could never have afforded. I realized then that Le Chaperon Rouge was meant to be.

First Halloween at Le Chaperon Rouge (1982)

Group photo at Le Chaperon Rouge (1982)

22

The key to happiness isn't magic, and it's not cold, hard cash. It's actually pretty simple when you stop and think about it. You need two important things to be happy – good, solid relationships and a career that you love.

If you wake up every day dreading your job, you're guaranteed to go to sleep every night with that same level of dread. Your relationship with your spouse, significant other or children is no different. If you can't stand them, you will never achieve happiness.

Both parts are required in order for the equation to truly work because even if you're surrounded by people you love, if you hate your job, that hatred will slowly eat away at your soul and the vicious cycle will worsen day after day, month after month and year after year, until one day you look around and realize you've pushed away the ones you love. Years later, you'll finally reflect on your life with a grim realization that you've wasted your opportunities for happiness, and no amount of money or other material wealth will have made up for it.

From the day I opened the doors to Le Chaperon Rouge my focus has been singular – to make a difference in the lives of the children we serve. It is an ideal I believe in wholeheartedly, and one I was well prepared to pursue. In college, I studied education and took numerous psychology courses. I speak several languages, including French, and taught at both a high school in Romania and a Montessori school in the United States. What I've tried to do was combine that Montessori experience with traditional education. It's one reason why our children are so successful when they leave us to go on to other schools.

For an immigrant, I've accomplished amazing things, both emotionally and financially. I'm a firm subscriber to the belief that if you believe in a concept, the money comes. I also believe that I don't do this just for me. I do it to make a difference because God helped me with my son, Alex. God also helped me come to America. And because God helped me become what I am today, I have to give back and try my very best to make a difference in as many people's lives as possible.

There are so many CEOs, entrepreneurs and other business owners I've met over the past 25 years that complain to me about how they work too hard or feel sorry for themselves because of the challenges they face. I have a difficult time empathizing with those people. My own journey has taught me that entrepreneurship isn't for everyone and that truly successful entrepreneurs, the ones that are both personally happy and financially prosperous, share a handful of common traits.

First, they love what they do. They do what they have to do each day in order to succeed. And because they love it so much, it doesn't feel like work. Second, perseverance is part of their core being. They put themselves out every day because they refuse to lose. Failure for them is never an option and setbacks are viewed as bumps in the long and winding road. Third, they are solutions-oriented. Every problem they encounter is met by a mindset where developing a viable solution overcomes any sense of self-pity or doom.

Finally, they combine a little luck with some smarts and intuition. I am very lucky, smart and very aggressive. I know how to complete deals and recognize which ones are the right ones to pursue. And when I see the right deal, I push and push and push until I make it happen. Further, I've always believed I have amazing intuition and relying on it has carried me many places I might otherwise have never gone. My mother used to say, "Since Stella was a baby she would get herself into trouble just to see how she would get out of it."

That may be an oversimplification of things, but she was right. I do like to solve problems. It may sound arrogant but I've come to believe that nothing is too hard for me to manage. When crises appear, people turn to me and ask, "What are you going to do to get us out of this?"

"Simple," I explain, "I'll just split the problem into stages and go step-by-step until I reach a solution."

The one time I can remember when I really did complain about the growing pains of my business, my mother pulled me aside and put it in plain terms.

"God has given you many gifts in life, Stella," she said, "Just take what you've been given and go do it."

Since then, that's been my approach. And when I've promised something to someone, I always have delivered upon that promise – no matter how challenging the solution was to develop and achieve.

So it didn't take long before the little school that could began to outgrow its space in the basement of the church. Word had spread, enrollment was on the rise and we needed more space in order to continue our expansion. I searched and found a building in Northwood Plaza on Lorain Road in North Olmsted that I had heard used to be a daycare center. It was just down the street from the church so I drove over, took a look and decided it might just do the job.

The plaza was owned by Ream Builders and despite not having much money I set up a meeting with the company's president, Bob Ream, to discuss whatever opportunities existed. We met in his North Olmsted office and he was very gracious.

"I'm interested in one of your Northwood Plaza properties," I explained.

"Which one?" he asked. Bob was a cheerful man with chubby cheeks, friendly eyes and white hair that was thinning on top. He wore a white polo shirt and a pair of khaki pants. He leaned back in his chair as we talked, rocking forward to put his elbows on his desk every so often.

"The one in the back of the plaza; I understand it used to be a daycare center."

"It did," he said. "But we converted some of the building to office space recently."

I let my eyes drift from Bob to the photos of houses, plazas and other properties that adorned the walls of his office. I guessed all of them were Ream properties or buildings they had built. "That's OK," I said. "I think it's what I need. Are there still smaller rooms in there from the original daycare center?"

"There are," he said. "So, Mrs. Moga, are you interested in renting some of the space?"

"I am. I have a daycare center and we've outgrown the current space we're in. I'm looking for something larger than can also accommodate future growth."

"And where is your current center located?" he asked, seemingly very interested in helping solve my problem.

"We're in the basement of North Olmsted Congregational Church," I explained. "Pastor Torb rents me the space. So what would it cost to rent your entire building?"

Bob thought about it for a moment then replied, "$5,000 a month."

I nearly fell out of my chair because I couldn't afford that much, but I didn't want to tell him that and end the conversation right there. "OK," I said, nodding as though the amount was something well within my means. "And are you willing to sell the property if I'd rather buy it?"

He smiled. "I am," he said, then leaned back again.

"And what would your asking price be?"

"$240,000," Bob said without hesitation.

This time, I couldn't hide my shock. "That sounds a bit high," I said. "Would you be willing to take less?"

Bob chuckled. "It depends how much less."

"What about $150,000?"

"No," he said. "I'm sorry."

The two of us spent more than a half hour talking about the building, its square footage, the zoning, how many rooms it had, what kind of work Ream would be willing to do on the building to get it in the condition we needed, before Bob finally said, "Look, I'd take $180,000, and not a penny less."

"You have yourself a deal," I said.

"What about financing," Bob suddenly interjected. "Do you have your financing already in place?"

"No," I admitted. "But I will go to the bank and get it."

"OK," he said. "Come back when you get it and we'll draft a contract and put together all the paperwork to make this happen."

We stood, shook hands and I left Bob's office without a clue on how I would be able to secure $180,000 from a bank.

The next day, I went to a bank and asked to see someone who could help me with a business loan. I was shown into a small office and sat down. After we introduced ourselves and I explained I was here to get a business loan for $180,000 so that I could buy a building to expand my growing daycare center business, the banker began asking questions.

"Do you have a business plan we can review?" he asked.

I shook my head. "No."

"What about your income tax statements? Did you bring those with you today?"

Again, I shook my head. "No."

The banker pursed his lips. "And how much money do you intend to provide as a down payment for the financing?"

"None," I said. "I didn't know I needed any of those things."

The banker sighed. "Well, Mrs. Moga, I'm sorry to tell you that without any of this, our bank will be unable to provide you with a loan. Thank you for coming in today and we hope to see you again when we can help you out."

That was it. The banker showed me to the door, shook my hand and I left, dejected. But I wasn't beaten just yet. I went back to Ream Builders the next day with an idea and a plan.

"Did you get your financing in place?" Bob asked as we sat down in the same office as before. His wife was present this time.

"Not exactly," I started. "Would you consider a land contract?"

I hoped Bob would do the same thing the woman who had sold me my condo had done. To this day I even like the phrase "land contract."

He thought about it for a few moments. During the awkward silence neither of us said a word. Bob seemed reluctant to get involved with a land contract.

"It's not something I would normally do," he said. "I'm not sure I like the idea."

His wife spoke up. "Bob, please help her out. We can put together a land contract with our lawyer."

Finally, Bob smiled and said, "OK. I'll tell you what. If you can give me $50,000 up front and pay the rest in installments, you have a deal. But do you have any money whatsoever?"

I had about $5,000 I knew I could come up with, not $50,000, but I was one step further along to buying the building so I nodded. "OK," I said. "Let me see what I can do. Go ahead and get the paperwork in order."

We stood, shook hands yet again then I left. Once more I left knowing I didn't have the means to complete this deal. But I also knew how I was going to manipulate the situation in order to get the deal done. I thought I might be able to give Bob the $5,000 I did have and then provide large chunks of money for several months until I paid him the entire $50,000 down payment. If he wanted to sell the building now, he'd go for it. If he had other options or could afford to hold onto the property without any tenants or a buyer, he wouldn't.

A few days later, Bob called and set up an appointment for us to meet again. His attorney had completed all the paperwork for a land contract. "Bring the $50,000 and we'll sign the papers and move forward," he said. "Can you meet tomorrow morning at 10 a.m.?"

I agreed to the meeting and as I did I began to get cold feet. Throughout the rest of the day and all night long I started to worry about what would happen when I showed up with only $5,000 and my crazy scheme. When the time came, I didn't have the courage to go and sent my daughter with $5,000 cash in her little hands and a written message: "This is the money for the building. If you want, my mother will talk to you about the rest."

Bob was livid.

"I wasted my time and my lawyer's time," he yelled at Dee Dee. "And this is what she does for me – send a little girl with one-tenth of the money! Tell your mother I'm very disappointed in her."

And then he sent Dee Dee on her way.

Dee Dee delivered the message, including the part where Mr. Ream yelled at her. I decided that rather than simply walk away from the deal I wasn't going to let it die. Besides, he was mean to my daughter. So I went back over to Bob's office and dropped the $5,000 on his desk.

"Look," I said. "I can raise the rest of the money. I'm not wasting your time. And you don't have to yell at little girls."

Bob stood and started to hand the pile of money back to me.

"No," he said.

I cut him off before he could continue. "I can do this," I insisted. "It's January right now. Take the money. Give me the building. If I can't pay you the other $45,000 by the end of December, you keep all the money I've given you, throw me out of the building and keep the school for yourself." Then I plopped myself back down in my seat, crossed my arms and waited.

It took a moment, but Bob finally sat back down and gave me a little smile. His wife walked into the room and stood near the door.

"You have spunk and confidence," he said. "I'll give you that."

I looked over at his wife. She was as scared as I was.

"Let's help her, Bob," she said.

Bob looked at his wife, then me; then he laughed.

"Fine," he said. "You have a deal. If you don't pay the full $45,000 by the end of December, you basically walk away and everything transfers back to me. I will have all the documents redrafted to reflect that."

"OK," I said. "Thank you."

"Don't thank me yet," he said. "If you fall even one penny short, you don't satisfy your end of the deal. Do you understand that?"

"I do," I said. "I do."

For the next several months I would give Bob large chunks of money – $1,000, $2,000, $3,000 – whenever I could. I also was able to expand our service offerings and put infants and toddlers in the school. It was something I couldn't do in the basement of the church, but with my own building, with more space and better facilities, it became a possibility. And because of that, business picked up considerably.

When December rolled around, I had paid Bob a total of $43,000 toward the down payment but was still $7,000 short. And on December 18, when everybody was thinking about Christmas and buying last-minute presents, I was desperate for money.

We were doing well, but not well enough. But because Le Chaperon Rouge was still an intimate place where I was involved with every child that came through the doors, I'd been able to forge relationships with several of the parents. A few I could even go so far as to call my friends. So I asked for and received a meeting with a small group of parents with whom I'd become the most friendly. Many of them had been sending their children to my school since the first year, when we'd been in the church basement.

The meeting took place at the school on a cold, blustery December evening. It was a last-gasp effort, I realized, but had a feeling that if we were delivering the type of childcare these parents wanted, the idea I had in mind might just work.

I thanked everyone for coming then explained the background of the deal I'd made with Ream Builders and what I had been doing for the past year, paying large chunks of money through cash flow to Mr. Ream several times a month. After all the bills were paid, everything else had been going toward that down payment.

"I need $7,000 to finish my down payment for the building," I finished. "If I don't have it, they will throw me out."

Choruses of "That's not possible," "It can't happen," "No way" and "Oh my God" echoed throughout the room.

"Does that mean the center will be gone, too?" one parent asked.

"Yes," I said. "I'm sorry to have to tell you this, especially now. I thought I'd make it for sure. I never thought there was any way I would get this close and not reach the full $50,000."

Again, a chorus of disbelief swept through the room.

"We have two possibilities," I continued, then delivered my pitch. "You can give me some money for tuition in advance. In return, I will give you a 20 percent discount. If we do that then I'm going to be able to pay my bill."

"What's the other possibility," another parent asked.

"Not a good one," I said. "If that possibility doesn't happen, the other one is that the center will be forced to close at the end of the year, as I mentioned."

I took a deep breath and finished. "I've taken a hard look at my books and know for sure that I will not be able to come up with $7,000 between now and December 31st through normal tuition payments. That's where we stand."

For the next several minutes no one said anything. Silence filled the room. And then, a wondrous thing happened. One at a time, every parent in the room rose and offered to give me money. It was as if something had just swept through the room and lifted everyone onto it. There were so many candidates that it totaled more money than I needed. In the end, I accepted only the $7,000 I needed and gave all of the parents who volunteered the advance payments the discounts.

And so, on December 30, 1984, I carried $7,000 in cash that I had collected from these wonderful parents of my students to Ream Builders and placed it on Mr. Ream's desk.

"Here you go," I said. "The final $7,000. Every penny."

Bob smiled at me. "Thank you, Stella," he said. "Please have a seat."

I sat down.

Bob tapped his fingers on the desk. He eyeballed me for several moments. Then he said, "I have an idea."

"Why don't I give you back the $50,000 so that you can go to the bank and apply for a loan?"

I shot him a puzzled glance. "Why would I do that?"

"Well," he said, "$50,000 is a lot of money. If your business is doing as well as it seems to be – so much so that you were able to raise the $50,000 for a down payment – I would bet that the bank will see things the same way I do and give you a loan for the remaining $130,000."

"You mean buy the property outright right now?"

He nodded.

And so I did as Mr. Ream suggested and went back to the bank. This time, I my paperwork was in order and the banker was very courteous. As Bob predicted, the banker saw the $50,000 as a substantial amount of money for a down payment and approved a loan for the rest.

My mother used to say "Everybody can make money when you have money. It's the creators of big fortunes that make it without any money that are the heroes in business."

The deal I made with Mr. Ream was the first lesson in business real estate. It's one thing to pay rent and to run a small company. It's a whole different ball game to own property. Your identity as an owner is everything. You can not fool around with a bank. You may be a very nice person to your friends, family, and customers, but the bank doesn't care about any of that. Having the credentials to look good on paper is a hard thing to achieve. As a newly arrived immigrant to America, I learned so much those first few years. Most American children knew more about banking than I did – from cashing a check to opening a bank account, to getting a loan for a big commercial property.

What had happened was pretty amazing. Mr. Ream was a real nice man. He saw the same flicker of light inside me that the General saw when he gave the approval for the passports to leave Romania. They felt that I had good intentions and passion. They wanted to help and be a positive force in the world. That's how I inspire people. They know that my motives are not selfish and shallow, and they feel good knowing that they've helped another human being with a dream.

Doing business with Mr. Ream was the first experience that demonstrated what I had learned in Romania dealing with the Communists I would be able to apply to doing business in America.

I have always stayed on the unconventional side of business affairs. It is one thing to ask for things and to practice honesty, honor, duty and general well being. But it is never OK to mislead someone and then to really mess their lives up by lying, cheating and stealing. Go ahead and ask for the lower interest rate or discount. Work harder than anyone else for your next promotion. Redo the business proposal six, eight, or sixty times until it is right. But be honest about it.

This was the first business loan I secured and became the beginning for a nice, successful journey with my schools. It was such a big deal for me, and it was such a big deal for my future dealings with banks. Suddenly, I had "brick-and-mortar" to use as collateral and the future of Le Chaperon Rouge looked much, much brighter.

Stella, Dee Dee and Le Chaperon Rouge
kindergarten graduation class (1982)

Stella portrait (1984)

Le Chaperon Rouge logo on the Rocky River school building

23

Nineteen eighty-four turned out to be a memorable, albeit stressful, year. My business turned a critical corner in its existence and its survival no longer seemed threatened. My personal life also underwent significant change. My relationship with John continued to sour, but on a good note, 1984 was the year I bought my dream house.

Getting the house, like everything else in my life up until that point, wasn't simple. I found a new development under construction called Bretton Woods on Sycamore Oval in Westlake and went to the model homes. At the time I knew I didn't have any money in my pocket and that I would have a hard time getting a house because I didn't have additional money for a down payment. But I had been able to secure the building for the business and thought I might just find a way to buy a house as well.

The agent, a young, attractive woman, walked me around the development and showed me the lots and what the houses would look like when they were completed. I pointed to one of the larger lots and said, "I want this one. How much?"

She looked me up and down then frowned. "$38,000. Are you sure that's the one you want," she said. "It's one of the most expensive in the development."

"Yes," I replied.

We walked back to the model home.

"And If I just buy a finished home, how much would the house be?" I asked.

"$178,000," she said.

"I'll give you $100,000 for it."

"What?" she said. "I can't do that."

"What if you don't paint my house on the inside, don't install the floors, don't give me a fireplace and I do all of it myself?" I asked.

"I'm sorry," she said. "I can't do that either."

I left disappointed but not defeated.

The developer was Bennett Builders. I set up an appointment with the owner, Don Bennett, and told him the same thing: "I want the vanilla house – doors, plumbing and electric. I'll do the rest."

At first, he refused. "Look," he said. "People don't want to see amateurs working on a house in a development where they're moving in or thinking about buying a house in. That would be bad for business. They would think their house wasn't built by professionals."

"But I would use tradesmen," I explained. "They're just friends of mine. It wouldn't hurt your business."

"What kind of tradesmen?"

"Romanian tradesmen," I said. "They're experts at floor and wall installation."

"I don't like the idea," Bennett said.

"Mr. Bennett, please. It won't hurt a thing. No one will know they're not your contracted men but you and I."

Finally, exasperated, Bennett relented. "OK," he said. "But for $113,000, not $100,000."

"Deal."

When I left it was with the realization that once again a deal had worked in my favor. Filled with confidence, I went to the bank with all the paperwork for the house – showing how both the land and house were appraised for much more than the $113,000 I was requesting for a mortgage loan. The loan was approved.

I remember how happy I was when I chose the colors of the walls and the colors of the outside of the house because I was so amazed that I was able to accomplish this and buy a house. But the actual work on my house quickly turned into a circus-like atmosphere. I remember how our neighbors came and saw the Romanians installing the floors. They were supposed to put a cement mesh underneath the tiles and they didn't know how to do it. In about a month, all the tiles were cracked.

The painting wasn't done right. Either was the basement. Water kept coming in. Eventually, we corrected everything but the basement. For the next several years, water kept oozing in at the unlikeliest of times.

On the day I moved in, I called my friend Piana. She had passed her exams and moved with her husband to New York to become a practicing psychiatrist. When she answered the phone, I said, "Guess where I'm calling you from, Piana? My dream house. Remember that model house we saw in the development? Well, I built something similar."

She was so happy for me.

Unfortunately, the same couldn't be said for John. We had had our problems for years, but our relationship was deteriorating as fast as my business was growing. We weren't getting along at all, and nothing either of us did seemed to change that. I shouldn't have been surprised. We were miserable. We didn't have anything to do with each other. I would drive around for a while, sometimes hours, before I went home, just crying.

John was also miserable and wanted out of the marriage, but he never directly said so. After Dee Dee was born, we stopped sleeping in the same bedroom. After Alex was born, we stopped having sex. In fact, we did not have sex even once during the last five years of our marriage. We finally ended the charade in October 1987, when we were divorced.

Overall, I truly believe that John is a good, smart person. I wouldn't have been drawn to him back in college if he hadn't been good at heart. Unfortunately, that wasn't enough. Being a good person didn't translate into being good for the people who were around him day and night. To this day, I still can't explain why John was never close with Dee Dee. At times, his disaffection for her even bordered on disdain. When she was in 10th grade, John wouldn't let her be a teenager and spent all his time criticizing her and telling her that America was a terrible place. That may help explain why to this day Dee Dee has never had much trust in men.

John didn't seem to like me either. The moment I became a mother, he moved into a different room. He was constantly annoyed with something. And if nothing real existed, he concocted something to complain about. John would blame one of us for every little problem he had. When it came to me, I was never smart enough, I was never pretty enough, I was never tall enough, slim enough or nice enough for him. But the more we fought, the stronger I became until I realized I needed to get away from the poison he had injected into our lives.

John was good with Alex, though, very good, in fact. Part of it was that he told me he felt sorry for Alex. Despite the reason, he was very attentive to Alex's needs when he was younger. Even then, after our divorce, every time Alex went to John's condo, John would sit around drinking and smoking while Alex watched television. John would promise Alex vacations to Canada and other things that he never delivered on. And throughout, John was critical of America.

From the time we arrived, John hated this country and planned to move back to Romania. Finally, he decided to move back the year when Alex was supposed to graduate from high school. John said he was going to leave in March, a few months before Alex's graduation. But I told John that he couldn't do that to his son and needed to wait until Alex graduated. That pretty much sums up John's viewpoint – him first, everybody else second.

In every action you make in your life, there is a deciding moment that precipitates that action. For the end of my marriage, it happened one day in February 1987 when Dee Dee was a senior in high school. She woke early and came into my bedroom.

"Mom," she said, giving me a nudge. "Wake up."

I did. "What it is, sweetie?" I asked.

Dee Dee sat down the edge of the bed and I sat up.

"Mom, do you know that I go to school every morning so sad because I see you and daddy so unhappy. When I see you in this big bed by yourself, I get so upset."

John had been sleeping downstairs in the den on a sofa.

"Oh, honey," I cried then gave her a hug. The two of us cried together for several minutes before I wiped my eyes. "Dee Dee, go get ready for school. I will take care of this."

I got out of bed and went downstairs. John was asleep on the sofa. I sat down beside him. "John," I said. "We can't live like this anymore. We should go to counseling and try to make this work. Our situation is destroying the children."

John sat up and gave me a glare that showed just how much he hated me. "You're the big businesswoman," he said. "I'm happy living this way. You solve it."

For one of the few times in my life I was speechless. Then I tapped him on his shoulder and said, "OK. I'll solve it."

I rose and went back upstairs. The next day, I went to an attorney and filed for divorce.

Stella and Alex at the Sycamore Oval home in Westlake, Ohio (1985)

Alex and Stella on a ski trip at Peek'n Peak Resort (1987)

Alex's Le Chaperon Rouge graduation party (1987)

Alex (1989)

Alex at four years old

Alex (1991)

24

By mid-1985, things looked good for the North Olmsted school. The waiting list was long and getting longer; and a number of prospective students' parents began pushing me to open a second school so they could enroll their children. As it turned out, running out of room was a good problem to have.

I looked around in the immediate area and found a suitable location in a Westlake strip center on Center Ridge Road near the corner of Canterbury. It was owned by Richard Valore and about 3,000 square-feet. It was a little tight, and the playground was very small, but for a second location it seemed good enough.

Mr. Valore's asking price for rent seemed astronomical, but I wanted the space and negotiated an equitable deal that provided me with nearly four months of free rent while I made all the necessary preparations to get the doors open.

Le Chaperon Rouge II opened in early 1986. Once again, my timing couldn't have been better.

Dagmar Celeste, wife of then-Ohio Governor Richard Celeste, had recently been making news for her efforts to promote affordable, quality daycare for working mothers. In April, on Liberty Day, she visited Northeast Ohio and scheduled an appearance at my new Westlake center.

"One of my friends told me about your home-like quality here," Dagmar remarked as she and I walked through the hallway from one classroom to another. Celeste's assistant accompanied us, silent. Behind us, several newspaper reporters and a photographer completed the procession.

"Is it true you've only been in the United States for five years?" Dagmar asked.

"Yes," I said, still in disbelief that Ohio's first lady had decided to come to Le Chaperon Rouge. "I escaped Communist Romania and came here in September 1979. I brought my family with me. We didn't have any money and weren't allowed to bring anything except for one suitcase each. But we made it."

The First Lady shook her head. "That's amazing, Stella. Simply amazing. And look at all you've accomplished today."

Around me, reporters gobbled up every word. The assembly had spent the past 15 minutes watching a group of children present a program in French, something we'd incorporated into the curriculum. Now we were headed to a different classroom to watch children participate in art class.

"The state has a small daycare center in Columbus for government employees and is planning another," Dagmar explained, half addressing me and half addressing the accompanying media. "This is something private businesses should be considering; setting up daycare for their employees."

I nodded in agreement.

"There are so many working women these days," I said. "Look at me. What's important, though, is that it can't just be any daycare center. It has to be one where the children are cared after well and treated with love. That's what we're all about here."

"I couldn't agree more," Celeste said, then stopped and turned to face the reporters.

"A place like Ohio can't afford to have more than 50 percent of its workforce without suitable daycare options," she averred. "We need to seek out options that can serve as examples."

She half-turned her body, lifted her left arm and gestured with a sweeping wave to the classrooms ahead. "Le Chaperon Rouge is a good example of what we need," she said. "Not only is Mrs. Moga a great example of the American dream and Ohio entrepreneurship at its best, but her center provides an educational program that is smart. She strives for a homey atmosphere with home-cooked meals, small personable facilities and plenty of staff. What more could you ask for?"

My heart raced.

"You have to keep daycare personalized," she continued. "That's the fine line we need to walk. You can't do it like you're making hamburgers."

Then she turned back to me. "Stella, you've shown us French and are about to show us art class, what else do you do here that sets you apart?"

I beamed and smiled my biggest smile. "We expose children to letters, numbers, everything they're going to need to be familiar with once they reach kindergarten," I said. "I feel it's important to do that now and give them a head start."

The First Lady nodded in agreement. "Well, you are certainly doing things the right way," she said. "You can tell you don't leave a stone unturned when it comes to children's education and providing them with a clean, nutritional and loving environment. You should be proud of what you've accomplished here."

I nodded. "I am."

The next day, Le Chaperon Rouge was featured in numerous newspapers. The publicity only helped continue spreading the word about my little center, and our notoriety continued to grow. And the most exciting part was that we were succeeding not by being followers, but by being leaders and trying to do things in ways that hadn't been done before.

A classroom in the Le Chaperon Rouge Westlake building (1986)

25

Such fast growth would have been fruitless if I hadn't been so committed to running the business ethically. It may sound trite but I've spent more than 25 years trying to run my business by example and being dedicated to my staff. I believe that you are only as good as your employees are, and if your treat them well, pay them fairly, provide them with good benefits and give them the same respect you expect yourself, they will want to excel for you and for the business.

It doesn't get more scientific than that, and there are no hidden secrets to success. My employees see me with a smile on my face every day, no matter how hard I work or what challenges I'm facing. They sometime tell me that they feel embarrassed when they don't work as hard as I do. I explain that I'm a person just like they are; no different.

As a company owner it's important for me to understand that my employees often do not have the same agenda I do. I'm building an asset, they're building a life. So to make up for that gap in goals, they need to know I value them and respect them. When I do those things, I've found I have built a very successful organization.

Further, dedication and enthusiasm are real; you can't fake those things. When you work with children, they can tell whether you care or not, and whether you love them or not. It's a very simple philosophy, and I tell this to my grandchildren all the time: If you put your heart into it, you can accomplish anything and everything. And then, when you accomplish your goals, you can measure success not just by dollars and cents but by the look on parents' faces when they see how well their children are treated and how complimentary they talk about you when someone brings up your name or the center.

That said, I admit that I'm not perfect and have made many, many mistakes over the years. I'm human, after all. One major leadership shortcoming of mine continues to be a wanting to feel indispensible. It's probably understandable because I've poured my heart and soul into this business, but it's not a good thing. Even if I delegate something, I sometimes go back over and over to check if the task I delegated was accomplished.

Perhaps it's because of my struggles in Romania, or the challenge I faced in the early days when if I didn't do it myself it wouldn't have gotten done, but whatever the root cause, even though I've gotten this far, I have to start learning how to trust people if I want to go even further. When I tell people to do something – or they tell me they'll do something – I need to believe they will accomplish it, even if it's not going to be the same as how I would do it.

The bottom line is that I've come to realize that my next personal level of growth will come when I start truly trusting people and being less involved in every level of the business. This doesn't mean I'm a control freak and keep everything close to the vest. It's the opposite, in fact. I strive to ensure that my employees do not work in the dark. I've spent years crafting and articulating a clear message and concise job descriptions for every area of the business – from janitor to top management. If you assume people understand what you want to accomplish within an organization or assume they know what you want them to accomplish, you're doomed to failure. At Le Chaperon Rouge, we've overcome this by providing regular training, communicating often and putting everything in writing. Then, when we are successful, we let everyone in the organization know about it. The more they know about what's going on, the more successful and committed they'll be.

Back in 1987, after we received favorable press from the Dagmar Celeste visit, my business life continued to hum along. I opened a school in Avon Lake in one of Kopf Builders' buildings. One day, after negotiations ended and I was preparing to open the school, an older woman stopped by the building and confronted me.

"Avon Lake does not need a daycare center," she said. "The mothers should stay home to take care of their children. I am going to stop you from opening this daycare center."

Calmly, I took the woman by the hand and smiled.

"Come with me," I said.

At first, the woman was apprehensive, but she nodded and let me lead her through the building.

"I am going to do great things for the children," I explained as I showed her the classrooms, went over the curriculum and described the nutrition program we used.

Eventually, she calmed down enough to sit with me and talk. We chatted for a long time and over time she and I became good friends. She even became a volunteer at the school, coming in and playing with babies in the infant room not long after we opened our doors.

The next expansion occurred shortly after I bought a new house. In December 1989 I bought a building on Pearl Road in Strongsville that had been an old office building. It was two stories high with offices upstairs and an antique store downstairs. It wasn't zoned for daycare but I bought it anyway. I figured I could get it rezoned later.

The owners wanted $260,000; I paid them $180,000. It was a good deal.

Afterward, I didn't have enough money to remodel it properly through a high-end construction company so I hired some Romanian immigrants I knew – an electrician, a plumber and a carpenter – and brought them all together at the building on a Friday afternoon.

They were a motley crew, but I figured they'd be able to get the job done quickly and cost-effectively.

"Tomorrow morning," I told them, "come here and we are going to gut the building. Take everything out."

"Everything?" the carpenter asked.

"Everything," I said. "All the junk, many of the walls, some of the flooring, I'll point out what needs to go. And make sure to bring enough people that we can get this all done tomorrow and Sunday."

The men agreed, and the next morning, they showed up with an all-Romanian crew and hit the job. We didn't know, and honestly I didn't know, that we needed a dumpster. I wrongly assumed that the city's sanitation department would come and take my garbage away. So picture this scene: We're in the middle of Strongsville, a high-end community, right on a main thoroughfare, Pearl Road. We gut the building and put all the debris, everything you can imagine, in the front of the building. There was even a pile of dirt as tall as the building. And then, at the worst possible moment, the wind started up and scattered garbage all over the streets.

On Monday morning, first thing in the morning, politicians and businesspeople from the city of Strongsville, including Mayor Walter F. Ehrnfelt, arrived at my building, angry. A line of cars filled the road next to my building and what appeared to be a mob of people stood there, all of them shouting. The mayor was quite literally bright red with rage. The building inspectors were fuming. People I didn't know or recognize were standing and pointing and gesturing wildly at all the detritus. And everybody was on my property.

"What in God's name is going on here?" the mayor yelled at me when he finally saw me approach the mob.

"We're getting ready to open a school," I said. I realized as I said this that I didn't have any plans that had been properly submitted or approvals received from the city for all the work we'd done.

"Not like this you're not!" the building inspector screamed, running toward me like he was going to kill me right then and there.

He jabbed a finger in my face. "You will never open a school in Strongsville! Never!"

It wasn't worth fighting, so I tried a different tactic – diffusion.

It took about twenty minutes to get everyone calmed down and their voices to a reasonable level. Once they were calm, well, at least as calm as they were going to get considering the circumstances, we stood in a little circle on the front lawn and talked.

"Why didn't you know you needed a dumpster?" Mayor Ehrnfelt asked. "What were you thinking?"

"I didn't know," I said. "It's an honest mistake."

"An honest mistake? Look at this place; it's a war zone!"

I looked around and couldn't argue.

"OK," I said. "It is. But now you have to help me."

The mayor's face began to take on its previously reddened hue. Then, instead of launching into a new diatribe he sighed.

"Fine," he said.

He probably didn't mean it, but really, what other choice did he have?

Within two hours, the city brought dumpsters, trucks and an entire crew of maintenance men in and cleaned up my property. The irony of the situation is that despite all the hoopla it caused, they never levied a fine against me for the trouble. I don't know why. But it was almost comical how upset they got. I don't blame them, though. I wasn't being a jerk; I honestly didn't know my responsibilities. But it was pretty funny seeing all those officials stop their cars, leap out and help clean up. It took most of the day on Monday.

The next day, guilt set in and I went to the mayor's office to apologize. His secretary didn't want to let me see him, but I insisted. I barely got his door open before he screamed, "Get out of my office! I don't want anything to do with you? Do you know what kind of trouble you've created?"

I stood there in the doorway and stared at him, unwavering.

"Mr. Mayor," I said, suddenly enraged. "I came from Communism and secret police, and they didn't scare me. Don't think for a minute that you are going to scare me. Your attitude stinks! You act like you're in the Nazi army. You're insulting me, a lady, by throwing me out of your office. If you don't want to hear my apology, shame on you!"

I thought the speech was pretty good, but he threw me out anyhow.

Undeterred, at 8 a.m. the next day I returned to city hall. Again, the secretary reluctantly let me in. This time, however, I spoke first upon opening the mayor's door.

"Look," I said. "I owe you an apology; you owe me an apology. Let's be friends. And let's try together to open a school in your city."

The mayor looked at me with disdain. I could see he wanted to shout at me again, but he was savvy enough to recognize that it wouldn't do much good. I was, unfortunately for him, here to stay and I would come back every day until he let me talk.

He sighed and let out a small chuckle, on the polite side of a scoff.

"OK," he said. "But you have to follow the rules. This is a very well-respected city. We cannot do what we want. We have to have building permits. We have to do things the right way. Do you understand me?"

"I do."

The mayor gestured me to come inside and sit, which I did. We spent the next half hour talking about everything that needed to be completed before the daycare center could open – rezoning, new permits, etc.

After the meeting, it didn't take long before everything was approved and the school opened. It wasn't the best looking building but it was a cute school. And the swift enrollment of new students underscored the need in that community for what we offered.

A few years later, when I needed a bigger school, I bought the property next door from a doctor. I got it at a very good price. And with that property I had enough commercial frontage to go to the city again, ask for approval to demolish both buildings and submit plans for the construction of a new building for a new school.

This time, I wanted to do it by the book and be partners with the city rather than accidental adversaries. So I let the city know I planned to leave the school in operation in the front and build the daycare in the back then demolish the front of the building and the next door building and put an office in the front.

"You can't do that, Ms. Moga," a zoning clerk explained when he saw my application. "You need public facility zoning for the school and general business zoning for the front. You cannot mix two zonings on the same property."

But I wasn't one to just take no for an answer. I was, after all, a person just like him.

"Guess what," I said. "We are going to make history because you are going to approve me. What do I need to do to get this done?"

The clerk told me I needed to file an appeal with the city's zoning board, and I went to the city and applied for approval. For almost a year I bugged them, so much so that they eventually tired of me and relented, granting for general business zoning in the front and public facility for daycare in the back. And with a permit in hand, I began demolishing the building next door.

Unfortunately, this project did not go smooth, just like everything else I'd tried in Strongsville. First, the company I hired didn't approach demolition in a normal way. Instead, of just knocking the building down, the workers started taking it apart piece by piece. And once more, the mayor came by, livid, and complained.

I acted quickly. The last thing I needed right now was to make an enemy of the city again. So to get the project back on track the right way, I fired the original demolition company and hired another firm. That didn't do much good because not long after this firm completed the demolition and began construction, the general manager of the company talked to people and I found out that company was going belly up and they would not be able to finish the project.

I was shocked. I got invoices that I'd been paying all along the way during this project. I was shocked by the news, so I fired the man on the spot, even though it was a fruitless move because he wasn't going to work for me anymore anyway. I later learned that his money woes were the company's own fault. Instead of paying the tradesmen, the owner used the money for other things.

Finally, exasperated, I hired a third builder. This time, he was able to complete the languishing project. By the time he was done, it was 2001. The project had begun in 1998. If there was anything good that came out of the process, it's that the Strongsville school in its larger facilities continues to be a strong contributor to my chain of daycare centers.

Unlike the builders that defrauded me and went bankrupt, I try to run my companies with little overhead and no greed. I treat money with a lot of respect – I work hard for it and try not to spend it unwisely. If I can do something with less money, I will.

Inside each and every one of us there is a moral compass. I've seen money come and go in my life. Money was never my driving force. If it was, I would've stayed in Romania. My family always knew how to work hard. We were never driven by greed or to show off to people. We wanted to own our land. Land for us meant security in an ever changing country. Money doesn't bring security to life. Hard work and dedication does. When circumstances take away all of your possessions, you still get to walk away with your life skills. And with these life skills, you can always rebuild what has been taken away.

Money is like water. Try to hold onto it and it seeps through your fingers. Putting money to good use is the only way to make it work for you.

Money is only a secondary priority to a primary passion. When you find your passion in life, money is the extra bonus of success. When you make a promise like I did to take care of children, you do whatever it takes to keep that promise. It becomes your zest and love for the cause. Money is an empty joy in itself. Besides, how much stuff can you buy when you know your higher purpose is still not known to you? People get lost in years in the thrill of shopping.

But this bad habit gone awry will lead you right into a brick wall at a high speed. Sooner or later, the price we pay for debt is with our spiritual integrity. The stuff we buy gets outdated and we end up selling it at a garage sale. Always start a path with the end in mind. Ask yourself many questions along the way. Will my present build or compromise my future? Am I investing in something that is going to reward me or destroy me? Are my children and even grandchildren going to benefit from the way I am living my life now or am I going to be their burden? What can I do to start living life with a higher purpose? Maxing out my credit at the local mall is not it. Life presents us with many choices. Choosing wisely is within our power. Making sure the small choices nourish our lives leaves the big choices taken care of.

I love to wheel and deal, negotiate and haggle. I look at it like a game where I try to get what I want. But I pass on the savings to the parents of the children we serve and don't take a lot of money out of the business. So for everything we offer, we're probably the best price in the industry. If you calculate the time one child spends in our school each week and all the services he or she receives – food, academics, activities, nice buildings, quality teachers and the like – it comes out to about $4 per hour. That's a pretty good bargain and one reason I've been able to be successful in a very competitive industry.

Original building for the Le Chaperon Rouge Strongsville location
(1989)

Sign outside the new Le Chaperon Rouge Strongsville building
(2000)

Le Chaperon Rouge Strongsville (2000)

26

Le Chaperon Rouge Child Care Centers and Private Elementary, the culmination of my life's work, has today evolved into a leader in the field of education. We pride ourselves on our ability to make service our competitive advantage by offering a full package to every student that attends our schools at a much lower price than our competitors.

We offer home cooked meals – breakfast and lunch; as well as a nutritious snack in the afternoon. We have worked to develop an innovative curriculum that is age appropriate with building blocks like social studies (artist of the month, country of the month, field trips and special visitors); science (animal of the week, senses, human body systems, color of the week, etc.); reading and writing; social emotional management; language arts; storytelling; dramatic play; math (number of the week, shape of the week, etc.); creative art; fine and gross motor skills; music; and circle time. We include extra curriculum activities such as French, Spanish, music and computers in the regular tuition. For an additional fee, children also receive classes like gymnastics, ballet, karate and dance.

Marry that with state of the art buildings that house our schools and we have created something that isn't offered anywhere else, and priced it competitively.

Our buildings were specifically designed to allow us to offer small classroom sizes for each age group of children, a large gross motor play area, a dance room, outside playgrounds with grass and rubber flooring for safety, a full size kitchen, a security system with cameras and keypads on all the doors, bathrooms in each classroom, and a comfortable size parking lot with easy access to the facility for convenient pick up and drop off times.

One thing I was careful to ensure was that each one of our locations was near major highway exits for convenience for our clientele.

From my years in education before opening the schools I learned that in order to succeed you have to offer value. Most of our competitors charge extra for meals and curriculum. They also do not have the beautiful buildings specifically designed for a daycare center. If they do have such a building, their tuition reflects it. It is usually much higher than Le Chaperon Rouge.

We have been careful to treat every client the same – as if they were our own children. In that vein, we do not have special customers. All of our children get the benefits that our program provides. We do have special customers like sports celebrities, radio and television personalities, and affluent members of the business community whose children go to our schools. However, everybody at Le Chaperon Rouge is a VIP customer.

Despite our success, I've kept the schools true to their humble origins and not forgotten what my struggles to get them started taught me. Because of that, our customer service transcends our service in one special way: we are owner run and operated. To this day, I remain involved in every aspect of the running of Le Chaperon Rouge, and my personal dedication and 'do whatever it takes to be the best' attitude has changed the standard in day care in the Cleveland area over the last 27 years.

What this means is that every detail of our operations is tended to and every concern is managed promptly. My staff is also inspired and trained to work in the same manner that I do.

I've developed systems that allow us to train our staff in the smallest detail, like smiling and hugging our children, to the biggest, like how to teach curriculum, keep each classroom organized, clean and, just as important, decorated with the children's work.

We also teach our staff to communicate with each parent and offer a report card a few times a year to track each child's progress. Our directors and teachers also know that we want perfect inspections from the State of Ohio, Health and Fire Department. Having perfect inspections is not a small task. Everything has to be perfect on a daily basis – paperwork in the office and in each classroom, ratios, all supplies and equipment in working order, and all staff following the state rules and regulations.

I'm a stickler for details. Le Chaperon Rouge trains each staff member not just in how to do their jobs but also how to offer great customer service to our children and their parents. The management team and I have written and continually revised every training manual at Le Chaperon Rouge. We make sure all teachers are well trained long before their first day on the job.

We also offer a CDA program, which is the equivalent of a two year college degree in early childhood education. One thing I've learned over the years is that in order to maintain good teachers, we must teach them in the best ways possible. This wonderful program is offered at a huge discount and we pay the rest of the fee. The teachers are trained at one of our facilities by someone that we hired personally. The State of Ohio also requires that teachers in a child care center take in service classes on a yearly basis to keep up with such topics like child abuse, CPR, communicable disease and first aid. Le Chaperon Rouge offers these classes to all of our teachers for free. At any other day care center, the staff must search out and pay for these classes themselves.

Because my life had been difficult and money was always hard to come by in America, I instruct my directors to help me keep a watchful eye on every detail at every school on a weekly basis. Our daily operations manager makes rounds at each school and has a multiple page report that encompasses every aspect of each school. This manager talks to every teacher, cook and director to maintain our level of excellence.

My company came about because I was unhappy with the care my son received and the disdain the center had for my concerns. So I built Le Chaperon Rouge in such a way that we are prepared to handle any concerns from our customers. Our directors have been employed at Le Chaperon Rouge for a long time and we always hire our directors from within. These directors answer directly to me on a daily basis. They keep in close contact with me and our daily operations manager. Any concern that arises is handled promptly. The number one reason Le Chaperon Rouge has maintained a fine level of success is because I have the highest of standards and me and my staff follow through on promises made. I am very proud that I've been able to make Le Chaperon Rouge into a brand that stands for the best quality child care with a loving hand at a very competitive price.

Each location of Le Chaperon Rouge is streamlined to run seamlessly. We treat our staff with the utmost respect and care. The teachers get praised when they are doing things right. When problems arise, we correct them right away and we help in the correction process. We follow up to make sure the problem is completely dissolved. The most important aspect is that we have a hard working group of people. When your company is strong like that, any new employee is going to blend in with a good working system. An incompetent new employee is not going to last long within such a thriving group of people and will be replaced quickly.

Because we treat our employees with the utmost respect, they like coming to work and being part of a positive work environment.

Our benefits package is unmatched by any other company in this field.

We offer paid vacation, six paid holidays a year, off for each teacher's birthday, free home cooked breakfast, lunch, and a nutritious snack in the afternoon, health insurance package, retirement package, CDA program on site and at a large discount, all in service training classes for free, partially paid college tuition, competitive wages, raises on a regular basis, and free or discounted tuition for the employee's children.

Our teachers have all the supplies needed to run successful classrooms. Because our teachers thrive in their working environment, they talk highly of the company they work for to everyone they meet outside of work. This is the way we've earned our reputation.

When I actually take the time to step back and look at how much I've been able to accomplish with my business and what it took to get here, I'm still amazed by it.

27

As my business continued to grow I focused on fine-tuning my leadership style. Things weren't so positive in my personal life so it only made sense to keep my thoughts on business. My personal failures with John had escalated to the point of no return and our divorce was finalized in October 1987. John moved out of the house on Sycamore and into a condominium.

The day he left, everybody cried.

It felt like someone was dying. Alex, particularly, was destroyed. He couldn't bear to watch his father leave. I didn't help matters along, and didn't thing about the consequences of my actions until much later. Because I wanted to make a clean break, I decided that as John was moving out, I would do the same. I put the house on Sycamore up for sale.

Alex took out some of his frustration on the "For Sale" sign that was planted in the front yard. A few days after John moved out and the sign went up, Alex pulled up the sign and threw it in the woods. When I confronted him he said only one thing: "I don't want anybody to buy the house we live in."

In retrospect, that was probably one of my biggest mistakes in helping Alex deal with the situation. I should not have moved him from house to house around the same time as the divorce. While the change was liberating for me, it was just too painful for him. And as if that weren't enough, during the divorce proceedings, themselves, Dee Dee graduated from Westlake High School.

The following year, after the dust had settled, I sold the house on Sycamore and netted $70,000 profit. As part of the divorce settlement I paid off John's condominium, bought him a winter car and a BMW. He wanted nothing to do with my business because he hated the schools so much. That was fortunate because it allowed me to move forward without him as part of the business equation. With the extra money I had left over from the sale of the Sycamore house, I upgraded homes and bought an in-progress custom-built house in a new Westlake development on Hilliard Oak Lane.

Most of the finished homes were already going for $350,000 and more, but I was able to negotiate a price of $212,000 just as construction began. That didn't get me many frills, but I didn't care. I figured like everything else, I'd make changes along the way and end up with the home I wanted.

This is where I met Michael Kennedy, my current husband.

Mike was one of the tradesmen building my second house. I'll never forget the day we met. It was February and I parked my Cadillac at the job site that morning, hopped out the car wearing a fur coat with high-heeled boots and strode into the midst of the chaos that was construction.

"Who is in charge of this job?" I shouted.

Mike looked up from his work on the house and met me before I reached the site, itself.

"Who's asking?"

I shot him a glance that said, 'I'm in charge here!' and said, "I am. I am going to be the owner of this house."

"OK," Mike said. "So what can I do for you, Mrs. Owner?"

"It's Ms. Moga," I corrected. "And I want you to make sure that every other beam is doubled in the basement. I don't want this house to move in the wind."

Mike nodded. "Anything else?"

I launched into a laundry list of demands and ended with the declarative statement, "And I don't want any plywood in the house at all. Do you understand me?"

For a moment, there was silence. Finally, Mike cleared his throat and in a calm voice said, "Lady, you're going to get what you paid for."

Then he turned on his heels and walked back to the job site and resumed his work. I watched him for a few minutes and right then, I knew this man was destined to be a major part of my future.

And as it turned out, he was, but not in the way I originally thought. My plans for the house on Hilliard Oak turned out to be written in red ink. After signing the initial contract at a bargain price I set out to make change after change on the project. The builder wanted me to pay for every change order and sent me bills indicating as such. I refused to pay and fought him every step of the way. Our arguments on the issue became somewhat funny after a while. I eventually didn't have to pay the change orders and even saved a lot of money on the overall project, mostly because of Mike. When the house was done, I probably saved about $80,000.

The house was finished and I moved in with Dee Dee and Alex in February 1989.

My relationship with Mike developed because the circumstances were right. I was newly divorced and I stood by myself for the first time in twenty years. I felt free and ready to face my future. I knew that if I divorced John, I would give myself a chance at love again. I had to find my strength and courage to do that. It was hard for me because in Europe divorce was still such a frowned upon concept. That was in my head as well. How could I be a divorced woman? Who would want me in my forties and a single mom of two children?

On the other hand, anything was better than being in a loveless marriage. I wanted to use caution in my new freedom. I had not dated since I was a teenager. What did I know about relating to men as a grown woman? Not much. I decided to approach dating just like I approached everything else. With a plan and a "do my best attitude."

I read books about being single in my forties. I asked my friends what to do on a date with American men. In other words, I got informed. So I started dating. Even as inexperienced as I was I knew one very important thing. I wasted twenty years of my life with a man who did not love me or appreciate me. This time, I wasn't going to make the same mistake.

I knew what I was looking for: A feeling when I met the right man; a feeling of something familiar, a bond of sorts. I knew from seeing other couples along the way that there was love out there.

My mother and father would say to me, "Stella, if you are going to divorce just make sure that this time you find someone that is going to see the light in your beautiful spirit. Not someone that is constantly going to disregard it and try to extinguish it."

And that's where Michael came in.

Michael is from a small town near Toledo, Ohio. He comes from a good family. His mom, Irma, was a piano teacher and his dad, Ernie, was an accountant. His family was the American dream in action for many generations.

Michael is a good solid American man. He works hard, has his feet firmly planted in reality and can hold a conversation with just about anyone.

In high school, he played basketball. His playing career prematurely ended when he cut his hand while working in a factory. As a result, he lost his scholarship and was forced to change schools and attend Bowling Green State University.

After college, Michael moved to Indiana, where he worked for a trailer factory as a manager of operations. Eventually, he ended up in Texas. The building industry was booming there, and he found jobs building cabinets.

In 1985, he moved back to Ohio. He met a woman and in 1987, married her. Back in Cleveland, he was working in construction on new developments around Westlake when we met.

Michael worked on my house until the day it was finished. I liked dealing with him because he was a no nonsense kind of person. I was in the process of building yet another school so I asked Michael if he was interested in some side work from his regular job. I told him that I needed shelves for the schools. Buying shelves would cost a lot of money, but if we would buy all the wood and he would build them, I could offer him a pretty good wage and I could save some money in the process.

We agreed, and Michael started building these shelves in my garage. We developed a nice friendship. We talked about books, politics and business. I liked his point of view on life in general because he knew how to cut through all the nonsense and get to the real part of the issue.

Eventually, Michael began to do more and more work for Le Chaperon Rouge. I would call on him whenever I needed work done. He always did it well and at a fair price. One day, he came to me and told me he was getting a divorce. I wasn't surprised. He had mentioned on a few occasions that he was not where he wanted to be in his marriage.

I remember that he smiled at me and it warmed me from my head to my toes. What was not obvious in the years that we had known each other was very obvious now. He gave me an 8" x 10" piece of wood that had a heart in it. It wasn't manufactured or anything. The piece of wood actually had this heart that was grown that way naturally in the wood. On the piece of wood he wrote these words "Happy Birthday. I am lucky to know a wonderful and interesting person like you."

We went out a few times and became inseparable. All those years I dated, I never felt such chemistry with any man. Also, our physical attraction for each other was like a magnet. When he would look at me or hold my hand, a jolt of electricity would run through my entire body. We fell in love and it was right. I was happy for the first time in my life.

Michael puts his heart into everything he does, just like I do. He works really hard and he's not afraid of physical labor. He is very good with his hands.

After a 10-year friendship and business relationship, our love was born and we were both sure that we were soul mates. Our relationship was based on friendship. The passion that we feel for each other comes from that. We trust each other.

Our engagement was really sweet. He took me to his old college and proposed by the fountain near the university seal right on campus. He told me that he loved me and that he waited for me all his life. We were glad that we had found each other.

I was very comfortable with Michael. I knew he would be by my side. A love that is based in trust is the purest love.

Michael and I moved in together after we got engaged. Because we were going to be together forever anyways, the pressure to marry was never there. Year after year passed and we just had a nice routine in our lives. We talked about a wedding, but somehow the idea for that never came to life.

In the interim, Michael managed the building of my Strongsville school. We had so many problems with the contractors of that school; it was like a revolving door to that project. He finished the building in spite of all the problems.

In 2001, my accountant and I went our separate ways. We had hired many people to manage the office. It was hard to find a good person to handle the huge workload. By the time the last one quit, we were in trouble. Our paperwork started to reflect the problems with our inability to keep a steady bookkeeper.

Michael took over the office in 2005 and he's done a great job. I no longer have to worry about the state of my affairs. Michael finally found his niche. He works very hard and all the teachers like him.

Michael is honest, passionate about life, loyal, dedicated to his family, an amazing son, father, and step-grandfather. He has a great sense of humor and makes me laugh every day.

His daughter, Kayla, has turned out to be a really nice young lady. She is heading for college soon. He was always there for her with a kind word and a hug every time she needed him.

Michael is our reality check. As much as we have on our plates every day, he keeps us grounded and checks us when we start to get too dramatic in the moment. He has a way to make us all feel loved and cared for.

He has an ocean of patience. He is well rounded and cultured. To me, he looks like a Viking that I fell in love with. I remember once a movie about the Vikings with Kirk Douglas and Tony Curtis that reminds me of Michael's looks and personality.

America gave me my John Wayne. He knows how to carry himself in any situation and he is undoubtedly my other half.

Stella and her Porsche at the Hilliard Oak Lane house (1988)

Stella inside the Hilliard Oak Lane house (1988)

Stella in the living room of the Hilliard Oak Lane house (1988)

Stella: The American woman she became (1989)

28

My father and I were always close. From when I was a child until I had children of my own, the two most important people in my life were my father and my grandfather.

Grandpa lit the original fire that burned bright within me to lead us out of Romania. Dad was the rock who provided the most important advice in my life when he said I'd be miserable if I went into business with Elizabeth. That counsel led to the creation of Le Chaperon Rouge.

So when dad got sick and was hospitalized in early 1992, the effect on me was devastating. I had visited dad the Sunday before, on a beautiful afternoon, but for only a little while. He said to me a few times during the visit that he wanted me to stay a little longer but I didn't.

I learned that complications from his diabetes led to the illness – he hadn't been receiving his insulin shots properly. That resulted in a worsening of his condition, which led to a stroke and a diabetic coma. He was hospitalized and we were all worried about whether he would survive.

One night at 4 a.m., I received a call from the hospital.

"Do you want your father on life support?" I was asked. It was one of my father's doctors; I don't remember which one.

Talk about your fateful questions in the middle of the night. I didn't know much about medicine and I knew even less about ventilators. Had I imagined the consequences of my decision, I would have given the doctor an unequivocal "No."

Instead, the only thing I was thinking about at that moment was the chance, no matter how slim, that my father could get better.

"Will it help?" I asked.

"It might," the doctor said. "We won't know until he's stabilized."

So I saw the ventilator as a short-term fix. It would give my father the time he needed to get better. How could I have known how wrong I was, even now, after living through all the grief and guilt that the decision caused?

"Yes," I said. "Do what you need to do."

And so they put my father on a ventilator, which kept him alive for two-and-a-half years. He never got better, and though he came out of the coma, he remained in a semi-comatose state, paralyzed and unable to communicate. The only movement he had was the ability to open one eye. I would go to the nursing home and visit my father, and he would open that eye and cry. And for two-and-a-half years I would cry with him. My life during that time was not very enjoyable, and I rarely got to relish the good things that did happen from 1992 to 1994.

My life was changing so rapidly. All the people that were by my side the first half of my life were now shifting chaotically. Emotionally, I was very unsure of myself. I divorced John. Dee Dee had grown and had a life of her own at college. Alex was healthy and content busy growing slow and steady and my father – my rock, had fallen ill in the worst case scenario.

So I concentrated on the one thing that never let me down – my business. At work, I knew what was happening and I could help and run things the right way. Le Chaperon Rouge was running like a well-oiled machine. There, life was still in good shape.

In early 1992, I recognized that the time had come to build a new center in Westlake. We had outgrown our existing location, and by that point I already owned two pieces of commercial real estate, the building in North Olmsted and the building in Strongsville. I was still renting the property in Westlake.

I found a developer that hired a construction company called Commercial Construction on Center Ridge Road in Westlake. The schools were doing very well but I still wasn't liquid enough to have a big chunk of cash for a down payment. So I sat down with the developer, a gentleman from Wooster, Ohio, and went to work on a deal.

"Sell me the property and build me a building, and I will pay you $5,000 a week," I proposed.

The man accepted.

At first, the arrangement worked well. I paid him $5,000 a week every week for four months. But I failed to consider all the other bills I had to pay and soon realized I'd overcommitted myself. Just more than four months into the project, I went back to Wooster and plead my case with the developer to restructure the deal.

"I'm not going to be able to continue paying you $5,000 every week," I explained.

"That's not good," he said.

I agreed. "But," I added, "I can keep making significant weekly payments. I just don't think it's going to be able to $5,000 every week."

We talked for a little less than an hour. It was agreed upon that I would pay him whatever I could on a weekly basis and, at the same time, go to a bank and secure the necessary financing to finish the deal.

So one week I'd pay $3,000; the next it would be $1,000; the following week, $4,000. This went on for a couple weeks until I felt I was in a good enough financial position to apply for the bank loan. I contacted several different banks and told them what I needed for the project. Rather than the traditional method of preparing all my paperwork, financials and laying out the business plan for the construction project I invited the bankers to come to Le Chaperon Rouge and see the operations. I explained how we were "one of the best."

Conventional methods have never been my strong suit. Having to devise a business plan on paper for me was not a good representation of Le Chaperon Rouge. My company was so much more than that. Banks and financial institutions never really care about the person they are lending to. They wait to make sure you are financially sound on paper and the rest is a nice bonus.

However, the rules are not always meant for me. So I bend them to get my plans through. Never in any dishonest way, though; I just like to offer up a more human approach to banking.

I convinced the vice president of a very reputable bank to come out to one of my schools and consider the deal. When he arrived, I showed him the operation. I gave him the same tour I've given to many new parents enrolling their children in our school. On our tour, I also explained to him how I got as far as I did in this country going back to arriving at J.F.K airport in New York City. I told him why I am different than most business people applying for a loan. And lastly, I asked for his help.

Needless to say, it wasn't the most appropriate approach and I was, admittedly, a bit arrogant about it. I still didn't realize what I should and shouldn't be able to do, and was convinced that whatever I put my mind to I would be able to accomplish.

After showing him the operations, we reviewed my financials, and I sat him down on a little chair in one of the empty classrooms. I went to the chalkboard and began to outline my requirements on the board.

"I want to pay this interest rate," I said, writing down a series of small numbers.

The man nodded, not so much in agreement as in acknowledgment.

"And I want this number of points, and this level of down payment," I continued.

When I was done the board was filled with numbers and I had the nerve to actually end by saying, "Take it or leave it."

Apparently, the vice president was both amused and impressed by the presentation. His bank loaned me the money I needed to buy the building in Westlake.

Unfortunately, shortly after completion the builder went out business – it was the second contractor I'd worked with that went belly up – and we had to use other contractors to fix all the late mistakes. Despite those minor issues the building was completed in early 1993.

When we moved our school from the little 3,000-square foot Canterbury location to the amazing building in Westlake that we had custom-designed and built, it was a very precious moment. Even in my sorrow I still had to pinch myself because I couldn't believe I had accomplished so much in such a short period of time.

During construction, the Daisa family suffered another huge blow. My father was in the hospital and my mother had become so sad that my sister and I began keeping tabs on her to make sure she was OK. Unfortunately, she and I got into a very heated fight about my father and I blamed her for not being diligent with his insulin shots. I told her she was the cause of his diabetic coma. From there, our relationship became very tense. That made the events of November 10, 1992, that much more difficult – both the recollection of them and to have lived through that evening.

My sister called late in the evening. Since the argument, my sister had been the one who had stayed in contact with mom and made sure everything was OK.

"I just called mom's house and she didn't pick up the phone," my sister said. Her voice sounded a little strained.

"Are you sure she's home?" I asked.

"Yes. She didn't tell me she was going anywhere."

"That doesn't mean anything," I said.

"But Stella, it's 10 p.m. Why wouldn't mom be at home? And why wouldn't she answer the phone? Please, can you try to call her?"

I agreed. There was no answer when I dialed my mother's phone number. I tried twice. And then I called my sister back.

"She didn't answer for me either," I said.

"I'm worried, Stella."

"Me, too," I agreed. "Do you want me to go over and make sure she is alright?"

"Yes," my sister said. "I'll come with you."

"I'll ask Dee Dee to join us as well," I said.

I called Dee Dee. She said she didn't want to go by herself and would bring a friend, Melissa, along.

"Your aunt and I will meet you there."

I arrived to find Dee Dee, Melissa and my sister nervously waiting outside. It was dark and none of us remembered to bring a house key with us.

"I'll take a look," I volunteered, then walked around the outside of the house. I crept up to several windows and tried to peer inside, hoping to get a glance at mom sitting on a sofa watching television or asleep. But the house was dark and no lights were on anywhere.

I returned to the gathering. "Nothing," I said. "It doesn't look like she's home."

"But she has to be," my sister said. "There's nowhere else she could have gone at this hour."

We postulated what could have happened for a little while and then I spied a brick near the back door. As I bent to pick it up my sister gave me a queer look.

"I don't see any other option," I said. "Everyone, stand back." Then I rammed the brick through one of the windows on the back door, shattering the glass.

Inside the house, nothing moved.

I reached an arm inside the broken window and unlocked the door. Then I let the four of us in.

The inside of the house was just as dark – and quiet – as the outside.

"This doesn't look good," my sister said. "Stella, what should we do?"

I shook my head and shrugged. "I don't know."

"Mom," Dee Dee said, "I'm scared."

I turned to her and put an arm on her shoulder. "It's OK, sweetie," I said. "Everything will be fine. Why don't we all just look around and see if we can find mom."

For about ten minutes the four of us searched the main floor. We didn't find her. But we did find her purse and keys. She definitely never left the house. It was strange. Finally, I suggested one last place.

"Let's look in the basement," I said.

We went around to the basement door and I found the door ajar. I pushed it all the way open and tried to look downstairs.

"Mom," I called.

No answer.

It was dark, and I tried the light switch. It flicked on and light flooded the stairwell.

Nothing could have prepared any of us for the scene that lay before us. My mother lay at the bottom of the stairs, bent at an impossible angle, her arm outstretched and lying in a pool of what appeared to be her own coagulated blood. Her head was sideways and as I ran down the stairs I saw that her eye was open and dried blood was all over her face. There was no doubt, mom was dead.

I howled and ran back up the stairs, pushing my way past the screaming group and then rushed outside. I ran up and down the street crying, for how long I'm not sure. It felt like hours but was probably only a couple minutes. Finally, I composed myself enough to return to the house where I found my sister, Dee Dee and Melissa holding each other and crying. I called the police from the kitchen phone. An ambulance came and took my mother away.

Later, we learned she must have been heading down the basement stairs in the dark to get something, lost her step and fallen down the stairs. She broke her head when she hit the basement floor and bled out. Most likely, she died on impact.

My mother's funeral was very long and very painful. Most Romanian funerals are that way. She had an open casket and hundreds of people attended. Dad wasn't able to come. Mom was just 66 years old when she died. She was healthy and full of life. She had been so upset about my father being sick that she had been distracted in everything she did. Her death was a tragic accident and an utter shame.

We buried my mother many years before we should have. And after the funeral, my sister and I began to fight about it. Each of us blamed the other for not paying enough attention to our parents – one now dead, the other semi-comatose in a nursing home.

This only added to the deep, unresolved problems between us. For most of our lives, my sister overtly envied me for everything I was – pretty, successful, my parents' favorite. She didn't help my parents out with anything while they were alive, up until the fallout between my mother and I, and I was the one who gave them everything they could have ever needed or wanted.

Both mom and dad had helped me out at the school. I gave them jobs to do as little or as much as they wanted. My sister said I killed our parents by working them too hard. I was insulted when she said that because it simply wasn't true. My parents loved the schools. They loved working there and they loved the children, who called them grandma and grandpa. They were also so proud of me and my success and the fact that they could share it with me.

I never went back to my parents' house after the night we found my mother dead. My sister went and took everything. I didn't care.

Our fights – and there were many of them – caused my sister and I to stop speaking. For about five years, neither of us spoke with the other. We only saw each other one time, and that was at my father's funeral in 1994.

In 1997, we finally reconciled.

My sister told me that she was wrong; I said the same. We got together again as sisters and friends. I regret those years because she and I missed a lot of special moments we could have shared during an important period of our lives.

She and I are very different people. She got married to a good man who loves her and has always taken good care of her. She had two wonderful boys that she raised with all the love she has. They are both successful, balanced human beings. The oldest is a doctor and the youngest is a lawyer. She had many jobs along the way and even acquired property in Cleveland and Florida. Overall, my sister's life was content and successful.

I was my father's favorite. He encouraged me to be aggressive and strong. He loved my sister too, but in a different way. His expectations of me were very high and I didn't disappoint him. I knew he was devastated when I married John. My failed marriage made me even stronger.

Over the years, my sister and I have learned to appreciate each other. We no longer delve in the history of our lives that sets us apart from each other. We cling to joyful memories and work hard at keeping the peace between us rather than winning the silly argument of the moment. Together we are strong and have built a bond that we waited to feel between us all of our lives. We spend time together just relaxing and sharing each other's company. In our hearts, we both solemnly believe that our parents are resting in peace knowing that our lives are content. This is all they ever wanted. And they know we are good.

As for my mother, I blamed her for my father getting sick. She was so strong and I wanted her strength to help my father. I never could go to the cemetery. I tried a few times. I would shake and cry and just couldn't get myself to see the grave.

I didn't make time for her. We should've spent more time enjoying each other's company, but we didn't. There is nothing worse than regret. Death is one thing. It's necessary, but guilt and regret are not. You have the power and time to spend with your family and friends. Once they are gone, it's so hard to look back and know you should've done it differently. After my mom died, I took every opportunity to tell mothers and daughters to be kind and giving to one another. You don't beat death by living a long life. You beat death by living life well and savoring every moment.

Losing my mother was the biggest shock of my life because she was so young and full of life. Nothing could've prepared me for this. Nothing. I questioned everything about life in general. I felt really alone. Nothing is supposed to end this tragically. I lived my life the way I wanted to live it. I made things happen that made our lives better and easier. I never stopped evolving into the person that God meant for me to become. I did God's work every day, keeping the promises that I made to him. So why did mom reach such a dreadful end? Why? Why? Why?

For a while I only had pain. I was stuck in this pain thinking for the first time in my life that I never would recover. The questions in my mind were endless. They all went unanswered. I just went through the motions in my life. I was insecure. Then I began to try to pull myself together. I found this strength deep within my spirit.

I began to take care of myself and spend more time relaxing and spending more time with my children. I prayed to God for peace in my heart. I surrendered to my fate. That was all I could do. I accepted what God had in store for her. At least she died quickly. She didn't have to suffer. Her duty had been paid in full. That's what I would tell myself over and over again.

I now had to finish out my days without her. Dee Dee and Alex needed me here strong and healthy. So that's what I worked on being. The natural progression of life was my only consolation. So I became more mature, serene and took less for granted. I began to see each moment as a gift instead of living my days, weeks, months and years in automatic.

Time passed and I learned to live with the good memories and banish her death. My mother had a great sense of humor. We would laugh together until our bellies hurt. She had a way of saying things and reading people that went directly to the bottom line. And she was right most of the time.

Stella at a ribbon cutting for Le Chaperon Rouge school (1992)

29

Dee Dee was always a good student. Near the end of high school, however, her preoccupation with boys took center stage and her grades began to slip. In college, she did well enough to think about law school. She got engaged, and then broke up with her fiancée and quit school. I took her on a cruise in early 1992 hoping the two of us could escape our problems and I'd be able to get Dee Dee back on track with her life. I was still reeling from my mother's death and getting away seemed like a good idea.

We ate. We drank. We relaxed. We talked. Things were great until Dee Dee met Kevin King.

I didn't like Kevin from the moment I met him. Something about him just didn't feel right. He came from a good family in Fayetteville, Arkansas, but Kevin didn't seem to appreciate much. He reminded me of young spoiled kid. And here was Dee Dee, who had watched me work so hard to put food on the table and clothes on her back. They were polar opposites, and I didn't understand what she saw in him.

For the rest of the cruise, Dee Dee spent time with Kevin. The more I spoke with him, the less I liked him. It turned out he was a heavy drinker. But Dee Dee soon fell in love with him, and shortly after our return to Cleveland she informed me she was moving to Arkansas to be with Kevin.

I'll never forget the day she left; it was one of the saddest moments in my life. My little girl looked so young and helpless. She wore a ponytail that day and was excited to go. I couldn't share her excitement.

Kevin arrived at our house in a pick-up truck and the two of them packed up all of Dee Dee's belongings and loaded them into the truck. I didn't like Kevin at all. Part of it was that he was taking my baby away from me; the other part was that I could see exactly the type of person he was, even if Dee Dee couldn't.

And then they just drove away.

After she left, I cried so badly that I couldn't even drive my car. It broke my heart having my little girl go 1,000 miles away from me. I was so upset that I vowed not to support Dee Dee financially. If she wanted to leave with Kevin then he would have to support her.

I probably should have known better.

Dee Dee had worked for me when she was younger. The only other job she had was at a mall during her junior and senior years in high school. She learned how to manage life from me. Everything I went through in life was with her by my side. She and I grew up together. So it didn't surprise me that she had herself quite a little plan before she moved to Arkansas.

Her boxes weren't even unpacked at Kevin's house when she started negotiations for a rental space in the heart of downtown Fayetteville. The space she wanted was a beautiful building that was mostly empty. The downtown area was full of privately owned little boutiques and it was doing quite well. The mall in Fayetteville on the other side of town had very few clothing chain stores at this time.

Dee Dee came home in late April and went resale shopping in Cleveland at the same store that she and my mom would frequent even long after we could afford any kind of clothes we wanted. Dee Dee went through a period in her life just like I did, when she wanted to keep up with her friends' style and designer labels. That was short lived for the both of us. We as women knew how hard it was to work for the money so neither one of us had the heart to spend it foolishly.

Dee Dee loved resale shopping. It was one of the things she and my mom loved to do together. She knew how to pick out great clothes and still dress amazingly out of those crazy, used clothes.

For several months, my disappointment kept me from supporting Dee Dee the way I should have. But she managed. And she soon realized what kind of person Kevin was and left him. She stayed in Fayetteville, though, and in June 1993 I received a phone call.

"Mom, it's Dee Dee," the voice on the other end of the line said.

"I miss you, Dee Dee, but I will not send you any money."

"Look, mom, everything is dead here. But I have an idea. I am going to open a used clothing store; a consignment store."

"And how are you going to do that?"

"The same way you did, mom. I'm going to take every cent I've saved up and open the store and work hard and put everything I have into it."

In that instant I realized that I could not be mad at my daughter. Yes, she left me. Yes, I was upset about it. Yes, I warned her not to go. But she was smart and she had our family's genes. She was like me. She was committed to creating a business from nothing. And I was proud of her.

"Then good luck," I said. "I hope you are big success."

So my daughter put her store together with the same care and passion that I opened my first school. She made it into a great success. She knew how to work hard and people genuinely liked her. Sales for Dee Dee came easy. She's a natural like me.

Dee Dee called her store A-line. She built her own shelves and racks. She made connections in town and filled the store with consigned used clothing. In no time at all, Dee Dee turned that little store into a success. It was so successful that in February 1994, just 14 months after its opening, Dee Dee sold it. Then she took the money from the sale, turned around and opened a second store, a new clothing store in downtown Fayetteville called The Source, in the same location, with new clothes from New York City.

By now, I was impressed with Dee Dee's business abilities. I visited her in Arkansas in the spring of 1994 to see what she had built. Dee Dee showed me her store, pride in her eyes, voice and manner as she did so. We walked along the street where it was located. As we strolled and I looked around, an idea struck.

"Why are you renting?" I asked.

"What do you mean, mom?" she said.

"Just what I said, Dee Dee. Why should we pay rent? We should buy this property."

"With what?" she said. "The store is doing well but not to the point where I have enough money to buy the building."

"I'll buy it," I said. "It's a good investment."

So Dee Dee and I met with the building owner, who wanted $1.2 million for the property. After a short negotiation, I bought it for $840,000. Suddenly, we had property in Arkansas.

Our joy was short-lived, however. On September 14, my father died. Two-and-a-half years of suffering came to an end. Knowing it was coming, however, did little to ease the mourning.

A few months later, in early 1995, I received an unwelcome letter from the Internal Revenue Service informing me that I was being audited for allegedly not paying payroll and unemployment taxes. Someone had apparently called the IRS and made the accusation. But it wasn't true.

Nevertheless, the IRS froze my accounts. I found myself without any ability to stay in business or even pay my personal bills. Luckily, friends loaned me money to pay the bills, buy food for the schools and pay my employees' salaries.

The entire affair was chronicled on the front page of a local newspaper,

West Life, where I was wrongly accused in writing of failing to pay payroll taxes. It was a crucial moment in my business life because parents started to look at me like I was a criminal. I knew I had done nothing wrong and needed to prove it to the parents and the IRS or else everything I had worked so hard to build would come toppling down.

The IRS came in and audited me. They pored over every scrap of paper I had. They looked at my books, rifled through my bank account records, flipped through cancelled checks and bills. And when they were done, after about a month, they found I hadn't done anything wrong. I had paid every penny I owed and they cleared me of the accusations.

But the entire affair took its toll on my health, and I began to feel very sick. I went to the doctor. They conducted several tests and at first, thought it might be my liver. Then they thought it could be my gall bladder. Finally, they settled on my pancreas, and decided to take X-Rays to find out for sure.

A radiologist read the X-Rays and diagnosed the problem in my pancreas. My doctor sat me down in his office, a grim look on his face.

"You have pancreatic cancer," he explained.

I was shocked. How could it be?

"What?" I said. That sure sounded like a death sentence. "How long do I have to live?"

"About six months."

I left the doctor's office in a state of shock and denial. And then I became lost and started praying. If modern medicine couldn't save me, perhaps my faith in God could.

Friends urged me to seek out a second opinion, saying that maybe the doctor was wrong. I did, and discovered my friends were right. The initial diagnosis was wrong. It wasn't a tumor on my pancreas after all; rather, it was an inflamed gall bladder.

I was relieved to learn that I wasn't going to die from cancer, but I was none too happy to have been misdiagnosed the first time. The doctors treated the correct problem and a few months later, I felt better.

It was about this time, around June of 1995, that things once more took a turn for the better. There must be something about the month of June that's good for our family. One year after opening the Source, Dee Dee called with good news.

"I'm opening a restaurant," she said.

"What do you know about restaurants?" I asked.

"Nothing," she admitted. "But didn't grandma and grandpa have restaurants in Romania?"

My family had run successful restaurants back in Cluj, so Dee Dee was right. The restaurant business was in our genes.

"They did."

"Well, if they could do it, so can I," Dee Dee asserted.

And so Dee Dee opened the restaurant in the building we bought. Within weeks of its June 7th opening it was bustling with people.

Dee Dee's restaurant soon became a destination place in town, drawing customers like Alice Walton and her brothers, who owned Wal-Mart; members of the Tyson family, which owned Tyson Foods, and the owners of J.B. Hunt. It was an amazing restaurant and a tribute to Dee Dee's business acumen that without any food service experience that she was able to develop such a successful place.

Dee Dee was a hard worker. She knew what she wanted. The restaurant experience taught her the most important life lesson – when you love what you do for a living, you give it your best and do whatever it takes to get the job done every day.

Everything changed a few years later, when Dee Dee's daughter, Isabella, was born. The restaurant, clothing store and the building were no longer Dee Dee's top priority.

I fell in love with Bella more than I ever expected. I was in Fayetteville to visit Bella every ten days. I would come home, take care of business and Alex, and like a loving grandma, would hightail it back to Arkansas to be with baby Bella.

Dee Dee finally looked at me five months after Bella was born and said the magic words I had wanted to hear. "Mom I'm ready to come home. Let's sell everything here and I want to come back to Cleveland."

Within three days I had two big trucks in front of the building, six men packed her entire life in Fayetteville in those two massive trucks and I brought my two precious girls home where they belonged. The restaurant we rented to new owners with all the stuff in it for a good price. The clothing store we sold to one of the tenants living in Dee Dee's building. Both A-line and The Source are still in business today and doing well.

My trips to Fayetteville, however, led me to look closer at it as a place with a lot of business potential.

Next door to Dee Dee's restaurant was an old historic hotel called the Mountain Inn. It had been built in 1866 and was owned by the Maharishi Mahesh Yogi, who had let it fall into a state of disrepair. The Maharishi had bought dozens of properties across the U.S., including one in Northeast Ohio, near where I lived. They were originally supposed to be used for transcendental meditation and peaceful enlightenment palaces, but few had turned out the way they were planned and most of the properties had not been kept up. But this hotel had a fascinating history. We heard that former U.S. President Bill Clinton and U.S. Sen. Hillary Clinton honeymooned there.

By 2000, the Maharishi's organization was selling the hotel. I found the phone number for the man handling the sale and gave her a call.

"What are you asking for the Mountain Inn?"

"$1.8 million."

"That's too much," I said. "It's run down. It needs a lot of work. How about $900,000?"

"I'm sorry," the man said. "That's simply not enough for the property. It's historic, you know."

"It also needs a lot of repairs on it," I countered. "If you take $900,000, I'll take care of all the repairs."

The man must have been thinking about the offer because there was dead air for a few moments. Finally, she said, "OK, I think we can do that."

And suddenly, I owned this old, run-down historic hotel.

So what do you do with an old hotel?

Well, I saw the need for an upscale hotel in Fayetteville, Arkansas, but I didn't know how to start. I also saw the need for a major project in that area, so I bought another property on the street, the Haufbrau Restaurant, for $300,000. That gave me most of the block to work with, and from there a plan began to form in my head. Soon, I bought the rest of the properties on the street.

With that much land to work with I decided to approach Holiday Inn headquarters. I didn't know where they were located and learned their headquarters was in Atlanta, Georgia. I called and introduced myself as Stella Moga from Cleveland, Ohio.

"I have a run-down property in Fayetteville, Arkansas," I explained. "I want to turn it into a Crown Plaza flag."

That was the upscale Holiday Inn property and I figured if I took an historic hotel and turned it into a high-end hotel, it would be a financial boon for the area. It could also be the anchor for a strong development project.

"Oh, honey," the lady said, "we don't go to Fayetteville, Arkansas, with Crown Plaza. But if you have properties in major cities, we can talk about Crown Plaza."

"Honey," I countered, "you are going to go to Arkansas because I said so. And thank you for your time."

I hung up the phone undeterred and set out to change their minds. I found a developer, a hotel guy, and enlisted his help. With his help and my determination, we reached the vice president of development in charge of Crown Plaza hotels for Holiday Inn.

When the executive heard we wanted to go with a Crown Plaza flag for my hotel in Fayetteville, Arkansas, he wasn't too enthusiastic.

"We're not real interested in that area," he said. "It doesn't make good business sense."

"What do I need to do to convince you?" I asked.

"Prove to me that we're wrong and that our prior look at that market wasn't correct," he said. "Show me that you can make our brand profitable in Fayetteville, Arkansas."

"OK. I will."

And so I set out to prove the company wrong. I conducted a thorough market study of Fayetteville and took it to the vice president in Atlanta. I was going to make him see the same potential of a Crown Plaza in Fayetteville that I saw, even if he was reluctant.

The study must have shown him something he hadn't previously seen because he agreed to fly to Fayetteville and see the area for himself.

Imagine this: the vice president of Holiday Inn hotels arrives in Fayetteville, Arkansas. I give him a tour of the city, walk him around the property and try to convince him that this was a good location for a Crown Plaza.

We must have done an exceptional job because he gave us his verbal commitment before he left and when he returned to Atlanta approved the flag for my property.

That was a very important moment in my business life. I had just become the only private individual – a woman – with a big company backing me up to own a Crown Plaza flag.

After receiving approval, I hired an architectural firm based in St. Louis to draw up blueprints for a world-class project. Then I convinced a group of Arkansas developers that this would be THE project of the decade in Fayetteville. We lined up the idea of condominiums in the project and made it an entire block. And I called the newspapers in Fayetteville and said, "I am having a Crown Plaza flag ready to go, and I have this amazing project on paper."

We received a lot of publicity. The run-down Mountain Inn hotel had been closed since 1998 and people were clamoring for something positive to happen in that area.

I paid a total of $2.14 million for all three properties – Dee Dee's building, the Haufbrau Restaurant and the Mountain Inn, and in 2003 with a lot of wind in my sails sold it to two local developers, Richard Alexander and John Nock, for $3.4 million.

That one deal changed my entire business financial situation.

Dee Dee with Kevin King in Arkansas (1992)

Dee Dee readies for her move to Arkansas (1992)

Stella, Dee Dee and baby Isabella in the
hospital shortly after Bella's birth (1999)

Stella and Michael Kennedy meet with the
Crowne Plaza corporate management team (2000)

Dee Dee's building in Arkansas (1995)

Tangos dining room in Arkansas (1995)

The Source (1995)

30

I have never been one to give in during a negotiation. Saying "no" and being willing to walk away is easy if the deal isn't good, but giving too much ground just to get the deal done isn't an option worth considering. That said, once I identify something I want, I work hard to close the deal on favorable terms, and without overpaying. My friends and family took to calling this "Stella's Way."

So what is Stella's Way?

Maybe it's a manifestation of my strong personality. Perhaps I'm blessed with a touch of good luck or timing. It could be both of those things. But I like to describe Stella's Way as a combination of tightly focused willpower, business savvy and dogged perseverance. Simply put, the rules don't apply to me. It is the last trait, perseverance, which has served as a guiding force in my life.

Perseverance makes me believe that failure is never the final result. Rather, failure is a temporary situation. It is something you deal with as a bump in the road on the path to success. How you face failure and view it as a learning tool and building block defines your ability to succeed. You face your failure, you figure out how to get past it and then you act. More importantly, you don't let anyone else define your successes and failures for you; you take control of your own life and affairs, and you achieve the goals you set for yourself.

It's as simple and difficult as that.

This is what Stella's Way means, and doing things Stella's Way has served me well throughout my life. If you had met me for the first time in 2001, you would have had a difficult time recognizing me for the struggling Romanian immigrant that I was when my family and I arrived in Fairview Park in September 1979. My English was much better. I'd divorced John and had two wonderful children. I'd become a successful businesswoman, owning a burgeoning chain of daycare centers and schools and nice houses. Simply put, I had completely transformed my life.

That year, expansion was on my mind. A few years had passed since we'd invested heavily in the new school in Westlake, and the investment had paid off. It helped that the Arkansas business ventures had proved so lucrative, as had my personal real estate dealings, and I was no longer satisfied with just the locations in North Olmsted, Westlake, Strongsville and Avon Lake.

Le Chaperon Rouge was doing quite well; the schools were filled with happy children. But I'd begun to recognize that the business model I'd created had a lot of unrealized potential. It still does today. The children who attended Le Chaperon Rouge were treated exceptionally well. We were "candy free" and focused on nutrition, education and fun. We had attracted and retained quality teachers because they received a good wage and generous benefits. We were standing at the precipice of something much grander, and I looked to the city of Rocky River for the next phase of Le Chaperon Rouge's growth.

Rocky River is something of a locked-land community. It has been for quite a while. There isn't a wealth of commercial land available for new development, and finding something suitable to build on is something of a snipe hunt. I finally found a closed gas station at the corner of Wooster and Hilliard that sat on a property I thought I might be able to work with.

In its better days, the run-down property had been a Marathon station. But it closed because Marathon didn't want to pay the exorbitant cost to renovate the underground tanks to meet with tighter EPA regulations on gasoline storage. It was just one of hundreds of gas station casualties at the turn of the decade because of more stringent regulations and the elimination of what the service station companies referred to as redundant operations, properties within a close proximity to other company-owned stations.

I contacted the real estate agent who represented Marathon and was told they wanted $495,000 for the property. That was too high. There was no way the deal was going to happen for that much money. I tried to negotiate a better deal with the real estate agent but ran into a brick wall.

That's when Stella's Way took over.

First, I approached the mayor of Rocky River, William Knoble. Getting a meeting with him was a lot easier now than my earlier mayor meetings had been. In 2001, I was a successful businesswoman with a history of developing daycare centers and schools that had a positive effect on the communities where they were located. I had long since shed the rough-edged style I'd started with. My assimilation to being an American was more than two decades in the making. This time, the mayor treated me with a high level of respect.

We sat in his office and discussed the vacant property I was trying to buy. Knoble was a charming man. He was very interested in economic development for Rocky River and the addition of a Le Chaperon Rouge location made good business sense for him and the city. Years later, in 2006, he got caught up in a nepotism scandal for hiring relatives on the city payroll and was forced to resign. But on this day, he was still thinking more about the city than finding jobs for his acquaintances.

"So why is the property still vacant?" I asked.

"It's a difficult piece of property," he admitted. "That is a challenging intersection and there are still underground tanks there. Clean up isn't inexpensive, and we won't allow a restaurant or fast-food restaurant to move into the space. That's the type of buyer that typically has the money to do the brown field renovations that need to be done."

"So you have not had any interested parties?"

"We have," he said. "They just have not been viable options."

The mayor shifted in his seat a little and leaned forward. "Tell me more about your ideas for the property, Ms. Moga. We might be interested in allowing you to build a daycare center there."

"That's good, Mr. Mayor," I said. "I haven't purchased the property yet but I'm still negotiating with the owners. Once I have the city's commitment that I can build, I'll try to complete the deal."

"Are you prepared to handle the tank removal and clean up?"

"Yes. That will be part of the final deal. Don't worry which of us will take care of it. It will get done."

"OK. What about our concerns about potentially increased traffic? As I mentioned, it's already a challenging intersection."

I nodded, smiled and reached into my bag. I pulled out a folder and handed it across the desk to the mayor. He took the folder, opened it and looked at the single sheet of paper inside.

"I've already done a preliminary traffic study," I explained. "As you can see, this outlines the general traffic that my existing daycare centers have. It's more or less early in the morning and in the evening, after the end of the typical work day."

He nodded.

"That's good," he said. "Very good."

The two of us discussed my proposed project for a while longer before the mayor clapped his hands together, stood and walked around his desk toward me. I rose from my chair. He reached out his hand for me to shake. I took it.

"Ms. Moga," he said, "I think you can consider the city to have a favorable opinion of your project. We can't approve anything until you're the property owner and put forth your official plans for the building, apply for any zoning changes and the like. But I don't see anything in your initial proposal that would cause us to oppose your plans."

"Thank you," I said, and left.

With that, I had the city's backing on the project. But that left the big problem – the price. The real estate agent wouldn't budge. I really wanted the property and recognized that continuing the path I was on would be nothing more than an exercise in futility. Once more, Stella's Way kicked in and I did what I thought was the best strategy for the situation – I bypassed the middle man.

Marathon Oil, the property owner, was based in Findlay, Ohio, so I decided to drive down there and meet with whoever could directly negotiate a deal. It turned out they were anxious to divest of the property and more than willing to move on the asking price. We agreed on $220,000, which I couldn't believe at the time.

And then I found out why.

When my developers came out and quoted me to clean the land – remove the underground tanks and replace all the dirt with new, clean dirt – the $60,000 price tag was a bit shocking. Luckily, Marathon and I hadn't completed all the paperwork on the transaction so I went back to them and told them they'd need to pay for the brown field clean up or I would walk away from the deal.

Once more they agreed.

After subtracting that $60,000 from the $220,000 price we had previously agreed upon, I ended up buying the land for $160,000. That turned out to be a very good business deal.

I hired Geis Construction Co. from Streetsboro to build the building. The owners assured me they could put up the building in three or four months. The company specialized in warehouses and commercial buildings, and I was skeptical they could build such a specialized building as a daycare center in the same timeframe.

But they came highly recommended, and Fred Geis convinced me that not only was their work very good but they could handle the job. Geis ended up completing the two-story building with in-and-out play areas and a full commercial in just 90 days. It turned out to be a decision that benefitted me far beyond the Rocky River building, which we opened in 2001.

Stella at Le Chaperon Rouge promotion event (1999)

Sign outside the Le Chaperon Rouge Rocky River building (2001)

Le Chaperon Rouge Rocky River building (2001)

31

During construction of the Rocky River school I built an amicable relationship with Kathie Geis. We became good friends and she helped a lot with my schools. Her company would go on to build the next three locations for Le Chaperon Rouge, in Avon, Independence and Hudson. The second of these, Hudson, which included our new interior and exterior prototype that we would use from 2003 on, came about in sort of a roundabout way.

I received a call one day in 2002 from a representative at Jo-Ann Fabrics. He explained the company was looking to develop an out parcel of land on its property as a daycare center. They had been talking to four national chains of centers, including the Goddard School, but hadn't yet found an operator that fit their criteria.

"Kathie Geis from Geis Companies spoke with our president, Alan Rosskamm, and recommended you as a good operator of daycare centers," he said.

"Kathie built my most recent school in Rocky River," I said. "That's very kind of her."

"If you're interested, we'd like to invite you to a meeting at our headquarters in Hudson to make a presentation about Le Chaperon Rouge."

The reality was that I hadn't even thought about Hudson as a location. It was in Summit County, not Cuyahoga, outside the region where I'd built other schools. But the mere fact that I was essentially being asked to present by the president of such a large and prestigious company because he wasn't impressed with my national competitors made my response easy.

"When?" I asked.

The meeting was set for about a week later. I arrived early in the morning with Cathie Geis, her son, Fred, all my paperwork, newspaper articles about Le Chaperon Rouge, photos and my brochure. The conference room was huge and there were about five people from Jo-Ann Fabrics in attendance.

I leapt into my presentation, explaining how our schools were better than others because of the type of education we provided, our commitment to nutrition and how our goal is to make a difference in the lives of the children we served.

About ten minutes into my presentation a gentleman walked into the room and everyone stood up. I thought, 'Who in the world is this guy?'

The man didn't say anything; he just sat down and looked at me.

"You are late," I said to him. "I will have to start my presentation all over again."

The man nodded.

"Who are you?" I finally asked. "And what do you do for the company?"

A hushed wave of whispers spread throughout the conference room. The man cleared his throat.

"I guess you will have to start that speech again," he said. "I'm Alan Rosskamm. I own the company."

Never in my life did I think the owner, Alan Rosskamm, would spend his valuable time to come see and hear Stella Moga, a little operator of daycare centers, give a presentation to his staff. But he did.

"Wow," I said. "Mr. Rosskamm, even if you don't do business with me, I'm going to make sure your employees know you took valuable time to look into daycare for them. That's very commendable." And then I re-launched into my presentation.

"At Le Chaperon Rouge we teach using educational play," I explained. "We make learning fun, and we do it in a positive environment where the children are nurtured, cared for and loved."

"We do this by offering many, many programs. We have infant care, pre-school, private elementary with a gifted student program, before and after school care, summer camp, French classes, gymnastics and a music program.

"Our children take field trips. We offer them computer training. They get lots of exercise through programs like ballet, tae kwon do, a physical fitness program, soccer, basketball and baseball.

"In some locations, we're offering Spanish instruction. And in every location nutrition is a focus. We have our own kitchens and provide nutritious, hot meals to the children."

"What about class size?" one of the people in the room asked.

"Children are placed in small classrooms," I replied. "They are grouped by age and aptitude. We offer separate classrooms for six weeks to 12-month olds, 12-months to 18 months, 18 months to 36 months, three-year-olds, 3 ½-year-olds, four-year-olds, 4 ½-year-olds, pre-K and Kindergarten."

More questions ensured.

"What about your teachers? What is the turnover ratio?"

"There is not a big turnover with our employees because they are happy," I explained. "Happy employees equal happy children. Our teachers are provided with a good wage, hospitalization, paid vacations, sick days, holidays, paid time off for birthdays, some college tuition reimbursement, free in-service training and a good work environment."

Nods went around the room as I said this. I've always put a lot of focus on my teachers. Without top instructors we would be no better than other daycare centers.

Other questions ranged from additional programs to the food we served children to my own personal involvement to our tuition fee structure. When I finished answering all of them, the group gave me a controlled round of applause.

After the meeting, Mr. Rosskamm approached me. He had a hint of a smile on his face.

"Very impressive, Ms. Moga," he said. "Thank you for coming out this morning and sharing all this information about your organization."

"Thank you for the opportunity," I said. "I know I am the best daycare provider and can provide the best choice for you. So how much do you want for the land?"

Rosskamm chuckled. "And you're to the point," he said. "I like that. OK, then. We have already received an offer for $425,000 from a chain school. Do you think you can match that?"

"Mr. Rosskamm," I said, "That's a lot of money. If a daycare center has to pay almost a half million dollars just for the land, then your employees will get what are you are looking for, not what they need. They will get lousy care, lousy academics and they will not be able to afford the daycare you want to put in the front of this property."

He frowned.

"But," I said, "if you choose my school, I'm going to give them a reasonable price, an amazing program, amazing food, and you'll be proud of this operation up in the front."

"Ms. Moga," he said disapprovingly, "if you cannot pay $425,000, then we do not have a discussion. That's the asking price."

"Fine," I said. "Thank you for your time." And I took my paperwork and left. On my way back to the west side all I could think about was what a waste of time this had been. At first I'd been impressed that Alan Rosskamm had spent time hearing my presentation. But in retrospect it seemed like his mind was already made up. He had already chosen a provider but wasn't completely satisfied with their programs. They had deep pockets but not everything else he was looking for. It appeared to me that unless somebody, meaning me, matched or beat the offer from the other school, he was going to go with them.

I didn't hear back from anyone at Jo-Ann Stores. Nobody sent a thank you note. Nobody called to tell me they had chosen a different firm. It was dead silence, and I began to forget about them.

But about a month later, on a Monday morning, I was visiting the Rocky River school. It was just after 9 a.m., and the school was buzzing. They were making pancakes from scratch in the kitchen. In the preschool program upstairs, a little girl in the three-year-old class was trying to imitate a picture from a Picasso. In another room they were practicing French. Downstairs in the gymnasium, a class of children were engaged in gymnastics. What a perfect morning to visit the school, I thought as I walked through it with a large smile on my face and pride in my heart.

As I passed by the front door again I noticed a large entourage of people approaching the front of the building. I rushed to the door and peered out. I gathered myself and opened the door to find a group of Jo-Ann Fabrics people standing there: Mr. Rosskamm, his mother, his wife and several representatives who were identified as being from the company's HR department.

I stretched out a hand to Mr. Rosskamm.

"Welcome to Le Chaperon Rouge," I said. "I like the fact that you came unannounced because now you are going to see a real school in action."

For nearly an hour I led the group through the school. We visited classrooms. I showed them the kitchen. We wandered through the gym. They spoke with teachers. They watched students in class. Mr. Rosskamm spoke with the director. When they were finished, I led the group back to the door.

"Ms. Moga," he said. "Thank you for showing us the school. You've got it."

"Got what?" I said knowingly.

"The deal," he said.

"But what about the $425,000?" I asked. "I've already told you that price is a non-starting factor."

"Yes," he said, then looked back at his mother and then at me. "I know that."

I peered over his shoulder at his mother. She was smiling. I smiled.

"So how much do you want for the property?" I asked.

"Can you pay $240,000?" he said.

I nodded and shook his hand. "Mr. Rosskamm, you have a deal."

Thus, we struck the deal for Le Chaperon Rouge Hudson on a proverbial handshake. We drew the paperwork up a few days later, and the doors to our fifth location, on Darrow Road in Hudson, opened in 2003.

Good thoughts, deals, intentions, actions, and life are like a train. They connect together and run on tracks that lead to your next destination. When you spend your whole life doing things the right way, your whole way of being follows this mindset.

By the time Jo Ann Fabrics and Mr. Rosskamm came to me, I had already been doing good deals for most of my adult life. Even though I was delighted by this great deal, it no longer blew me away. My life was attracting these deals now on its own. The way of the future was no longer to build and struggle with my company. It was now just to practice and use what I learned the hard way all those years building my business without going to business school. I could teach courses in the most prestigious business schools and the students would learn more from me than from the books.

As an entrepreneur in my field, I realized once you've built your business, there is a next step. This important step is to maintain what you've built with the same passion, strength, and faith that it took to build it. If you don't learn this very important lesson, you will not be able to keep your business successful. Most people think if they created a business, put it on the market and have thrived with it, the work load can be lessened and they can relax. This could not be further from the truth. If you don't maintain the quality of your business with the same standards that you worked so hard when you opened it, your business will not survive. So building a business is like climbing Mount Everest. Maintaining a business is the magic formula to success.

Hudson school open house (2003)

Stella in front of the future home of Le Chaperon Rouge
Independence (2004)

Stella with the sign for the Hudson school opening (2002)

Le Chaperon Rouge Hudson (2003)

32

It was around 4 p.m. on a Tuesday in early March when the phone rang in our Rocky River office. I was out and about, travelling between different locations. One of my employees, our bookkeeper, answered the phone.

"Hello," she said. "Le Chaperon Rouge. May I help you?"

"Hello," a female voice said, not identifying herself. "We are looking for Ms. Stella Moga."

"She is not here right now," she replied. "Can I take a message for her?"

"Yes. We would like to invite Ms. Moga to join the President on stage tomorrow morning."

There was a slight pause before she asked, "President of what?"

"President of the United States," the woman said.

My bookkeeper scoffed. "Ms. Moga doesn't have time for jokes," she said, then hung up the phone.

Less than a minute later the phone rang again.

"Hello," my bookkeeper said. "Le Chaperon Rouge. May I help you?"

"Miss," the woman said. "This is not a joke. This is real."

While my employee sat stunned for a moment, the woman reeled off a telephone number in Washington, D.C.

"Please give Ms. Moga this phone number to call as soon as possible," the woman said. "We need her full name and social security number so that we can get her clearance to appear on stage with President Bush tomorrow morning."

And then she hung up. For a few minutes, my staff member sat there in a panic. And then she proceeded to track me down and recount the entire conversation. When she was finished, she said, "I'm so sorry, Ms. Moga. I thought it was a joke."

"That's OK," I said. "How could you have known?"

After getting the message, I sat there wondering exactly what was going on. And then I called the number the woman in D.C. had provided.

"Thank you for returning our call, Ms. Moga," the woman said. "We would like to invite you to sit on the stage tomorrow morning with the President."

She asked for several pieces of personal information so that the Secret Service could clear me for the appearance then said, "You'll need to be there at 7:30 a.m."

"It would nice if I had more notice," I said. "I have a full day of meetings."

"Ms. Moga, do you want to sit with the President on stage or not?" she said.

"Of course."

"Then be there no later than 7:30 a.m.," she said, and hung up.

I quickly called all my appointments for Wednesday and cancelled them.

The next morning, on Wednesday, March 10, I woke up early and got dressed. I arrived at the Cleveland Convention Center for the Women's Entrepreneurship in the 21st Century Summit a little before 7:30 a.m. and found a long line of people waiting to get in.

After my phone call with the woman in Washington I called around to find out what exactly the event I was invited to was about. It turned out to be a summit for women entrepreneurs, and more than 1,000 women were expected to attend. The President was coming to speak with a key constituent group – women – as part of his re-election campaign.

So I became aggravated when I saw the line. I hadn't solicited the President to appear with him. I hadn't signed up for this event. And quite frankly, I didn't have time to stand in this line when I was supposed to check in at 7:30 a.m. to sit on the stage. I began looking around for event organizers. Instead, I found a couple of Secret Service agents. They were busy guiding people in and searching purses and bags.

I walked up to one gentleman wearing a dark suit and sunglasses, just like in the movies, and said, "I can't stand in this line. I was invited by the President to sit on the stage. Where can I go check in?"

He didn't miss a beat. "What is your name?" he asked.

I told him. He checked a sheet he had and said, "Ms. Moga, come in on please."

I was ushered into a large room filled with women and news reporters everywhere. A man directed me to the stage, where there were many tables and seats set up astride the podium. In reality, it didn't seem as special as it sounded but it still was very flattering to be invited to be up there. There were more than 1,000 people and only a handful up on the stage.

I took my seat at an assigned table and began listening to the speakers, successful women from all over the country. The President was supposed to speak at 10 a.m.; he didn't arrive until noon. Instead, we heard more speeches – mostly prepared – from successful female entrepreneurs and other women who held powerful positions at large companies.

After about an hour, I looked around my table and said to the other women there, "Do you feel how I feel? These ladies are wasting our time. These are mothers and grandmothers who left their businesses to attend this and hear something meaningful. And guess what, they didn't say anything meaningful."

I raised my hand and said, "Excuse me. Can I have your microphone for a second?"

At first, the woman at the podium didn't understand me. She continued her speech.

I repeated myself and asked if I could use the microphone.

Finally, the woman said, "Yes, of course. You have a question?"

I stood up and took the microphone. "Thank you," I said. "I'm very sorry to interrupt your presentation, but all these people here – mothers and wives and grandmothers of America – they have questions. We have questions. We need answers. You talk with no substance. We have questions for you and the President."

And then I launched into a series of questions, like a Russian machine gun. "What about education? What about so many children in classrooms? What about terrorism? What about people taking our factories and our industries abroad? And what about not having jobs?"

The audience applauded.

The woman – I can't remember her name – began answering some of the questions. And then she opened the discussion up to other women in the audience who continued to ask questions.

I looked around. It seemed like the women on stage, including those who were sitting at my table, were glaring at me with either hatred or disdain in their eyes. But the women in the audience, at least those I could see clearly from the stage, were smiling at me. I looked back at my table and their glares. I didn't care. The questions needed to be asked.

Finally, around noon the President arrived.

He shook hands with all of the women on stage before approaching the podium. He was smiling and laughing. I wasn't that impressed with him. I thought I would be but I wasn't. You would think that when a person like the President of the United States came and you shook hands with him that you would feel amazing. But I didn't feel that way at all. He didn't have that presence I had expected. He was just a man, and I treated him as such.

Once he reached the podium, a member of the Secret Service came over to our table, leaned close to me and said, "Miss, if you say a word or move during the President's speech, we'll take you out."

I felt like I was in communism. If those people hadn't stood by me and made sure I didn't speak, I would have. And when the President began to speak, he confirmed my ambivalent feeling.

"There are people who doubt our ability to compete," the president said. "There are economic isolationists who surrender and wall us off. It's bad for the economy, bad for consumers. It's bad for workers. We'll prove the pessimists wrong again."

It sounded like a typical stump speech. "I know there are workers here concerned about jobs going overseas," he said, looking over at me. "I understand that."

Then the president publicly acknowledged that Ohio's unemployment rate, 6.2 percent, was higher than the national average, which was 5.6 percent, and argued against trade barriers and higher taxes.

"They don't explain how closing off markets, closing off markets abroad, would help the millions of Americans who produce goods for export, or work for foreign companies right here in the United States," he said, adding that new jobs were on the horizon. "Economic isolation would lead to retaliation from abroad, and put many of those jobs at risk."

When the President was done the crowd gave him warm applause. I didn't bother. I also didn't stick around once we were allowed to leave.

Ironically, later that year I was named the Ohio Republican of the Year for 2004. It certainly didn't come about from my appearance with the President that day. And so, in late May 2005, after the President had been re-elected, I was invited to Washington, D.C., with the other 2004 Republicans of the Year.

It was a good opportunity, not just to go to D.C. and have dinner with President Bush and his wife but also to meet with senators and congressmen to talk about all the issues with education and daycare centers in America that had been bothering me for years.

I filled out a stack of paperwork close to a half-inch thick that asked for more information about myself than I had filled out to get a bank loan or buy my house. I invited my sister to join me.

When we finally left for the event in June I left all the documents and my invitation on my desk at home. I had a dull ache in the back of my head on the plane, as though I'd forgotten something, and then realized I didn't have the paperwork. I thought I'd put them in my carry-on suitcase but I quickly found they weren't there.

"We have a small problem," I told my sister on the plane. "I forgot my invitation and paperwork for the dinner."

"What!" she yelled. "Are you crazy, Stella? Do you think they will let you in just because you show up at the door?"

"No," I said. "We'll call the White House and get it all straightened out."

For the rest of the plane my sister thought I was crazy. When we arrived, we caught a taxi to our hotel. My sister continued to ask me what I was going to do when the White House told me we were out of luck.

"We'll take care of it," I kept saying.

I was wearing a pair of shorts and a T-shirt when we arrived at our hotel. I went up to the reception desk and introduced myself. "I need your help," I said. "I have to talk to the White House because I was invited to a reception with the President. But I don't have the invitation to prove it. Who should I call?"

The woman at the desk looked at me like I was nuts. "Let me get the manager," she said. "Maybe he can help you."

A few minutes later, the manager approached us. "Ms. Moga," he said. "Let's see what we can do. Do you know to whom you spoke from the White House?"

Luckily, I did. "Yes," I told him, and he called the main line and began to explain our situation to one of the White House receptionists, who connected him to the woman who I had spoken with before.

"I'm sorry, Ms. Moga," she said. "It's too late to do anything. You don't have any of the documents we sent you for the reception? None of them?"

"I left everything at home," I explained.

"I don't think we can print you a new one," the woman said.

"No," I said. "You need to find a way to help me."

"I'll see what I can do," the woman finally said then gave me a phone number. "Call me back in an hour and I'll let you know where you stand."

I called three more times before the powers-that-be finally agreed to make me a new invitation. The White House sent it by courier over to the hotel, and I received it three hours before the dinner reception.

While I dressed for the party my sister started laughing. "Stella," she said. "I've never seen anything like that in my life. I can't believe you were able to push people at the White House around like they had nothing better to do than make you a new invitation."

"What do you expect?" I said. "I wasn't coming all this way so that we could not go."

Picture this: At the dinner reception a few hours later everybody was dressed in black and beige. Black ties everywhere. Here I am, Stella Moga, from Cleveland, Ohio, the Republican of the year for Ohio, dressed up in an amazing red dress, red purse and red shoes. Le Chaperon Rouge, right? I looked like an eyesore in the whole place.

They checked our purses and our persons very thoroughly upon our arrival. The security was unbelievable. The room was enormous. And the Ohio table was in the far corner of the room, about as far away from the President as possible. My sister and I walked all the way across the room and found our seats. I looked around and was disappointed with how bad our seats were.

But then I had an idea. I hadn't actually donated any money to President Bush's re-election campaign. And I'd only given a total of $2,500 to the National Congressional Republican Committee. So how good a seat were they really going to give me?

There was an interesting looking commemorative clock at each place setting. I picked it up and showed it to my sister. "This is nice; we should pick up a couple extra at the end of the night and take them home as presents."

She nodded. I looked around again.

"I need to use the bathroom," I said. "I'll be back in a little bit."

I walked away from our table and began peering around the room. I didn't see any signs that pointed toward bathrooms so I approached a Secret Service agent and asked him where they were. He directed me back toward the entrance where my sister and I had come in.

"They are outside the main ballroom," he said. "If you leave the room, you will need to get back in line and go through security again."

I thanked him, went back to the table, retrieved my invitation so I could get back into the room and headed off toward the bathrooms.

After clearing security again, I decided to scout out the rest of the room. The Ohio table was just too far on the other side of the room for me to go sit at. I had made this long trip to Washington, D.C. for the event and wanted to at least have a good seat at the dinner. I slowly began wandering around the room instead of going back to join my sister at the Ohio table.

I walked for a few minutes, nodding at people standing and sitting throughout the room. And then I spied a table by the front of the room, near the stage, that had one open seat at it with no purse hanging off the back.

Slowly and cautiously, I approached it.

When I reached it, I smiled at the seated group and sat down myself. The other guests at the table looked questioningly at me but no one said a word.

Finally, I broke the ice. "I know I wasn't invited to sit here," I said. "But I came from Ohio and don't want to sit in that far corner. I cannot see or hear anything from there. Was anyone sitting here?"

They looked at each other then at me. I'm sure they thought I was crazy. Oddly, though, they told me that no one was seated there and didn't ask me to leave. And then, before anyone could approach and ask me to move, the President and First Lady were announced and everyone stood. A few moments later, dinner was served.

I had an amazing experience at that table. We talked about many things. It didn't take long before the other table guests warmed to the crazy Ohio interloper clad all in red.

After dinner, President Bush and his entourage rose and began moving from table to table. He came over and remembered me from his appearance in Ohio. I shook his hand. His chief of staff, Andrew Card, came over and I had my picture taken with him.

"Mr. Card," I said. "What are we going to do about education in this country?"

Card actually gave me a few minutes to rant about my concerns. Then he invited me to come back to Washington to discuss it in further detail. He had somebody take down all my information and assured me someone would call in a couple of weeks. Of course, nobody every followed up with me. That was a bit disappointing because I was just trying to help make a difference. I learned then that everything in U.S. politics is pretend. Nobody listens. Nobody cares. I became sick and tired of politics after that.

My sister caught up with me about 15 minutes later. She was holding three clocks.

"What happened to you, Stella? You just disappeared," she said.

I recounted my tale and that evening the two of us had a good laugh about my forwardness. "You never cease to amaze me, Stella," my sister said.

"What do you expect?" I said. Then we wandered around the ballroom and picked up a couple more clocks each until we had a total of 10. Finally, we left and went back to the hotel.

The next morning, when we were packing, I told my sister she should probably pack her five clocks in her checked luggage rather than her carry-on bags.

"They're strange clocks," I said. "They look like little bombs. Do you really want to have to explain to the inspectors how you took five clocks from the White House reception if you get stopped?"

My sister shrugged off my warnings. "Who is going to stop us for having clocks?"

True to my prognostication, at the airport my sister's bag drew suspicion when it went through the X-Ray machine. They saw five identical clocks hidden in her bag and pulled her to the side.

I had already been passed through the check point and was waiting for her on the other side.

"Stella," she cried. "Help me!"

She spoke in a heavy accent, which drew attention to her. I shrugged at her; there wasn't much I could do to help.

The security personnel began asking her questions about her bag. I couldn't hear what they were saying but I noticed my sister getting more and more agitated and moving about nervously. I realized this couldn't be good.

So picture my sister with her dark hair and heavy accent trying to explain away the clocks. She didn't realize they didn't care that she had taken five of them from the reception; they only wanted to know what they were and why there were five identical ones packed together in her bag. To the security guards they looked like bomb components; the timers.

My sister got more nervous and talking very loudly.

"It's nothing," she said. "It's not what you think. They're just clocks. I took them from the White House. I'm sorry I took more than one."

The more agitated she became, the more concerned the security guards got. They called the Secret Service, who arrived quickly and together escorted her away toward a little room to, I assumed, interrogate her.

As they led her away she screamed at me in Romanian. "Stella, tell them we're sorry," she said. "Tell them it's all a mistake. Help me!"

But there was nothing I could do. I was already through the check point and knew they weren't going to arrest her once they got her alone and looked at the clocks and she calmed down enough to explain what they were and where they came from.

About half an hour later, my sister was released and we headed through the terminal toward our plane home.

"I can't believe you didn't come help me," she said.

"What was I supposed to do?"

"Tell them they were clocks from the White House."

"And they would have believed me? No, they'd have dragged me into the little room with you and we'd probably still be there."

The whole incident was pretty funny, although my sister didn't think so at the time. To be fair, I did tell her in the hotel to pack the clocks in her checked luggage. It wasn't my fault she didn't listen.

Stella in Washington, D.C., surrounded by a bevy of
American flags (2005)

Stella at the President's Dinner in Washington D.C. (2005)

33

These days, I'm often asked about my definition of success. I've built a chain of daycare centers and private schools. I own commercial buildings, residential properties and for a Romanian immigrant that arrived with pretty much nothing have done very well financially. But you can have all the money in the world; if you're not happy you're not successful. And, it's not really up to you to determine whether you're successful or not. It's up to others. When people recognize you as a success then you are a success.

Recognition comes in many forms. You can be recognized by third-party organizations. You can be written about or given awards by the media. I've been lauded by both groups. But the best type of recognition I've received is when I go places and parents, children, former clients and current clients approach me and offer thanks for what our daycare centers and schools provide them with. That's probably the most personally satisfying form of recognition.

Between the years of 2004 and 2007, my business successes were recognized by numerous organizations and media outlets. The awards were flattering but even today remain hard to believe. I didn't start Le Chaperon Rouge to achieve glory or become famous. I founded the first school out of necessity. I was frustrated with Alex's daycare situation. Everything I found was subpar. I'd wanted to make a difference; to do it the right way. And it had worked. But, who was I to turn away the free publicity for the business that accompanied the accolades?

In 2004, I was named a finalist for Ernst & Young's prestigious Entrepreneur Of The Year Awards. That same year, I was featured in a weekly news journal, Crain's Cleveland Business, which wrote about my organizational growth in a niche market. Then in 2005 I was invited to participate as a panelist at Smart Business' "Perspectives: Women in Business Conference" and featured on the cover of the magazine, a monthly management journal for CEOs.

That was a very rewarding and humbling experience. I had the opportunity to speak in front of more than 300 people from the Northeast Ohio region, many of them my peers. I was on a panel with the president of a media Web site, the president of a college, the owner of the nation's pre-eminent immigration law firm and the director of women's health from the Cleveland Clinic.

I had a ball.

When I spoke, the audience laughed, cried and applauded. I told them stories and they were captivated. It was truly a magical morning.

Two other great honors that came my way were in 2007, when I was chosen as one of the Top Ten women-owned businesses by the Cleveland chapter of the National Association of Women Business Owners' (NAWBO) and Le Chaperon Rouge was recognized by Lorain County Community College as one of the Golden 30 recipients in Lorain County in the established business category.

At the Lorain County Community College event, I didn't know in advance that I would be asked to give an acceptance speech. Again, I captivated the crowd with a couple stories about our early days. In the organizers' description of my business that accompanied the award, I was called "the Cadillac of daycare." That was very rewarding.

I've also learned the importance of giving back to the community when you're successful. In 2008, I got very involved with University Hospitals' Rainbow Babies & Children's Hospital, a world leader in the treatment of children with heart disease, cystic fibrosis and other disorders. The hospital is considered one of the top five children's hospitals in the country, and I helped raise money for it during the summer and fall.

In 2009, I once again received numerous accolades for my business acumen. Le Chaperon Rouge was named one of 30 organizations honored with a World Class Customer Service award. A few weeks later, I was once again named an Ernst & Young's Entrepreneur Of The Year finalist.

That same period of time saw the most recent growth phase of the business. In 2004, I purchased a plot of land on Rockside Road in Independence and we built that location. It opened the same year. I also sold the North Olmsted school and building that year for $475,000.

By the end of that year I was in the market for a new house to buy. My schools were doing well and I had money to invest in residential real estate. I lived in Westlake and liked the city, so I drove around it looking for a new neighborhood under development.

Near the Cleveland Metroparks I found a street with no name that appeared to be the beginnings of a new development. I couldn't find the developers names anywhere so I approached the city of Westlake and asked them. They told me the project was being developed by a company called Charles Morgan Co., which was comprised of Mike Chambers and Steve Schil, who had worked with Valore Builders, a very reputable development company in the area.

I approached the gentlemen and found they were building only nine homes on the property, expecting them to be priced at $1 million and up.

"I'm interested in one of the lots," I explained.

"We're not quite ready to start building," Steve told me. "We're still in the planning stages."

But as with most other things, I was adamant about it. I offered $190,000 for the land, about one acre. And then I made them another offer.

"What if you guys build me the home and I let you use it as the model home for your development? That way, you won't have to build a model home because I'll let you use my house."

They were intrigued.

"But I want you to charge me only $300,000 for the house," I continued. "And it should be about 7,500 square-feet."

"We can build it for $378,000."

I was shocked. I fully expected them to come back with a price tag of about $500,000, especially considering what I was asking them to do. But they didn't. I accepted the deal.

Finishing the house was pretty comical. The builder wanted $18,000 for the type of fireplace I desired. I did it for $3,000. I bought some pillars from an antique store and worked with a carpenter to build it. A manufacturer wanted between $100,000 and $150,000 for the cabinets I was interested in putting in. I was able to buy them for the entire house for $28,000. And I was able to do them in a very high end cherry wood.

My builder probably lost weight and some hair because of me. Every time he saw me coming his face would drop and he'd think, "What now?" He tried to quit three times during the process. But in the end, we hugged. Also, I promised him and every member of his team – all the tradesmen – that if they did a good job on the project and handled all my crazy requests, that we would have a big party to celebrate the "moving in" of my new house.

They did a great job, and I delivered on my promise. We had a huge party with 100 people – the tradesmen, their families and my family. I cooked Romanian food and everybody had a great time. And today, my home on Woodlyn is appraised at $1.2 million. It turned out to be a very good deal.

Once my house was done I couldn't just sit still. I turned my attention to another school opening in Avon. I heard the city was developing rapidly and needed daycare. I approached the mayor, James Smith, and asked his advice on where to locate.

"Don't buy land," he said. "Buy the church at the corner of Chester and Route 83. That's your best bet."

I went and looked at the property. The church was vacant. The lot was big. The mayor had told me that I could probably acquire the lot next door with its building, assembling a six-acre lot that was perfect for a new school. I was so excited. I began making plans for how to transform the church into a daycare center. It had a big kitchen. It had amble rooms. I wouldn't have to knock it down and start from scratch.

So I purchased the properties for a total of $850,000. On a high, I called my Romanian relatives and told them the news.

"I bought a church!" I said.

The question they all asked was: "What are you going to do with it?"

"I'm going to transform it into a daycare center."

They were all opposed to the plan.

"No way!" they said. "Do you remember when Communists touched the churches back home? They demolished them. They were cursed for life. Don't do it."

So here I was. I'd paid $850,000 paid for the properties and I was desperate. I realized my relatives were correct; I couldn't simply let myself be cursed. For nearly eight months I weighed my options. Finally, I went back to the mayor and asked for help.

"You need a bigger city hall," I said. "Why don't you buy the church and I'll give you two acres along with it. I'll sell it to you for what I paid, $840,000."

After going back and forth a few times the city agreed.

Then I solicited the remaining property – four acres and the smaller building – to a developer. I asked for $1 million; they offered $985,000. It was a pretty unbelievable deal. The church ended up being a wash, but for a $10,000 investment I made close to $1 million. I went and bought one acre of land elsewhere in Avon and built my Avon school. I used the remaining balance for other projects.

My next project was in Amherst, close to a Cleveland Clinic satellite office. It was 2007 and with the exception of one thing, pretty uneventful.

We'd finished the building, itself, and were finishing the outside. We were working on the playground and the freight company that was delivering it called to let me know it was en route.

They explained that the equipment weighed several tons and could I have a crane waiting at the school, along with someone to operate it, so that it could be removed from the truck and placed on the playground.

I didn't have a crane. I didn't even know where to get one on such short notice. They hadn't told me before, and I hadn't handled the installation of playground equipment at the other schools; the project managers and developers had handled all of that. But I figured that between the truck driver and me that we'd be able to handle everything.

The driver arrived. He seemed to be in a hurry. He stopped the truck on the street because he wasn't able to turn it into the office space where the daycare center building was located. I sensed trouble was brewing, so I parked my Cadillac in front of his truck so that I was blocking him in.

I got out of the car and walked over to him, a big smile on my face. I knew that if I had pulled around him and parked either behind the truck or in my parking lot that he'd look around, notice that there was no crane around and leave. There was no way that I was going to let that happen. He was there with my playground and he was going to deliver it.

"Where's the crane?" he asked as I approached.

I did a kind of half head tilt, shoulder shrug and said, "I don't have one. Why don't you and I just push it off the truck and onto the playground? I'll get someone else to help me set it up later."

The man's eyes narrowed and his face reddened.

"You're kidding me, lady, right?"

"No, I'm not. Let's see if we can get the playground off your truck."

"That's not going to happen," he said. "Not if you don't have a crane."

The two of us settled into a short stalemate for several minutes before I noticed something I hadn't seen when I'd arrived a little earlier that day – a construction project down the street. Lo and behold, there was a crane on the project and there were people working on the job.

"Hang on a second," I asked the driver. "I'll be right back." Then I rushed past his truck, to the end of the street and across it, where I saw a team of people working on a road project. I flagged down one of the men.

"Excuse me," I said. "I need your help."

"What do you need?" one of the men asked.

"I need to borrow your crane."

I explained the situation and begged them to bring the crane across the street, into the development and to help us take the playground off the truck.

"We can't do that," the man said. "We'd have to get permission from our company, which probably would take days, even if they entertained the idea."

But I begged and begged and finally the lead worker agreed. While he was manipulating the crane to bring over I rushed back to the truck driver and explained what was happening.

"You're one crazy lady," he laughed. "But OK. I'll need to turn the truck around."

I moved my car. He moved the truck. He was able to back it up near the rear of the building and still leave room for the construction crew, which by now was ambling up with the crane in tow. It was a funny looking scene, rather surreal, but worked.

Together, the group of us removed the playground equipment from the truck with the crane, lifted it up and placed it in position on the playground, itself. The truck driver left chuckling and mumbling to himself. I'm sure he had never seen anything so bizarre.

Once he was gone, the construction crew finished and moved the crane back to their worksite, letting me know that we needed to keep this "special project" among ourselves. If their parent company learned what they had done, they would all be fired.

I wanted to pay them something for their efforts but I had only $33 in my pocket. I gave $13 to the driver and $20 to the two men that operated the crane. It was so comical; absolutely ridiculous; but we'd done it.

"I've never seen anything like this or anybody like you, lady," the lead worker told me. "You are something else. But this was an interesting experience I'll remember for a long time."

I thanked him and his crew again. The next day I went to the bank on my way over to the Avon location and withdrew more money. I found the same group of men working on the road and paid them a lot more money with a hearty thank you for their help. We were able to open the Amherst school in 2007.

Stella with the Woodlyn house plans sketched out on a paper
towel (2004)

Stella on location with the Woodlyn house homebuilder (2004)

Stella and Dee Dee inside the partially built Woodlyn house (2005)

Bella outside the Woodlyn house (2006)

Cover of April 2005 edition of *Smart Business Cleveland*

SERVICES   2005 ENTREPRENEUR OF THE YEAR®

FINALIST   STELLA MOGA | Principal | *Le Chaperon Rouge Child Care & Development Center Elementary Schools*

Outside the box

How Stella Moga's creative thinking saved Le Chaperon Rouge   By Amanda Wurzinger

Creativity and outside-the-box thinking are key assets for any entrepreneur. Combined with a little business savvy, they can save a business on the verge of collapse. Take, for example, Stella Moga and Le Chaperon Rouge.

Moga, a Romanian immigrant, began her first Le Chaperon Rouge daycare center in a church basement with just three children. Nine months later, she had 89 enrolled, and a long waiting list. But when she tried to expand, she ran into problems.

Rent on any building large enough to house her budding business was expensive. Knowing that if she raised her fees, her center might become unaffordable to some clients, Moga decided to buy a place. She found the perfect building and presented a $5,000 down payment to the owner. However, the owner wanted $50,000.

No bank would give Moga a loan; she had few assets, little savings and only a year of business experience.

Never one to be deterred, she struck a deal with the building's owner. She would give him her $5,000 and pay a monthly rent for a year. If, at the end of the year, she didn't have the $50,000 down payment, she would give the owner everything she had saved and shut down the business. If she had the money, the building was hers.

On the morning of Dec. 31, the day before her down payment was due, Moga found herself $7,000 short of her goal. So she struck another deal, this time with her clients — anyone who paid for two or more weeks in advance would receive a 20 percent discount.

By the end of the day, Moga had the full down payment, and the building was hers. Without her creative dealings, Moga would never have become the successful entrepreneur she is today.

HOW TO REACH: www.lechaperonrouge.com

Copy of an article in the July 2005
edition of *Smart Business Cleveland*

Stella with other finalists and winners at the 2005
Ernst & Young Entrepreneur Of The Year awards

Opening of Le Chaperon Rouge Amherst (2007)

Stella at the Ernst & Young Entrepreneur Of The Year awards (2005)

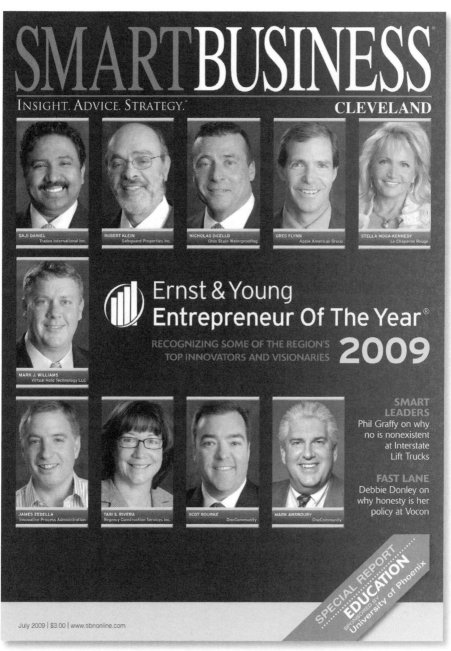

Cover of July 2009 edition of Smart Business Cleveland (2009)

Woodlyn house (2007)

34

In your business life, you can cope with most everything if it is fair and makes sense to fix it. If you try hard enough, it works out all of the time. Sometimes, you make many mistakes. When you do, you learn from them and say, "I tried my best" and you go on.

But what happened to me and my company in 2007 didn't make any sense. It wasn't fair to me. It wasn't fair to my family, my employees or the thousands of children we serve and take care of like precious angels every day.

Things were looking pretty good in March 2007 on the day when I received a call at my Rocky River location from a lawyer who told the director, Sandy Thomas, that he needed to speak with me.

Sandy tracked me down and told me a lawyer was on the line and said it was important. I picked up the line and introduced myself.

"Ms. Moga," he said. "A class-action lawsuit has been filed in federal court against you and your company."

I was momentarily paralyzed by the news, then my different mechanisms went into high gear and I responded. I knew I'd never done anything wrong that was against federal law but I quickly learned that in this country, anybody can sue anybody else for anything they want.

"Explain," I said.

"Look," the man said. "I need to see you right away. This is a very serious matter because a former employee filed a class-action law suit against your company. Can I come over now?"

When he mentioned the employee's name I remembered that she was one of the worst employees I'd had in the 25 years I'd been in business. She missed a lot of work. She created many problems with the company. Nothing was good enough for her. She lied about her background training and was very unhappy and controversial from the time she started until the day she left, which was after only a few months.

The lawyer explained that the class-action suit alleged I didn't pay my employees overtime or for short breaks or open houses with parents. It also said I didn't pay them for training, such as first aid classes, child abuse classes, CPR or sessions on how to deal with parents, creativity with arts and crafts, or how to get children interested in letters and numbers.

I was shocked. All these classes, and others, were necessary to work in a child care center, and most other daycare centers make their teachers actually pay a lot of money to take the classes. I offer them for free to my teachers as an incentive for perfect inspections.

She also claimed I didn't pay teachers to take out the garbage and throw it in the dumpsters in the parking lot.

"The lawsuit claims teachers should have been paid overtime for all these things," the lawyer said.

It was unbelievable and I didn't know how to respond. "Everything's not true," I finally said.

"That may be the case, but it's not as easy as just saying it," he said. "You have to prove it in a court of law."

My director, Sandy Thomas, looked at me. She had overheard my end of the discussion and had a pretty good idea what was happening. "What now?" she asked.

"We fight," I said to her, covering the mouthpiece. "It's not fair. Nicole is not getting a piece of this pie."

"OK," I told the lawyer. "Come talk to me."

The plaintiff in this case was hired in May 2006. She left in November of the same year. And when she left, I knew she was disgruntled. I later learned she said to other employees to come join her in the lawsuit so they could be as rich as I was.

It didn't take long for the lawyer to arrive. He stopped in front of my Rocker River school in a very fancy car. I looked at his car and thought about the people in my wonderful school that worked hard and deserved every penny they made. Staring at this lawyer in his fancy car and shiny suit I wasn't sure whether he deserved the money he made.

As he walked up to the door he wore a triumphant smile that screamed, "Lady, you're in trouble now, big trouble, and I'm going to save you!"

I welcomed him in and showed him around the school to prove how professional everything was run. Then Sandy and I sat down with him and he started once again to explain how serious this issue was and how we would need to deal with it.

I stopped him mid-sentence. "Look," I said. "This woman has a lot of personal problems that she brought with her before I hired her."

"That doesn't really matter," he said.

"Sure it does," I countered. "How was she able to bring a class-action suit against my company? I worked very hard for this company and built it from the ground up. What right does she have to do this?"

"I don't know," he said. "But she filed a class-action suit and is being represented by a reputable law firm."

I was astonished that in this country anybody can contact a lawyer and without any proof that lawyer can start an avalanche that can destroy something so valuable – a school that takes care of children 12 hours a day to the best of its ability. While researching class-action lawsuits later I learned that many small companies went out of business because they faced class-action lawsuits and didn't fight. They didn't have the courage or the means to defend themselves.

"You need be careful," the lawyer said. "You can't take this lightly because many companies like yours have been demolished because they didn't have the right representation. I can help you."

"I didn't do these things she's saying I did," I said, and tried to explain how everything she claimed were lies.

But the lawyer didn't want to hear. He was focused on scaring me to death so that I would hire him for the noble cause of him saving me. What he didn't know was that I was not going to give him a penny unless it was justified. He didn't know what kind of fighter I was. He did not know Stella's Way.

Rather, he saw my blond hair, my prominent chest, heard my accent and thought I was going to be scared to death.

"How much, in general, do you think this lawsuit will cost me?" I asked, expecting a range of $25,000 to $50,000.

"In good cases, this might cost you between $400,000 and $500,000," he said. "It depends on your payroll records. Oh, and I would need $150,000 as a down payment."

I was stunned. This was not the America I knew, I told myself. This was extortion. This was an unreal situation that couldn't be happening.

"OK," I said, pulling myself together and not so much agreeing to his terms and acknowledging the gravity of the situation. "But none of what she is claiming is true. If I wanted to deprive my people of short breaks or overtime or any other payments that they deserve I would not give them so many benefits."

"What kind of benefits do you give them?" he asked.

"Hospitalization, paid vacation, sick days and holidays," I explained. "I give them time off for their birthdays and pay half of their college tuition, half of the tuition for a master's degree. I give them free day care for their children, free meals and free in-service training that would cost them more than $500."

"I also have a CDA course in-house that gives them the equivalent of an associate's degree in early childhood education that would normally cost them close to $4,000 to earn," I said. "They only have the pay the $250 registration fee."

"Anything else?"

"Yes. I have a pension plan I match. And last but not least, I offer them money if they are in financial distress. Many of my employees don't ever pay back the money and I've always been OK with that."

The lawyer nodded, almost absentmindedly. I wondered whether he even cared that I was giving him all this information. I kept thinking that he saw my blond hair and heard my accent and figured the lawsuit was enough to scare me into hiring him whether I was innocent of the charges or not. But he didn't know how feisty I was or how resilient I am when somebody corners me. In those moments I remember my mother trying to fight those Communists in their gray suits, who wanted to make her give up the land her grandparents and parents worked hard to accumulate.

"I will call you back after I look into the lawsuit," I said. Then, instead of feeling sorry for myself I stood up tall – I'm only 5 foot, 2 inches – and guided him to the door. Then I came back and, in front of my employees, acted like nothing happened and this was no big deal. I decided to take it one day at a time and knew I would prevail.

But instead of calling this lawyer back I called my own lawyer, Brent English, with whom I had worked before.

Honestly, I did not realize just how serious and detrimental this lawsuit would be. I thought I was going to be able to meet with a federal judge and talk freely and explain that everything in the lawsuit was a big lie. For God's sake, this was a free country. The judge wasn't a Communist judge. He would, of course, listen to my side and agree with me that the plaintiff was wrong and that I was right.

How naïve I was. I learned that you do not have the right to talk to anybody but a lawyer who charges a lot of money for every second you talk to him. And I learned that a lawsuit didn't need to be filled with facts; lies worked just fine to get the ball rolling.

So the next day, after calling Brent, I began collecting information about class-action lawsuits. To my astonishment I found out that these were like cancers for small companies. A company can hire a lousy employee who can go to a lawyer and, just like that, file a lawsuit in the name of all your employees without their permission. Many of my employees were appalled that this happened; that someone had filed a lawsuit in their names without asking.

The lawsuit was filed on March 20, 2007, and my life wasn't the same after it. I came to learn that many employers get scared when they're sued because they do not want to fight. They end up paying exorbitant amounts of money to lawyers that don't wait to have proof that everything is not a lie before filing suit, or to employees who make up lies because there might be a discrepancy or two in payroll.

Nobody cares about the facts when it comes to suing people. This is what I cannot understand. How come you can take a company to court for a class-action lawsuit before all the employees agree to it and without proof that somebody did something wrong?

I learned that the sharks want their prey – the money – and you often are forced to settle the case, pay money then go on with your business or else you'll end up losing everything you've worked your entire life to build.

All of this happens while somebody like this labor lawyer that called me up and arrived on my doorstep becomes richer. The entire situation reminded me of a Kafka novel or an episode of the Twilight Zone: You are not guilty. You do what's right. But no one wants to hear. It's unreal.

I tried to explain all this to Brent, as well as other people, but no one wanted to hear my reasoning. Instead, I was forced to pore over three years of payroll records to prove that I paid – and sometimes overpaid – my employees for overtime and everything else that was alleged.

Shortly after they filed the lawsuit, lawyers at the opposing firm filed motions for conditional certification of the class-action part of the suit and expedited opt-in discovery, essentially asking the court to allow them to send out letters to all potential plaintiffs.

Despite opposition from me and my lawyer, in August 2007 Judge Ann Aldrich, who had been assigned to the case, conditionally certified the class-action suit and the plaintiff's motion to move forward. In response, the plaintiff's law firm sent letters of acknowledgement to almost 500 employees who had worked for me between 2004 and 2007, inviting them to opt-in to the lawsuit. The letter essentially said if they did they would be able to recoup a lot of money in back pay.

Many of my employees were furious and very frustrated. They wanted to write letters to the court saying the opposite of what the letter alleged; that I took good care of them and paid for everything they did, and sometimes more. I was asked repeatedly during September 2007 why no one asked their opinion before the lawsuit was filed.

"What about our voices, Mrs. Moga?" they asked. "We want a chance to explain this is nonsense."

The other lawyers were sure they would get hundreds of unhappy employees to opt in for the lawsuit. Mike and I were out of town for some of that month, but our trip wasn't as relaxing as it should have been. We spent hours on the phone talking with Brent and people in his office, trying to determine who was going to opt in for the lawsuit and what that meant for the suit.

As it turned out, from almost 500 employees who were eligible, only nine opted in to be part of the suit. The plaintiff's lawyers were livid and very upset. They began calling my employees at work, peppering them with unrealistic questions. The answer from my people was almost universally the same: "Leave us alone. We do not want to be part of this nonsense. Mrs. Moga is a good boss that takes care of us."

Finally, they didn't convince anyone else to join. Nine wasn't enough to validate a class-action lawsuit so the judge invalidated the class-action part and allowed the suit from just the nine of them to continue.

My family and I experienced a lot of unnecessary stress because of this lawsuit. We had a lot of sleepless nights. But I didn't lose my faith or trust in God, or my belief in my people. I knew I was going to prevail. Stella's Way was in full swing and I was up to the fight.

In November 2007 we were finally given an appointment with Judge Aldrich. The months leading up to it were filled with more anxiety than I cannot believe I survived. Before the meeting, Brent laid down some ground rules.

"When we meet the judge you can't say anything," he said. "This is only a meeting about the scheduling of the lawsuit. We're not here to discuss whether it's true or not."

"But that's not fair, Brent. I don't get a chance to defend myself?"

"Not today, Stella. This is a scheduling meeting."

Reluctantly, I agreed to keep my mouth shut.

When we arrived at the Federal court building it was an imposing place. I quickly understood why some people settled and gave in. Just the thought of dealing with a lawsuit under these conditions was enough to make most people want to give up the fight and pay, even if they weren't guilty.

Brent and I found the waiting room outside Judge Aldrich's chambers and sat down. We waited nearly an hour before we were finally able to see the judge. As we waited, the other lawyers arrived and sat down across from us. They barely acknowledged our presence. Brent warned me not to speak to them when we saw them but I was so angry I couldn't help myself.

"Gentlemen," I said. "God put us today finally face to face. I have a question for you."

As I spoke I watched out of the corner of my eye as Brent nearly leapt out of his skin to stop me.

"I want to know something," I continued. "Before you filed this class-action lawsuit why didn't you come and ask me if I paid all this money that you're claiming I didn't?"

They looked at each other, then at me, before one of them said, "That's not the way the system works."

"But it is not fair for a company to be taken to court before it is proven they're guilty," I said.

The men shrugged. They didn't care. They only thing they wanted, apparently, was money.

"So how much money do you want?" I asked.

"Hundreds of thousands," one of them said. He was smiling.

I was upset, and Brent put a hand on my arm and whispered, "Let it go for now."

I shut my eyes and tried not to look at the men. Moments later, it didn't matter as we were ushered into the judge's chambers. The room was enormous and very impressive, filled with ornate, detailed woodwork. Normally, I would have enjoyed it, but today I didn't care. I didn't want to be here and that's all I could think about.

The judge walked in, sat at her desk and didn't look at any of us. She just flipped through the file and treated us as though we were just fixtures in the room. Then she looked up and began talking about how the case was going to proceed.

Suddenly, I felt like I was back in Communist Romania where no one allowed you to say anything, where you obeyed and listened and did nothing that wasn't presented to you as allowed. I couldn't take it and spoke up.

"Excuse me," I said, and as I spoke all eyes in the room shifted my way. "Excuse me, your honor. In the name of all families and children in my daycare center I need one minute of your time to listen to me and what I have to say about this unfair lawsuit."

Brent hit my foot under the table and glared at me. He turned pink and started to perspire. The opposing lawyers began to grin.

The judge looked over at me and said, "You know, this meeting is not to discuss the case. It is only to figure out the schedule for the proceedings."

"I know," I said. "But please listen to me for one minute."

The judge pondered my request for a second or two. She had a slightly puzzled expression on her face. Finally, she said, "OK. Go ahead."

I began to speak but it wasn't easy. The judge's secretary kept popping her head in to interrupt, saying the judge had phone calls waiting for her to discuss other cases. I couldn't get past my opening statement to dive into the details.

Finally, the judge put up her hand and said, "Hold all my calls for a few minutes. I'm going to be busy for a little while." Then she looked at me and said, "Go ahead."

I took a deep breath and began talking like a Russian machine gun.

"What is happening to my company isn't fair," I said. "I paid everything to my employees that I had to pay. I have hundreds of employees who will testify about this in my favor. I cherish every one of my employees and respect them and pay them well through payroll and extra benefits."

I continued on about all the good things I offered my employees at the daycare centers for several minutes.

The plaintiff's attorneys tried to interrupt. "This isn't proper procedure," one said. "We're only here to schedule."

The judge put up her hand to silence them. Then she motioned for me to continue and listened intently to what I had to say for 30 minutes. She probably understood that this case didn't have any merit and that because it was already in court it was up to me to prove my innocence. The fact that I was given the opportunity to speak to this federal judge probably made a difference in the final outcome of the case.

When I was finally finished, Judge Aldrich spoke again.

"OK," she said. "I am going to approve mediation for this case to figure out the facts."

"What?!!" one of the plaintiff's lawyers screamed. "You are going to do what?"

"Mediation," the judge said. "We're going to send this to mediation to figure out the facts."

The opposing lawyers were livid. They hadn't wanted to hear my speech in the first place and now that the judge had actually listened and was making a decision based on my words, they were beside themselves.

"Assemble your information," the judge instructed me. "Show a mediator that the lawsuit is without merit, Mrs. Moga, and you'll prove what you say is true."

I thanked the judge for her decision while the plaintiff's lawyers continued their protest.

The next day, my husband Mike and others in my company sat down to start assembling all the documentation we needed to present. We went through payroll files. We looked at records about open houses. We reviewed extra activities that we had employees attend. We set out to prove that we paid our employees for everything that we were supposed to pay them for. It was a cumbersome job, and Mike, who is in charge of the company's main office, worked hard for many extra hours to find everything we needed to prove our case.

He didn't let me down.

Dee Dee assisted with paperwork as well.

"Mom," she told me, "we went through hard times together. Now we are going to solve this huge problem together, just like we did with everything else in our lives."

Shelly, my assistant, and all the directors, Beverly, Kim, Cassandra, Veronica, Sandy and Marie, also put in many hard hours to help out. All of my employees were there for us and I would not have been able to make it through this if they hadn't been. I felt love and dedication, which ultimately gave me the strength to prevail. Brent and his assistant, Wendy Barcik, worked tirelessly to prove our innocence. I felt just how much people believed in me and cared for our company.

The paperwork at Brent's office was in folders with all of the people that had participated in the lawsuit against Le Chaperon Rouge. It was difficult for Brent to decipher the 15 boxes that we gave him of original documents. I am a savvy business woman and do not put much money or attention in technology, so most of the paperwork was still done by hand. Unless, someone was truly familiar on where to find the documentation needed for this case, well, it was quite buried.

By January 2008, I was at a loss. Nobody seemed to care about the facts of this case. Both sides were talking about amounts of money that were conclusive by general estimates of $500,000. I tried and tried to tell them that these amounts were outrageous. It was like I was speaking a foreign language. Dee Dee was busy writing her own program and managing the schools. Finally she said to me "Mom, let's go to Brent's office together. I just want to make sure he has all your documents in order. The old fashioned way that we keep records, I bet he's had quite a time trying to put this big puzzle together for us."

Brent's a good man and a good lawyer, but he's not a miracle worker. Dee Dee and I went to Brent's office. We found that Brent had only been able to decipher about 60 percent of the information that we needed from the original files.

We realized that we needed to pick up the pace and get all of the remaining files deciphered. The following Monday morning, I sent our manager, Shelly, and Dee Dee to Brent's office, thinking that it would only be a few more days before everything was finished.

We were so wrong. It took six weeks to get all the paperwork together, but we crossed every t and dotted every i. Dee Dee and Shelly took over one of Brent's conference rooms. They worked every day for six weeks from 10 a.m. to 4:30 p.m. When we were done, that paperwork was like a masterpiece. On the last day there, they celebrated and were satisfied with all the documents. Dee Dee and Shelly concluded that we owed the other lawyers nothing and had the documentation to prove it.

We left Wendy, Brent's office manager, with every break, meeting, overtime, in service hours etc. documented on a chart that could not be disputed. Wendy could now spend another zillion hours to come up with the proper documentation needed to prove that we owed those girls nothing, and that, in fact, they owed me money for classes, or money that I had loaned them that they never paid back.

After the paperwork was completed and we were 100 percent

sure that we were right and they were wrong, I went on the offensive.

Brent delivered the completed documents to the opposing counsel and filed every motion necessary to finalize this case. I think they were shocked to see the final numbers. They were compelled at how we were able to come up with every document they requested. It looked like they made a terrible mistake and they knew it. They counted on the fact that my company was thrown into this predicament and would get scared and pay without looking through the facts.

But they were wrong. I went back to mediation and stood up for my employees and business. We won and they lost. I even had the judge make the other lawyers write a letter of no fault and apologize for what they did to me and my beloved Le Chaperon Rouge.

At the end of the fiasco, the opposing counsel barely got enough money to cover their paperwork fees. The woman who sued me got almost nothing. I had to pay Brent a lot of money, but only a fraction of what the other shiny suits wanted. Brent and Wendy were amazing putting up with me for a year and a half.

A big lesson is at hand for every business owner or CEO faced with such a big dilemma. Even the best lawyers are only as effective as the paperwork you, the client, provides for them. Check your lawyer's progress. Make sure he knows every inch of your case. You must be as informed as he is. If you leave anything to chance, that blind spot will determine the outcome. Not the real truth, but what they can see out of your evidence and documentation. Be aware to persevere. Be the best client and stay informed and up to date.

Meanwhile, in February 2008, after our meeting with Judge Aldrich, the plaintiff's attorneys contacted a local weekly tabloid publication. The lawsuit was included in an article the publication wrote about unfair labor practices.

Parents started calling the schools after the piece ran, asking me what was happening. Can you imagine having to explain that everything was a lie and that I had to defend myself? Sandy Thomas, who was also included in the article, was so furious that she called the publication and said it was a nonsense lawsuit.

The next day, on the publication's Web site blog, they published her denial.

We were finally assigned to another judge for the mediation, U.S. District Court Judge Dan Polster. Wendy, Dee Dee, Shelly, Veronica, Beverly, Kim, Cassandra, Marie and Sandy Thomas put together a set of Excel spreadsheets that proved that the plaintiffs, all nine of them, had no rights to claim our company owed them anything more than they'd already been paid.

The plaintiff's lawyers asked me to settle the case for $150,000. I was so angry with them.

"Over my dead body," I replied. "You don't have a class-action lawsuit against my company anymore. How dare you ask for this kind of money? Your clients don't deserve any money at all. I'll see this thing through to the end."

My response didn't do much to inspire goodwill from their side, but that didn't matter to me.

When we finally had our mediation appointment with Judge Polster he arrived with a big attitude and tried to intimidate me. He seemed in a hurry to have me settle the case.

"I don't want to hear about why you don't think this case has merit or what you see the facts as," he said. "I just want you to settle the case."

"But," I started.

"Just settle this case, Mrs. Moga. If you don't pay the lawyers and your former employees and decide to continue with this lawsuit, you are going to end up paying $500,000 or more in lawyers' fees. Just settle the case and move on."

I was stunned. I felt he was acting as a collector for those lawyers and their lying clients. I couldn't believe my ears. I couldn't believe a federal judge would do this without hearing my side. Before the appointment I had high hopes for the end of the case. But now I saw the judge's attitude and no longer saw my ordeal coming to its conclusion.

"I thought you were supposed to be prepared and know the facts," I said. "You're not even willing to listen to my side of the story."

"Mrs. Moga, you need to watch yourself," he said.

"It's evident that you have no idea about this case," I continued. "You better listen to me because you're trying to intimidate me just like the Communists did."

"Mrs. Moga ..."

"Your honor, this is not going to fly with me. I was not scared of the secret police in Romania. I am not going to settle this case."

"Mrs. Moga ..."

"You are going to learn about this case and you are going to solve it in our favor," I said.

"Mrs. Moga," he said loudly and forcefully enough to stop my diatribe. "No!"

And then he got up and walked out of the room, leaving us there with our jaws wide open and Brent as pale as a sheet of paper. We sat there for several minutes. The judge didn't come back. So we left, devastated. No one was willing to listen to us yet again.

The next morning, around 8 a.m., the judge called my lawyer.

"She's something else, isn't she," he said. "She's a fighter and she is not going to settle this case. Am I right?"

"That you are," Brent said. "She gave me a message for you. She wanted me to tell you she's appalled by the way you handled the meeting yesterday. She plans to talk with the Judge Aldrich about it."

"Well," Judge Polster said, "here's what I'm going to do. I am going to schedule another meeting for you and your client. And I'm going to listen to her. You can tell her that."

When Brent called me and recounted the conversation I was ecstatic. Finally, I would be able to tell my side of the story.

We met a few days later in Judge Polster's chambers. I began to tell him my side of the story. And then, because I just couldn't help myself, I launched into my complaints about his behavior during the first meeting.

"I'm unhappy with you," I said. "I'm appalled that you tried to collect money that those people didn't deserve. I expect an apology from you, as well as those shiny suited lawyers. They're extortionists, leeches, and you tried to help them get money they don't deserve."

I later learned that no one ever talked to a federal judge this way in his chambers, especially not a defendant in a lawsuit. But I didn't care. I was upset and felt mistreated, and I was certainly not keeping it to myself.

Judge Polster nodded. I could see that he wasn't too pleased with my outburst, but he'd promised to listen to my complaints and my side of the story, so he did.

"OK, Mrs. Moga," he said when I was done. "Here's what I want you to do. I want you to pay the lawyers what they want because they worked hard on this case on their client's behalf."

"No," I said. "I won't do that."

He looked at Brent, hoping to impart to my attorney the gravity of his words. Then he continued.

"If you go to court and continue to fight this, it will probably cost you more than $500,000 in lawyers' fees. I want you to understand this."

"I didn't know that federal judges were collectors for unjust lawsuits," I interjected.

Brent went pale and began to sweat again.

"OK," Judge Polster said. "That's it. I can hold you in contempt of court for speaking to me like that."

"Go ahead. I don't care anymore," I said. "Do whatever you need to do. I can't believe how unfair this is."

The judge sighed. He saw how determined I was and realized in that moment that he could hold me in contempt but it wouldn't solve anything, and it certainly wouldn't bring the case any closer to ending.

"I'm sorry that I wasn't ready for this case," he finally said. "We will hold another meeting with the plaintiff's lawyers and bring this case to an end."

At the final meeting I agreed to pay the plaintiff's lawyers for copies they had made and court costs they had accumulated. From the original $500,000 they thought they would get from me they ended up with, after taxes, less than $10,000 each.

The amount of money that the plaintiff received was around $100. The expense I paid my lawyer to represent me in the case was astronomical. And for what? If I would have given in, I would have been a stupid, scared employer who would have cost herself hundreds of thousands of dollars.

The plaintiff's attorneys were furious with the final outcome, but they didn't have much choice in the matter.

I said to the judge, "OK, that's good with me. I will pay this money if they write me a letter of apology saying that I didn't do anything wrong to my employees."

The judge agreed. He hammered out something that in effect said "Stella Moga and Le Chaperon Rouge did not do anything to the employees" and then ordered the plaintiff's lawyers to craft a letter from their firm mirroring those sentiments.

When I finally received the letter from the plaintiff's attorneys, it was as good as gold. It vindicated the entire ordeal that everyone had to go through.

Since then I've spoken with several small companies and shared my experience. I tell them that I want this story to be an example for the hundreds of small companies that are being taken to court every day. If employers know they paid their employees, they shouldn't give up. Don't pay. Don't settle. Don't be scared. Just prove your side and the truth will prevail. Fight the system, which needs to be fixed. The current approach to class-action lawsuits must be changed so that an investigation occurs before a class-action lawsuit is allowed to move forward.

In the end, I knew that America wouldn't let me down. I knew that I would prevail because I believed in myself and everything I do in my business every day. And it wouldn't have been possible without the hard work of Brent. The opposing counsel wasn't as prepared as he was.

And I wouldn't have been able to make it through without the hard work of his assistant, Wendy. God bless her and her baby, and Dina and Joe and everybody else in Brent's office. They really gave this case their attention, which it needed.

My husband, Mike Kennedy, was there for me 24 hours a day, seven days a week to hear my frustration and put together the paperwork that this case needed to be successful. I learned a lot about the people who work for me because of this ordeal. They put their hearts into helping me fight and never stopped believing in me or the business. And for this, I'll never forget them.

35

Every year at Le Chaperon Rouge we administer the Iowa Tests of Basic Skills to our kindergarteners to see how the curriculum we've designed stacks up nationally. The ITBS covers several areas, including math concepts, problem solving, social studies, science, geography, map use, source use and English language use. In 2007, our kindergarteners scored above the national average.

This is just one more measurement that says everything we've set out to do is working. We are achieving our goal to improve the quality of daycare and education. But the reality is that the journey has really just begun. I am currently working on opening our next school, in Solon, Ohio. After that, I plan to expand this concept nationally and build a chain of Le Chaperon Rouge schools across America.

My personal life has also come full circle. The same year that our students ranked high academically and we were opening the Amherst school and dealing with the lawsuit, Michael Kennedy and I decided the time was right to get married.

We had been engaged for eight years and together as a couple for more than a decade. Michael was nothing like John. Where John was a quiet academic who never got excited about anything, Michael was a tradesman by profession with an accountant's mind for precision and a lust for life. He made me happy; I made him happy. It was and continues to be a good match.

Earlier in the year I began looking for a wedding dress. I didn't find anything I liked that cost less than $3,000. I went to Naples, where I own houses, and searched the little boutiques there. In one, I found a dress that was perfect. It was beautiful – silk with pearls and beaded pearls. It was priced at $2,000, but there was a rip in the material, down the side. I brought the dress to the clerk's attention.

"How can you sell this dress for $2,000 with a rip like that?" I asked.

"Miss, it's on sale," was her reply.

"Well, why didn't you fix the dress?"

"We're not allowed."

"What does that mean?"

"We cannot fix the dress. But we can discount it."

"That doesn't make any sense," I said. "Why can't you fix it?"

"We just can't," she said. "But we can sell it for $1,070 because of the rip."

"That's too high," I said. "I'll give you $150 for it."

"I can't do that ma'am. It's a high-end designer dress. Even with the rip we need to price it at $1,070. If you want it, that's the price."

"I'll tell you what," I said. "Let me talk to the manager."

The clerk began to speak but stopped herself. She shrugged and disappeared in the back room. A few moments later she reappeared with a slightly older woman who was smiling. She approached me.

"You asked to see me. How may I help you?"

I showed her the ripped dress.

"I'd like to buy this," I explained. "But it is ripped and your clerk said you can't fix it."

The woman took the dress and examined it for a moment. "That's correct," she said. "We have to sell it as is. Once it's sold, we can fix it. We just can't repair the dress and then pass it off as undamaged."

"Now that makes sense." I eyed the manager. "So how much can you really sell the dress for? I'll fix it myself."

"Give me a moment," the manager said. "Let me look it up in the computer." She began typing on her computer behind the counter and nodding as she did. Finally, she looked up. "I'll tell you what. We paid $178 for the dress. I've been told you offered $150 for it and that we had it priced at $1,070 with the rip and $2,000 in new shape. How does the same $178 we paid for the dress sound? But you'll have to fix it yourself."

"You have a deal," I said.

And with that I was able to buy one of the most beautiful dresses I'd seen in my life for pennies on the dollar.

As we planned the wedding, I turned to Mike one day and proposed an idea.

"Let's have our honeymoon this summer, before the wedding."

"Why not wait?" he said.

"We can relax, get a nice suntan and then return ready for the wedding," I said. "Think about it, Mike. It's been a long and challenging year."

He agreed. The two of us were tired, and summer seemed like the perfect getaway time. We decided on Mexico. We found an amazing hotel in Cancun called Le Blanc Spa Resort. Le Blanc Spa is a high-end hotel that promotes itself with the tagline "As close to perfect as humanly possible." You have to be somebody to get a good room; President Bush stayed there when he visited Mexico. When we arrived, I had to pinch myself because it was so elegant.

Mike and I spent a lot of time on the beach reading when we weren't on the phone with Brent discussing the lawsuit. During our stay the ocean was very, very rough. They had red flags all over the beach and in the water that signified we should not go in the ocean. You were allowed to go in the ocean when the flags were yellow.

One day, all the flags were red but I really wanted to go swimming, and not in the pool. I saw a couple people swimming in the ocean and looked over at Mike.

"I think I'm going to go in," I said. "There are people in the water over there." I pointed at the group. "It must be OK now."

Mike glanced up and down the beach.

"I only see a few people over there," he said, pointing at the same group I'd seen. "No one else is in the water. But if you go where they are, maybe it's OK."

I acquiesced and headed down by where the other swimmers had been. I like to think of myself as a decent swimmer. When I was younger I had once trained every day thinking I would swim across the sea to freedom from Communist Romania. So I figured a shallow ocean with a rough current probably would still be child's play.

When I waded into the water the other swimmers were heading back onto the beach. In retrospect I probably should have viewed that as an omen. But I didn't. Instead, I began swimming. The water was choppy but I still thought I could manage.

For several minutes I swam and played in the ocean. It was warm and felt wonderful. I looked toward the shore and saw Mike reading a book. I waved, but he didn't look up and see me.

Suddenly, a wave rushed in and pulled me away from the shore. In a matter of only a few seconds it swept me a few hotels down the beach. Then, just as quickly, it swept me further out into the ocean, far away from the beach. I realized that this might just be my death.

Before I could react, the waves dragged me under the water. Water and sand filled my nostrils and mouth. I choked. Then I bobbed back up to the surface. I threw my arms up and waved them. The ocean was rough, very rough, and it dragged me down again and bobbed me up again. I was scared. I was sure I was going to be swept out into the ocean further and then drown. This was it.

In a panic I looked toward where the lifeguard was but he wasn't in sight. I screamed. No one reacted. I waved my arms in the air again and screamed louder. This time, a couple saw my arms and heard my voice. As I struggled to keep my head above the water I watched them rush down the beach looking for help. Mike looked up from his book, saw me and began to panic. A lifeguard popped into view. He grabbed a small motorized vehicle and dove into the water. He reached me in seconds and grabbed my arms. He pulled me aboard his vehicle and then back to the beach and safety.

I expected a lecture about swimming in dangerous water once we reached shore and I calmed down, but it never came. The lifeguard was apparently just as relieved as I was. Mike comforted me and for a while I was pretty freaked out. Needless to say I didn't get in the ocean again during our trip, even when all the flags were yellow.

My September wedding could easily have turned into my funeral. Luckily, it didn't. Unfortunately, Aunt Aurelia didn't share my guardian angel. By 2007, Aurelia was hospitalized with Alzheimer's and had been ill for several years. She died on October 7th and didn't get to see how happy I was on my wedding day.

Aurelia was 87. She had been in the United States since 1932 and lived a full life. My own life wouldn't have been the same without her. I took a moment of silence to think about her on my wedding day and reflect upon her impact on what had happened in my life since my family arrived on her front step.

On the day of my wedding, Mike went off with his family to get ready. I got up early and began to tackle the myriad tasks that still needed attention. The greatest of them was the floral arrangements. I had decided to do them myself. A florist quoted me $3,000 just for the flowers on the table. Instead, I went to Marc's and bought vases for $9 each. Then I bought flowers from Costco for $8 per arrangement. I spent a few hours putting them all together and setting them out on the tables. When I was done, I was very proud of how beautiful they looked.

Around noon, I came home. I saw the luxurious house, my wedding dress, everything so perfect in my life. I was so happy. I didn't want anybody in the house, so I was alone. I wanted to enjoy the quiet and the moment. I put on some music and just listened. Then I started to do my hair.

Halfway through, the curling iron broke. I spent about 10 minutes looking around for a replacement but couldn't find one. I was able to use a brush to do the rest. I put on my make-up and put on the veil. The only thing left to do was put on my dress, which I had lovingly repaired to perfection.

The limousine was scheduled to arrive and pick me up at 3 p.m. to take me to the church. It was about 10 to 3 when I started to put on the dress. I stepped into it but when I tried to zip it up the zipper wouldn't zip.

I began to panic. I didn't have another option. There were no more cream white wedding dresses in my closet. This was it. I began to panic.

There were two options: ask my neighbors for help, assuming they were home, or ask the limo chauffer when he arrived. I decided to go with the second one.

When the doorbell rang I rushed to the door. With one hand on the door and one hand on my dress I opened it. Standing there was this very large chauffer. He was African-American with a big round face. In one large hand he held his hat.

"Good day, maam," he said. "Are you ready to go?"

I tried to give him my friendliest smile. "Not exactly," I said. "I actually need a little help. My dress zipper won't zip."

The driver looked at me. Then he looked down at my dress. I pulled a hand away where the zipper was stuck and gave him a half-grin. "Do you think you can help me zip it up?"

I'm sure he didn't know what to make of the situation. Slowly and reluctantly he came in. I noticed he was perspiring. The man cleared his throat and said, "This is going to cost you extra ma'am."

I couldn't tell if he was serious or just trying to break the awkward ice.

I chuckled. "It should cost me less," I said. "Look, you are doing something I cannot do. I appreciate the help."

For several minutes he tried to zip up the zipper. It wouldn't budge. Finally, he said, "I don't think this is going to work, ma'am. We need pliers."

I didn't know where any were. Mike had some in his toolbox, but I knew his toolbox was in his car. "We're just going to have to keep trying," I said.

The man nodded. For another ten minutes he tugged and tugged while I pulled the dress as straight as I could. Finally, the zipper dislodged and the dress zipped up. By now, the man was sweaty. I gave him a towel.

As he wiped his brow he finally chuckled for the first time since he'd arrived. "In 20 years of driving limousines I've seen a lot of things," he said. "Things you wouldn't believe. But I have never had an experience like this."

"Me either," I said, and we had a good laugh.

Needless to say, we didn't make it to the church on time.

The wedding, however, was beautiful. We held it in the same church that had welcomed me to Cleveland all those years ago. And we held the reception at a nice reception hall near our house. I wanted both the wedding and the reception to be not just celebrations of Mike's and my wedding but also celebrations of what I loved the most – America.

My flower bouquet was comprised of red, white and blue flowers, matching the U.S. flag. I attached a nice American flag ribbon to it. The cake also represented America – on top of it I put little American flags. We had an ice sculpture that was an American flag. And when Mike and I came in as Mr. and Mrs. Kennedy the song they played was "God Bless America."

It was truly an amazing day that represented much more than just a wedding. It brought everything that had happened since September 1979 full circle.

And when you stop and think about everything that I've accomplished since that day, it's pretty humbling.

I started with nothing.

In 1982 I started my business with $1,800 in that North Olmsted Congregational Church. Today, I have a successful business worth many millions of dollars. I own a lot of real estate, including seven buildings that comprise the school chain.

I own three houses in Westlake – mine, Dee Dee's and another one. I also own four houses in Florida. Together, they are worth millions.

The Florida homes came about in an interesting way. I was at the airport going to Florida in 2005. I bumped into my friend, Edgar. I knew that Edgar lived in Naples and commuted to Cleveland for business once a week. He and his wife had a beautiful home in Naples. Just in passing, he gave me the names of some people to talk to down there since I was interested in real estate. The Naples real estate market was still pretty fluid and being a buyer's market you could get some pretty good deals.

I couldn't wait to get off the plane. I called around for some information about the lead Edgar gave me on a new development called Horse Creek Estates. I found the address and went directly to the president's office.

As usual, the secretary gave me the once over and reluctantly agreed to let me see Alan Schiffman. Alan was pleased to meet me. He probably thought to himself that here comes the gravy train with blond hair and a heavy Romanian accent. Wrong. Just as wrong as all the dealmakers I had met before him.

Alan and I stayed in negotiations for about three weeks. By the time the deal was sealed, I had five lots at Horse Creek Estates. The best part is that I got them for the price of three lots. These lots had luxury homes ready to be built on them.

The Southern lawyers from Arkansas had just given me my money back from the hotel and I had a very short time to reinvest the money in real estate so that I would not pay capital gains taxes.

I eventually sold three of the lots for a good profit and built two homes on the remaining two lots. We loved going to Naples and staying at the Ritz Carlton. I found out that the Ritz properties were selling lots for homes right on the hotel's golf course. I knew I wanted to buy a lot or two. I went to talk to the people at WCI sales office and I wanted to buy a lot. I went to see a builder and I said that I wanted a house on the Tiburon lot. The architect was from the Ohio area and he gave me a very good price. The WCI people told me that this house was going to cost me $2.4 million. I went back to the sales office. They wanted $725,000 for each house. I told them that I wanted two lots and was willing to pay $675,000 for each house.

They were offended and told me that WCI does not bargain. I told them that they have to start bargaining now.

Eventually, they agreed. I told them that I needed this deal in writing. The guy who was supposed to give me this price was not there the same day. I was supposed to leave for Cleveland that day and I told the people at WCI that they are going to be in big trouble with me if they didn't deliver the paperwork to me at the Ritz.

I signed the deal on the hood of the rental car.

Once I got back to Cleveland, I wanted to go back to Naples and build a second home for the same price. They had to give me a huge discount. I let them cool off a little bit and I went back and told them that they had to give me a membership to the Ritz as part of the $625,000 package. They were beside themselves. But I wore them down and they did it.

The membership is valued at between $75,000 and $125,000. I guess the price of the house went down to $575,000. It was a steal of a deal. After the homes were done, I put them on the market for $1,800,000 each.

Before they started construction they wanted to buy me out. They knew they had made a raw deal. They offered me peanuts for a buyout and I told them that they insult my intelligence. They have to do a very good job because I am watching every step.

Now I have two amazing homes in Tiburon-Naples' Marsala

development worth $3.6 million. I put only $2.4 million into them. And WCI held true to the Ritz standard.

When you think that I started with nothing, it's safe to say I did pretty well for myself. I followed my own path doing things Stella's Way. It wasn't always conventional but it worked. I've said it over and over again but it's worth saying once more: God Bless America. This is truly the most wonderful nation in the world to raise a family.

Bella at Stella and Mike's wedding (2007)

Stella and Mike at their wedding (2007)

Stella at her wedding (2007)

Wedding party (2007) (Marcus and Bella in the front row)

Stella with Dee Dee at Stella and Mike's wedding (2007)

Stella and Bella in Florida at the land bought in Tiburon (2006)

Stella and De Dee at the construction site for the house at
Marsala in Florida (2007)

Stella, Bella, Marcus and Dee Dee at the house in Horse Creek in
Naples, Florida (2006)

Stella after receiving her engagement ring from Mike (1999)

Stella and Bella at Stella's wedding (2007)

Stella and Marcus at Stella's
wedding (2007)

Stella and Mike cutting the
wedding cake (2007)

Stella and Mike at their wedding (2007)

The wedding cake (2007)

Stella and Mike's wedding
reception (2007)

Stella and Bella next to the Marsala sign in Naples, Florida (2007)

36

My granddaughter, Isabella Maria Moga, was born on March 3, 1999. I was 52. She came on a beautiful spring morning. The trees and flowers in Arkansas were already in bloom. It is such a happy time when a baby comes. Everything about life is renewed in a pure way. Dee Dee was working hard running between her restaurant, clothing store and managing her building. Dee Dee was quite settled in her routine of working one hundred plus hours a week. I was really worried about her. She loved what she was doing. The only saving grace is that her home was in the same building as her restaurant and clothing store so she was always at work or at home.

Lee, Isabella's father worked for Dee Dee at the restaurant for four years before Isabella was born. They knew each other well and she counted on him. He was a big help. Lee is a chef by profession. His passion in life is rock climbing. He would give her notice that he was leaving on climbing trips all over the United States. He would be gone a couple of times a year for one or two months at a time. But he always came back and she welcomed him back because he was good at his job. During the months that he was gone, she would somehow manage.

Dee Dee didn't tell me she was pregnant. I guess she wanted to be sure about the baby. I finally got a phone call from her. She was frantic.

"Mom, I'm pregnant and I have problems with my cervix, the doctors cannot do anything for me here. She said the cells are too advanced. I don't know who to go see or what to do."

She blew me away. My blood ran cold.

"What do you mean you are pregnant? Who is the father? My Lord, you are a wild child."

"Lee is the father. I didn't want to tell you. I'm sorry. I know I have disappointed you."

"Lee in your kitchen? Oh my, my, my," I gasped. I didn't know anything about this man.

"We got together briefly before he left for his climbing trip to Las Vegas. When he came back in June, we got together again and I got pregnant by accident. You know I wanted to have a baby, but I'm not ready to get married to anyone, including Lee. So I am having the baby and I will raise it myself. He wants to be a part of this, but I don't care about any of that. He can take it or leave it. I'm not getting married."

"Are you in love with him?" I asked her.

"No. I know he's a good guy. We've been good friends for years. He's okay. It's too late to worry about the details of it now it's a done deal."

We hung up and my head was spinning. This was so unexpected. I wanted my sweet daughter to find a man that would be good to her and she would be good to him. All of a sudden, I found myself sitting on the other side of the fence in a haunting conversation that had taken place between my father and I almost 30 years earlier. It jolted me deeply. I only imagined how devastated my father was that day when I told him I was pregnant with John's child and that I wanted to get married. Now, and only now, did I understand my father's pain – the pain of a parent seeing a child make a permanent mistake.

I had forgotten what she said about her cervix problems for a moment. Then I got really scared. The "what if's" started to race through my mind. Like a warrior, I pushed them away. No, no way. I will fix this. I leapt into action and started making many phone calls. I got a number to a Dr. Maki. He would see us in two days. I made Dee Dee a plane reservation back to Cleveland.

When I picked her up at the airport, I looked into her eyes. She was so happy and glowing. How could she be so happy? I wondered. It was like looking into a mirror from 30 years earlier. She was happy like I was happy to be having my baby. What an uncanny chain of events.

We went to see Dr. Maki. Here is a story that I must share because it's one that Dee Dee and I have shared and laughed many times over the years. We were in the waiting room at Dr. Maki's office. I am a careful money manager from the smallest detail to the biggest of deals. It is natural for me to save money. In our turmoil, we both had to go to the bathroom. There was only one toilet in the bathroom at Dr. Maki's office. I went first. Then I said to Dee Dee, "You go next and then we'll flush." She broke in total laughter. We both laughed so hard we cried.

"What are you doing, Mom? Are you trying to save the hospital money on their water bill? You goofy girl!"

To this day that story tickles both of our spirits.

Dr. Maki helped Dee Dee. He was the only doctor qualified to do this type of procedure on a pregnant woman. He was our angel and we are very thankful for that.

Dee Dee went back to Arkansas and the rest of her pregnancy was uneventful and happy. She worked until the day her water broke at 1 a.m. on March 3, 1999. At about six in the morning I received a phone call from Arkansas. It was my sweet daughter telling me that her water broke and that they were performing a C-section. The baby was breech.

In my most polite tone I said, "Couldn't you have called me sooner?"

I went to the airport in a frenzy and boarded a plane to Arkansas.

As I was boarding, I told the pilot to hurry up because my granddaughter was being born today and I absolutely had to be there.

As we landed in Fayetteville the pilot came on and said, "We've landed fifteen minutes early for the beautiful young lady who is becoming a grandmother today."

Lee's mom, Rosa, picked me up from the airport. We were meeting for the first time. She was a pleasant woman, very young looking for her age. I was relieved to see that she was normal.

I got to the hospital and the nurse could barely contain me to put sterile garments on before I entered the nursery, scanned it and zeroed in on a beautiful baby girl in the corner. I said to myself, "Please God, let that be our Isabella."

The nurse pointed to the same beautiful angel and said, "That's Isabella."

Every wish, every choice in my life, was right at that moment. The seas parted. The skies were all blue. And the Earth stopped. That's how I felt. My heart was open to love and God filled every corner of my soul. I felt complete for the first time in a really long time. There was my sweet Isabella, born healthy and strong in America. I felt my parents and grandparents there with me in my heart. Their lives were not sacrificed in vain. Isabella reaped all the rewards of all of our hard work and perseverance. There she was, my soul's gift, delivered and paid in full.

Dee Dee was still recovering from her surgery. I heard someone screaming down the hall, "Bring me my baby!"

It was Dee Dee. She was laughing and carrying on. From the moment they put that child in her arms, my daughter changed. She did not let them take Isabella back to the nursery not even once. The nurse would come in and tell us that she had to take her vitals.

"Bring her right back to me. Please don't take your time with her. You have ten minutes and then I will start calling. Please don't make me start calling."

The nurses took Isabella and brought her right back. It didn't matter to Dee Dee that she just had major surgery. Isabella was held from the time that she was born.

Isabella was a really happy baby. Dee Dee never left her with anyone. I would have to beg her to leave baby Bella with me even for a couple of hours. I would tell her to go find something to do and let me enjoy some time with my granddaughter.

She would reluctantly agree.

Bella, as we like to call her, is a gem. She is mild mannered and sweet like a fawn. She loves to please people and make them feel good about themselves. Ever since she could talk, she would compliment people. She is also very feminine and we spend hours playing store, restaurant, beauty spa, and pet store together. She is not afraid of hard work. She learned how to do her chores as a little girl and now she can clean up anything like a grown woman. She is also detail oriented and knows how to follow through and finish what she starts.

Bella loves people and asks all kinds of questions in conversation. When she was just four years old, her teacher at Le Chaperon Rouge wanted to put her in "time out" for talking during nap time. She went to the teacher, put her little hands on her hips and whispered, "Miss Susan! What am I going to do with you? You don't put me in time out. I am part of management here. You don't put management in time out."

Bella grew up with Dee Dee and me. She's listened to our conversations. It has certainly shaped who she will become as a grown woman. Isabella is my life now. We spend a lot of time together. She and I have gone together on many vacations. She loves me with all her heart. Dee Dee says I spoil her. But I just don't think that a child with so much goodness in her can be spoiled. Even though we can afford to give her whatever she wants, she is not a greedy child. She sets her own limits and knows what is right from what is wrong.

I know that Bella is going to continue on with the legacy of Stella's Way. As soon as she was able to talk in full sentences, I taught her my number one phrase: "When you put your heart in it, anything is possible."

My grandson, Marcus, was born September 25, 2001. He came to us in a turbulent time in American history. Dee Dee was very pregnant at the time of the 9/11 attacks. She had him by C-section, just like Isabella. He was a beautiful baby.

When Marcus was about three weeks old, he developed colic. He would continue to cry for the first eight months of his life. Dee Dee was beside herself. Bella was such a quiet child. Their entire world was turned upside down.

My daughter managed to keep her wits about her. She dedicated her life to raising two children by herself. Lee was around, but he was not very good at dealing with a colicky baby. Dee Dee couldn't even go out to dinner. She didn't leave town for four years after Marcus was born.

What was a hard baby turned into a stubborn and strong willed toddler. It was either his way or the highway. Dee Dee wouldn't leave him with anybody until he was about 18 months old. She would carry him around to the schools with her to make her rounds at Le Chaperon Rouge. Finally, she took him to day care and got a little break.

Marcus is a very smart boy. He has a witty personality and is quite a character. He is very athletic and took to all sports and physical activity like a fish to water. He loves an audience and likes to do skits from movies he's seen. His laugh and smile could launch a thousand ships. He is very social and can make friends easily. People are drawn to him. He is also very handsome.

We started him in dance class. At his first class, the teacher brought in an audience of all girls from one of the other dance classes to judge a contest for the best boy dancer. Marcus got out there and performed his little heart out. He won by unanimous vote. The girls were giggling about how adorable he was. He ate up all the attention like ice cream.

He is also a swindler. He makes deals with his teachers for the work he has to do. During one summer, he had lost a tooth. He went outside to play and took the tooth with him. He rushed home to inform us that he had lost the tooth outside playing and what are we going to do now? The tooth fairy will never give him his money without the tooth under the pillow.

A minute later, his wheels started spinning and he announced that he was going to write the tooth fairy a letter. In the letter he apologized to the tooth fairy that he had lost his tooth with a 'very, very, very, very, very, sorry'. He ended the letter with, 'so can I please have the money, anyways???'

This is my grandson. All of the personality traits from generations passed are alive and well in him. We absolutely adore him even as tough as he is.

My son, Alex, is the pinnacle of goodness. He couldn't even tell a white lie without getting sick to his stomach until he was a teenager. He went to Bowling Green State University and majored in psychology. He then went on to get his master's in counseling. His GPA for his master's was 3.8.

Alex is a hard worker and a mild-mannered human being. He has a very easy disposition and a strong belief in God. He married his college sweetheart in 2007 in a beautiful wedding in Southern Ohio. I didn't like Jennifer at first. She is a shy person and I didn't think Alex was ready for marriage.

As time passed, I forced myself to get to know Jennifer, Alex's wife, and we now have a good relationship. As always, when you don't agree with fate's issues, you should look deep into your heart and align your feelings with what fate wants. It is so much easier to surrender to these big choices in your life than to fight them every step of the way. Discontentment only wastes precious time away from your loved ones and you disregard what fate is trying to teach you. Once a lesson is learned, you can move on and get back to the love that we all deserve to feel for our family.

I am so proud of the man and husband my little boy has become.

Bella (2000)

Bella (2000)

Bella (2000)

Bella (2000)

Dressed as Snow White, Bella signs autographs at Disney World (2002)

Stella and Marcus during the holidays (2001)

Stella, Alex and Micky Mouse (1992)

Stella, Alex and Dee Dee buying Alex his first car, a Ford Mustang
(1998)

Stella with Alex at his college graduation (2004)

Alex and Jennifer's wedding (2007)

Stella, Dee Dee and Alex in Europe (1995)

Alex, Stella and Dee Dee in Cluj, Romania (1995)

Marcus' kindergarten photo

Marcus' kindergarten graduation photo

37

One of the benefits to being successful has been the ability to not just give back but to truly get to know people and make a difference in their lives. I used to do this with fellow immigrants, who would arrive in the U.S. and stay with me for several weeks before finding their own apartments and houses. Most of them were professionals – doctors, engineers, computer hardware engineers – as well as other well-educated people. Some of them weren't.

I was their sponsor, and as their sponsor, I picked them up at the airport, brought them to my home, fed them good food and took them shopping at grocery stores. We took them to the Social Security department and accompanied them to the bank to explain how American banks work.

In Communist Romania we didn't put money in the bank. There were just a few banks and all of them were government-owned. We never went to the banks in Romania because we used cash all the time. If you wanted something, you needed cash to buy it. So I would take my recently immigrated friends and relatives to a bank and walk them through the deposit and withdrawal procedures, tell them about checking accounts and then, once they had jobs, explain the importance of savings accounts.

We would also go to garage sales and to Goodwill, where I bought them things they would need to get set up in their own homes – silverware, glasses, plates, pots, furniture, comforters and sheets. And they would stay with us until they secured jobs and were able to move.

Getting jobs in one's trained profession wasn't easy when you were an immigrant who didn't speak fluent English. So many of my friends first took work doing physical jobs such as cooking and cleaning homes. That was OK with them. They all understood that here in America you had to go through the early stages first. Then, if you really wanted to do something, you would find a way to do it. They looked at me for inspiration.

I explained how I started – and failed – in a restaurant. Then I worked in a factory and in an office, then in a school as a French teacher. Finally, after I'd improved my English and saved a bit of money, I opened my own business. In every instance, I stressed my belief that if I could do it so could they.

The funny thing is, I don't know who was happier during these experiences – me, because I helped my friends and family, or them, because they were here in America.

I was in heaven because I could afford to do this. That's not to say it was easy, but by the time I began sponsoring families I had already moved into a nice house in Westlake, Ohio, and my schools were doing well. Needless to say, it was worth it. When we saw the expressions on their faces the moment they stepped into a grocery store or when they walked into my house you could tell that at that moment they were not just awed but thinking about the fact that their lives were now very, very different than they were back home in Romania. It wasn't too easy, but it was OK; we managed. It was worth it when we would see their faces the moment they stepped into grocery store or when they first saw my house.

Over the past several years, I've been lucky enough to make many people very happy by helping them succeed in this country. There are many success stories I'm very proud of.

Sponsoring immigrants was an amazing experience. It was an opportunity to give back the way that my own sponsor, Aurelia, did when she went above and beyond any real responsibility she might have had by taking care of us when we arrived.

In retrospect, though, I can't take credit for any of the things I've done to help others. It's not that those acts weren't honorable. And it's not that I did them with selfish motives in mind rather than out of the goodness of my own heart. No, I can't take credit for these things because the older I get, the more time I take to reflect back on my life. And as I do that, I think about my parents and grandparents and all they went through to provide a better opportunity for my generation. And more important, I realize that the person I am today is a direct result of the types of people my parents and grandparents were and what they taught me about who I should be.

It is because of this that I was so shocked by my experience within the U.S. justice system. My court case revealed how the system works and how unfair it can be. I never knew that someone could lie about you in court and, because of the way the system works, force you into settling the case when you weren't guilty so that you didn't rack up astronomical legal fees in order to clear your name.

And it is because of my upbringing that I've become disillusioned with politics. I had supported the Republican Party and President Bush and they let me down. The Democrats aren't much better. So what have their actions brought us? America's middle class is shrinking and facing financial distress.

Worse, the American family that I dreamt about as a child is suffering tremendously. Families spend less time together and our children are starved for attention from their parents while those parents focus instead on accumulating more material possessions. And what happens is that no one is happy.

I've learned that we have to stop accepting that this is just the way of life in America, and instead make significant changes with our approaches to money management and how we view the family.

It starts with women, who drive the economy with their spending habits. Many women go out and buy clothes to fill an already overstuffed closet when they don't really need anything new. They buy their children toys they won't play with and which will eventually end up being sold at a garage sale. And yet, many American women just aren't happy. If they only understood what it was like in other countries they might view things in a new light.

When I was growing up in Romania, women did all the work in their households. Men didn't help around the house or raise the children. But here in America, things are different. I have found American men to be extremely hard working, help with the children, and are phenomenal providers.

So I'm often surprised to find that there are so many divorces based not on the type of marital problems I had but rather based on husbands or wives who are simply bored and choose not to try to work on their marriage.

One of the most important gifts parents can give their children is to try to create a happy household for them. Back in 2006, when I had the honor of being part of a panel discussion with four successful women entrepreneurs and executives, I was asked by a member of the audience who I considered as my hero. I didn't hesitate to answer, "American women."

When you think about who has been responsible for so much of the dramatic change in America over the past 50 years, you'll realize that much of the credit should go to American women. When the men went to war during World War II, women stepped up and entered the work force. That generation of women laid the groundwork for today's women and the feminist movement of the 1960s and '70s.

American women paved the road for their peers worldwide to find their inner strength and persevere. So it should come as little surprise that there are so many women presidents, prime ministers and executives. That is why I am so proud to be an American woman.

Beyond preserving marriages, another important thing parents can do is realize the importance of nutrition. Our diets here in America have so much processed food in them. We eat too much white flour and corn syrup. And when children begin to eat this rather than healthy food, they end up obese. That's why at my schools we make nutrition a critical part of what we do.

Education is the other key component of both my schools and my belief in what it takes to succeed in America. Our children lag behind other nations' children when it comes to reading, science and math. And when foreign students arrive here, they're often more advanced in these areas when they enter local school systems.

Ensuring that these things are part of Le Chaperon Rouge wasn't easy, but they seem like common sense things to do. Learning to manage my business was really the more difficult part, and has been something I've worked on for years. Even as experienced as I've become, life teaches me something new every day. That's no exaggeration. I really do learn something new every day. The learning never ends. The element of surprise is a concept that should be alive and well inside each and every one of us every day.

I love what I do. I've aligned myself with my passion for work. a long time ago. Finding my higher purpose has afforded me the luxury to wake up every day and feel like I am making a difference in this world.

My best advice is to make sure you find your higher purpose. It will give your own life meaning to do God's work and feel good about yourself. No other solution will deliver this kind of impact in a life like the one you receive when you finally discover your higher purpose.

Most of the time, we are so busy and overwhelmed with our current circumstances, that it's hard to see embarking on a totally different path to reach our dreams. Not only that, but most people don't have the life skills and the 'do whatever it takes' attitude to carry these dreams to fruition.

So why try?

Because we live in a country that offers us the opportunity to try. The life skills and passion grows as you put your plans into action. God will show you the way if you are willing to be the hands for His work. Trying and failing is not the end. Picking yourself up and dusting yourself off to try and shift again and again until you reach your goals is the magic.

What if I would've given up in the basement of that church when I didn't have enough children in my school to even buy toilet paper? I would not have fulfilled my destiny and the fate of generation after generation would've been altered. You are not alone in this world. You are like a long chain connected to your past and future. What you do now determines who you will become.

The last decade at Le Chaperon Rouge was totally different than the first fifteen years of business. I now have the skills to do great business decisions and I also have the money to carry it through.

What I didn't collect over the years is a management team. I've relied only on myself to manage my business. And manage it well I did. I know how to talk to my employees. I inspire them or correct them when something is not going right. I know how to present my school to customers. I know what the parents expect of my staff and I each and every day they drop off their children at my schools. Whenever there is a complaint, I handle it with top priority.

I've tried over the years to hire managers to help me run my schools. Even though these people had the best intentions and credentials, I never learned to let go and let them manage. They could never do it like I could so I got flustered and disappointed by the results.

When Dee Dee came home from Arkansas we had four schools. I knew every parent and every teacher was trained by me personally. I knew what we bought at every school as far as food, milk, paper supplies, classroom materials, the hours of every teacher and director, and I signed all checks myself for payroll, bills, and taxes. Nothing got past my careful eyes.

We doubled in size so quickly that I was unaware of the changes that were about to sweep over my company. The new teachers I hired came from other day care centers and their skills were nowhere near Le Chaperon Rouge standards. My training, though good, was not uniform enough and I had a hard time being in multiple places at once.

Dee Dee became very involved in the management of the schools. She took to it like a fish in water. She had plenty of day care experience growing up in the business. Her eye for what needed to be done on a daily basis was sharp. She stepped up to the role of 'daily operations manager' like a pro. I didn't have to train Dee Dee. She knew my standards and what I expected my schools to deliver. Together, we managed fine.

I was able to concentrate on building and opening schools and Dee Dee concentrated on making sure we have good state inspections, minded the inventories and ran the classrooms. She also improved a curriculum that was designed to fit our high standards of educating the preschooler. We had written many versions of our daily curriculum over the years. Dee

Dee took all of our old ideas added some new innovative concepts and streamlined them into an incredible program. The teachers now have a solid foundation to run an extremely successful classroom.

In 2006, my daughter and I wanted to take Le Chaperon Rouge into a new direction. We knew that twenty-five years of experience working with children was a strong foundation for educating people on how to teach preschool academics. We saw an opportunity to enter a market in desperate need of a makeover-the stay at home parent. In her spare time, Dee Dee began to restructure our successful curriculum ideas to suit the needs of the American household.

My daughter and I became very passionate about this new project. But as passionate things do, it took over our time and energy. Le Chaperon Rouge had four young schools that needed constant nurturing and guidance and so did the Makeovers life project, as it has come to be called.

"Makeovers life" is a collaboration of many generations in our family. My parents were in the restaurant business for decades back in Romania. My daughter, Dee Dee, wanted a restaurant every since she was a child. That was one of her favorite games to play as a little girl. Dee Dee got her wish when she opened her own restaurant in Fayetteville, Arkansas. Her restaurant experience taught her how to cook and organize a kitchen in an efficient way. When she returned to Cleveland, Dee Dee instinctively set up her own kitchen to run like a commercial one – efficient in producing really good food with healthy ingredients.

This is how the Makeovers life Food program was born. She set up many kitchens to run like her own with great success. The system is simple and easy to maintain. Once you set up your kitchen for cooking the Makeovers life way, you will always be able to turn to it when you want to cook.

The Makeovers life Fitness program is based in having a walking routine. One of the simplest ways to stay healthy and active over a lifetime is to spend some time outside going for a walk every day. We all need a little time to clear our heads and get some fresh air daily.

Another good way to keep your body healthy and your mind joyful is to practice yoga. Yoga does not have to be a mystery. It is learning how to keep your body still in certain poses to make your core muscles (back and abdomen) strong. The most important practice in yoga is breathing. Taking deep belly breaths is really good for you. This kind of sitting still to work out is a great way to also clear your mind and create pockets of peace in your brain so you can relieve stress throughout your day.

Another part of the fitness program involves doing repetition exercises divided into arms, legs, and abdominals. These repetitions are designed to work out each area of your body to build strength in each muscle group.

The fitness program also encourages playing a favorite sport and dancing in the privacy of your home to your favorite tunes. Together, these daily fitness exercises keep you in good shape so that you can enjoy living in a healthy body.

The third part of the Makeovers life program is about meditation. Meditation is learning how to slow your thoughts way down in order to create pockets of peace in your brain. We all have busy lives and sometimes things come at us at one hundred miles per hour. The key to learning how to meditate is to show us the strength within that we all have in how we react to our daily events. It's not what happens to you in this world that you have any control over. The power lies in how you deal with it. Meditation helps you to deal with daily events with a much healthier outlook. The Makeovers life Meditation section of the program offers fifty meditation exercises to aid you with your life in action.

The forth and last part of the Makeovers life program is appearance. Appearance is how you present yourself to the world every day. When you look good and you've put yourself together, you feel good about yourself. It's not superficial to want to present yourself in a positive way in your daily life. The Makeovers life Appearance program has specific instructions on how to organize your clothes, grooming tools, and whatever else you may need for a successful image in your everyday life. Use these simple tips and tools to be the best you can be.

We've been running a successful preschool program at Le Chaperon Rouge for 27 years. Eight years ago, we took the time to create our own worksheets and project ideas that are like nothing that exists on the market today. The program – called the Makeovers Home Preschool Curriculum – is well-balanced in all subjects to introduce the young mind to the beginning blocks of science, math, social studies, reading and writing, music, fine and gross motor, language arts, and so much more. Introducing these topics early to a child forms connections in the brain that will make learning in the important school years much easier.

We took the successful curriculum program that we've used at our schools and reorganized it to be used as a guideline for the stay-at-home parent, the in-home caregiver or nanny.

The most important thing to remember as a parent is that your child needs to be on a daily schedule to thrive emotionally. Children do best when they can count on what's going to happen next. When your child naps before 2 p.m., he or she will be able to still be tired for their regular bedtime at 8:30 p.m. or 9 p.m. If your child is off schedule and takes a nap at 4 p.m. or so, he or she will never get to bed at a reasonable hour. As simple as this sounds, the schedule is simply the cornerstone of raising a balanced human being.

All of the wonderful building blocks from our curriculum have been organized to fit the young child's schedule at home. You can count on our program that it has been tried and true for almost three decades.

So while we were focused on developing this program, my daughter and I realized something: we are balanced human beings. We've both put in our time working ridiculous hours to make a business successful. However, now we both knew better than to try to make it alone. A plan is only as good as the people who carry it through. We had to get some help. But we were only burdened with past managers. Our skills to train and delegate were poor. As usual, when you are ready, fate delivers exactly what you need.

Not long ago, Dee Dee received a phone call from one of our previous directors, Shelly. Shelly had worked for Le Chaperon Rouge for about four years when she left to open her own school. Shelly was calling Dee Dee because her financing for her daycare center had not come through. She was looking to come back to work.

Shelly had been the director at two of our locations and had the management skills, daycare experience, people skills, work ethic, and expertise with state inspections to really do a good job for our growing company. And the cherry on the cake, she was used to working with me and my high standards for my schools. She had also helped Dee Dee with the curriculum reorganization a few years back.

Dee Dee really liked Shelly and felt like she could trust her with the management of our schools. So Dee Dee came to me and said, "Mom, I found us the manager we've been looking for! Shelly called me and wants to come back to work."

I just couldn't bear one more huge time, money and energy investment in one more manager that was going to disappoint both of us. I categorically said "No."

But Dee Dee insisted. Again, I said, "No."

My daughter knew Shelly really well. She picked Shelly to help her with the curriculum out of all of our teachers. Shelly was mild mannered and fair. So Dee Dee went to talk to Shelly and they sat down and devised a management plan. Dee Dee and Shelly knew the day care business like the back of their hands.

Dee Dee brought Shelly to me at one of the schools one morning by surprise. I was mad at my daughter.

"How could you put me in this awkward position?" I said in a harsh tone.

"Mom, give us three months. Please, I beg you. I know Shelly and I really like her work ethic, her people skills, and her experience speaks for itself. And besides you always said that the person who can help us has to have all of these qualifications. Shelly knows you and you two have worked together before. You're not going to scare her away."

What was I supposed to do? I reluctantly agreed.

Shelly and Dee Dee got to work. The three of us sat down and went through every page of our new management plan. Dee Dee worked alongside Shelly for 14 months. Things were going good. We finally found the help we needed.

Managers are only as good the owner's ability to manage them. I wanted Shelly to manage Le Chaperon Rouge well, so I kept in very close contact with her daily. And now, Dee Dee and I have found the time necessary to take our new idea, Makeovers, national. Because of my being able to delegate some of my responsibilities to a competent manager, I've had the luxury to share my story so that I can pay forward what this beautiful country has allowed my life to be.

Sponsoring and picking up immigrants at
the airport in Cleveland, Ohio (1985)

38

A Letter from Destina Moga

Hello, my name is Destina Moga. I am Stella Moga's daughter. My mother is my best friend, my teacher, my leader and my soul mate. She is everything to me. I love her with every bit of my being. She is a part of every aspect of my life – past, present, and future. I feel that we share the same spirit with my grandmother and great-grandmother.

We are a different kind of woman. A woman created solely to rely on God and ourselves to make things happen in our lives. Self empowerment as a woman in this world is a great gift and a tough practice. Drawing our strength from God creates a world where everything is possible. We persevere where others may not. We get what we need and use it as a tool to spread God's goodness and love to the people we love and the lives we touch. It is no coincidence that their strength is inherited and embodies both my mother and me. I also undoubtedly see this in my daughter as well.

My daughter, Isabella, has the same spiritual strength that my mother and I share. Isabella is wise beyond her years. She understands honor, duty, passion, and strength like she has already lived ten lifetimes. It shows in her words and actions. Life for us has a higher purpose. Being aware of this higher purpose drives all of our choices.

As a little girl, I felt my mother's love like a warm light flickering in my soul. The source of this love comes from God. It comes through my mother to me and through me to my own daughter like an ever-flowing river of unconditional love. Having the kind of love to carry us through all of life's ebbs and flows makes anything endurable.

As a child in Communist Romania, my world was sheltered from the hardships of the political regime by my mother's entrepreneurial spirit. She always found a way to provide a western lifestyle for me through her wheeling and dealing. She made friends and business connections with a lot of foreigners. I always had clothes, shoes, toys, and candy from Western Europe. How she got her hands on these items only she knows.

My mother is a teacher at heart. Education is her super highway to a better life. She instilled the importance of a good education in every aspect of my life. I've learned from her how to absorb information like a sponge.

My mother is tough. Actually, she is toughest on herself. She feels that with great power comes great responsibility. In Romania, our family created a comfortable lifestyle. We had everything we needed – homes, cars, clothes, food, and each other. The driving force behind leaving Romania was my mother. She was unwavering in the gigantic process of getting us out of the country. As a child, watching her do whatever it took to get the job done was amazing. I knew that my mother was very different from other mothers. I instinctively knew that this was a woman with a mission.

When we came to America with our entire family, I looked to my mother to lead us in the right direction. We had been living in the United States for a couple of years when my brother was born. My brother, Alex, was the greatest gift America had given me. I watched my mother scared and sick after she gave birth prematurely. She would cry over the fate of our new baby boy, but there was no desperation in her demeanor. She had soothed us all by stating that Alex was alright because he was in an American hospital and that he would pull through and be fine. Today, Alex is fine, and sometimes I think it's because my mother was so amazing. Our love and prayers pulled him through.

When she opened Le Chaperon Rouge, I was 12 years old. I had gotten used to her ways by then and knew that if she set her mind to do something, it would get done. She worked so hard at this business. She put on the business personality like a beautiful outfit. She learned to be professional and answer every need of each and every of her customers with a willing "Yes! Now what is your question?"

People are drawn to her. Her words first surprise them then inspire them. People want to help her because she is so capable to help herself. She learned business not in a classroom at a university but by doing business with real money and real deals. It's in her blood. Her mom and dad had fought the Communists. She did not have to in the United States. The ability to have a business here in this beautiful country for my mother is pure luxury and bliss. It's an entitlement that she never takes for granted and it shows in her every day. She gets up with a sheer hunger to strike a deal. I am her daughter and I can tell anyone that the stories she spins still blow my mind and surprise me at every turn.

Because she is so determined, our lives here have been easy and pampered.

As I got older and became a teenager, I was ready to get away from my parents. I explored philosophy and meditation. I read somewhere that some people believe that you pick your life – a predestination of sorts. Of course, that made me question my choice and I asked myself on many occasions why, if we do get to pick our parents, did I pick these two such different individuals?

The answers came at many different times in my life and in many versions. The overall one that has stayed with me and fits best over the years is that it is good to know both sides of everything before making choices in your life and swim between these opposing viewpoints as if they are made of the same piece of fabric. This is the deeper life lesson that my two wonderful parents have taught me.

With this sort of lesson learned, life becomes a series of experiences from a higher perspective that is anchored in my higher spirit and the positive forces in our world-unconditional love, surrender, honor, duty, passion, strength, and above all else, faith.

So, thank you, mom and dad and the legacy of the generations that have come before us and the generations that I will shape with the gifts that were bestowed upon me without the sacrifices and perseverance of everyone in this family.

As a final note, I want to thank my family for all their passion, strength and faith. From generations past, I am the way I am today because of them. I will take these gifts of the spirit entrusted to me and make sure that they are passed down to the new generations to come. I hope that you are able to take away something of value from the stories of our lives. I know that I certainly have.

Stella and Bella in Chicago (2008)

Stella and Marcus on vacation in Miami (2008)

Hudson school sign (2009)

Le Chaperon Rouge indoor playground (2009)

Le Chaperon Rouge kindergarten classroom (2009)

Le Chaperon Rouge outdoor playground (2009)

39

The 10 Lessons Learned During My Life

1.
When you put your heart into it anything is possible.

When I sum up my life, this one sentence stands apart from all others. This mantra has shaped my personality, from when I was a little girl growing up in Romania all the way to my current position as a successful American woman entrepreneur. It has trained me to persevere in my toughest moments and has given me the experience to push through when most people would have given up.

I trust this phrase. God for me lives in this phrase. He protects me and cradles me in this phrase. This phrase has taught me to lead by example. And I passed this personality trait down to my granddaughter, Isabella, who could utter this phrase even before she could speak full sentences.

When you learn what this concept feels like inside your heart, you will feel a passion like no other. Your spirit will participate in your life to create a new way of approaching the present and, therefore, reshape your future. The minimal everyday task will have a higher purpose and your milestone choices will be rooted in love.

2.
Nothing is more important than your children.

I've been blessed with many gifts in my life – health, peace of mind, a good family, good work ethic, strength, passion, and most important the gift of all my children. Everything that I have ever done and all that

I will ever do is for my children. I became a mother early in life. I know that every purpose from that moment on was set in stone. Watching my children grow into successful human beings has fulfilled me at every level.

Life has not always been easy to maneuver when it came to rearing my children. At every stumble or bump in the road, at every wrong turn, I was there for them. My strength was their strength. Their joy or sorrow was my joy or sorrow. I had faith that through my unconditional love, they were going to succeed in life and reach their own vision of happiness and contentment. I never gave up even when I was hit against insurmountable odds. I stood in the storms of our lives and I bent like a willow in the wind. I knew that God would work through me. I had faith sometimes blind faith that the best would come. And it did.

In present times, I see my daughter parent her children with the same fierce passion. I taught her that. Therefore, the legacy that I have instilled in her will live on in the next generation – my grandchildren. And this is the greatest gift of all to pass on – the ability to love unconditionally and the strength to carry it through.

3.
Follow through on everything you do.

A promise is a commitment to do something – to follow through on a task, or to finish a job. The concept of a promise is that once you've said "I promise" to yourself or others, you are bound to keep it. When you say "I promise," it means you can count on yourself to do whatever needs to be done to fulfill that commitment. If you do not keep a promise, you are not being responsible. You will not be able to count on your own word, and others will not trust you. This is first and foremost a matter of trust.

My family, friends, business associates and employees all trust me. It's that simple. All of these people trust me because I follow through on my commitments. When I make a promise, it's as good as gold. I learned this lesson early in life. And it has led me down the path of success, love and trust. I trust my instincts because I've learned that following through on my commitments I make leads to all the wonders this world has to offer. This is one of the main ingredients to being a successful business woman and a fulfilled human being.

When you have done your best and cannot follow through with a promise, be remorseful, be sad. It is not that you failed; only that you failed in your promise. People want to see remorse when a promise is broken. They want to feel that even though the commitment is questioned, that they can trust you will do your best the next time you make a promise.

Cultivate inner trust and it will expand outward to every person in your life. Make promises wisely. It is the calling card of your character.

4.
There are no failures in life; only lessons that lead you towards success.

There is no right or wrong when it comes to the things that happen in our lives – there are only lessons. This concept reminds us that everything that happens to us in life happens for a reason – to teach us our lessons. Life in action is made up of two kinds of events that tend to be viewed as either right or wrong. In every situation your brain reacts. When something happens in our lives, it is more important to find out why it happened than anything else.

When we reflect on the topic at hand and we figure out the lesson that we are supposed to learn, we can manage the incident easier and with much less stress. Also, when we discover the lessons that life is trying to teach us, we shift our view and become a student of life rather than the victim. The universe presents us with new lessons daily. When we don't know to even look for a lesson in these times, we miss a great opportunity to learn about ourselves.

Life comes at us fast. How we react to it determines how our days, weeks, months and years on Earth will play out. There is not much time for contemplation and most of us just react. Contemplation time is very important, though, but not at the time that our lives are spinning by us.

The time for contemplation is when we are relaxing – when we set aside time for meditation. This gives us the time to open our minds and train ourselves to react calmly in the face of our daily chaotic events.

Our brains learn these relaxation techniques and can turn to them to diffuse our emotions in times when our 'Not so good Mondays' are running at full speed. We learn to turn to our quiet meditation exercises instead of reacting to the stresses of the day. These exercises soothe us in our time of need. Our brains begin to trust this new pattern in handling stress. In times of meditation, we learn to reflect on the events of our lives and ask questions on how we can do things differently. It trains our minds to have a bird's eye view instead of staying within the bubble of any event. Training your brain takes practice.

In Romania, the concepts of modern psychology aren't really well known and least of all practiced. When something bad happens, people just react in total drama. They get stuck in this negative place in their minds. Therefore, they never learn. Mistakes get repeated and the process never evolves. The entire country's mindset is like this. My family was different in this regard. Why? Because my grandparents had lived in the United States. They knew that life could be different if viewed from a different perspective. The American perspective. The American way. Logic will not serve you well in Romania. This part of the world has not evolved much with globalization. People don't take responsibility for their failures. Successes are also over inflated and short lived.

As Americans, we know the importance of awareness in a situation. We value humility. The "own it so you can change it" phrase comes to mind. Only from this important belief of taking responsibility for all of your actions can you fix what's gone wrong in your life. When you place blame on circumstance or other people, you also give away the power... the great strength in your own ability to fix it.

I knew this from my family. My grandparents had been Americanized in their ways of thinking and not a million Communist regimes could take that gift away from them. This gorgeous and fruitful American mindset also affected my parents' generation as well. We were American in our spirits. It trickled into every one of our choices and ran through our veins.

I always saw my mistakes. Instead of being stopped in my tracks by them, I learned what not to do the next time I was presented with the same scenario. I have faith in God that whatever fate threw at me, I was able to learn a valuable lesson to guide me through other areas in my life.

This is a big lesson. Fate only gives you what you need, not necessarily what you want at the time. Fate knows that in order to succeed, stumbling and failing is a part of each person's personal process. Always look for the lesson. It's there. Find it. Learn it. It's the most important thing of all.

5.
Don't be afraid to put your faith in a higher power.

Every culture spanning our planet has some view on spirituality. In the last century or so, science and technology have made the belief in a higher power like God almost dismissive. The universe we have discovered is a highly organized system of being, so how can something that is only felt and not proven possibly exist? Well, to those who have felt that they have a connection with God, regardless of what religion or spiritual training they may have, the answer is quite simple. It exists because I feel it. Faith is real. The universe produces miracles every day. We have to believe it to see it.

In other cultures besides our over-technologically advanced one, the science of the spirit is real. People have been practicing it for thousands of years. We know that every religion has its code of ethics and that they are all based in good deeds not bad ones. We live in a world of dualities. Right vs. wrong. To be able to have balanced lives, we have to transcend these laws of duality and see our lives with the spiritual third eye inside our own hearts and minds. Love for our families and our world live in this thing called faith. Ensuring that the new generations have what they need financially, morally, emotionally and spiritually is important only if we have faith and love.

At the base of all of our emotions there are only two guiding forces – fear and love. Make sure you know which one you operate out of. When you operate in fear, your whole life has been a series of lost and chaotic events. When your life has been based in love, it has been driven by your connection to your higher self – God. Faith always leads you to love.

Having a strong faith means different things to different people. However, that's where the differences end and the bottom line is the same for each and every one of us – a flicker of hope, deep inside each of us. Our connection to that tiny flame that is untouched by our life's circumstances determines everything. Trust and strength is built when we are aware of our connection to our higher selves. Only from the strength of this connection can we create positive outcomes in our lives. Surrendering to what fate has to offer us is the magic of spirituality. When something happens to us that throws us into imbalance, it is not fate's responsibility to change. It is our responsibility to do whatever it takes to align ourselves with fate's wishes and bend like willows in a storm.

Put your faith in God's hands and he will cradle you and carry you through your life's greatest disappointments and highest glories as if they were made of the same fabric.

6.
Be passionate about everything you do.

Passion in life is like a muscle. The more you use it, the stronger it gets and the better it serves you. To have passion for the big things in life, you must practice passion for the little things. As children, our zest for life is insatiable. Children find excitement and inspiration in their own imaginations that trickle in their games and conversations. "I am going to the moon in the rocket I built." Or "Did you see me jump? I jumped from here to the end of our street."

As teenagers and young adults, some of that passion begins to fade. For some of us, it almost disappears altogether. Some of the lucky ones out there find passion in their profession, in a business, in being a parent, in a hobby or in a cause. As adults, we must find the passion that is buried deep within us to have a balanced life.

Some of the most successful people in the world have always had passion. It never dwindled in them as they grew. I am one of those people. Passion grows inside me in abundance. Whatever I set my mind to, I achieve it. It does not matter if it's a small daily task or getting a building permit after a city's told me it's not possible year after year. Passion is learned in the small details; the insignificant daily tasks that don't really matter. It's like the gymnast preparing for the Olympics – all of those floor exercises that those men and women do for years and years for one shining moment in front of a panel of judges and the whole world to watch.

Just like in life, preparing yourself to make milestone decisions with fierce passion, you must learn to do a lot of practice runs in the daily decisions. That's how you grow your passion muscle. If not, the big decisions somehow mirror the little ones. The way we handle the little decisions it seems we handle the big ones exactly the same way.

The business owner or the executive of a major company was not always in the position he is in today. He worked his way to the top. His work ethic drove his passion with an intended goal in mind-to succeed. He worked at a steady pace until he reached his final destination.

I've had the same passion in every area of my life. I've always wanted to move forward at a nice even pace. When I was young, I created my life with passion out of instinct. For example, "I want to go to America. I don't know what I'm going to do when I get there, but I will figure it out." Now that I'm older and my building era is over, maintaining my present condition takes just as much passion as it took to build it.

Some people believe that if only they can get that great job, the right spouse, the nice home, they will be so much happier and they will work hard then. No, the common consensus is to put your passion in everything you do now. Not years from now, but now. Our lives only improve when we become present and give today the best of ourselves.

When we find our passion and infuse it in our daily lives, things begin to flow. Find your passion.

7.

Common sense leads to innovative fresh ideas and new approaches to the same old stuff.

Common sense is a gut instinct. Gut instinct is a way that your higher spirit guides you through life's choices. Our world is based on universal truths. These truths are based in logic and choosing to be normal in the face of controversy and rebellion. These universal truths stand strong no matter where you live or where you come from. Character traits like seeing the normal way to run a business, support a friend, apologize first, learn to keep your mouth shut even though you're scared or angry, parent a child, deal with a heartache.

I always ask myself at the beginning of a project, "What is the final goal? What do I want the outcome to be?" I work backwards from my answer, always keeping the end in mind.

This working backwards from the end approach allows me to never lose sight of my goal. No matter what the necessary steps entail to finish the task at hand. I don't get weighed down by details. I say to myself, "Even though it seems impossible because of this I know the big picture is what I want and need to accomplish next in my life." Therefore, I stress less than another person in the same circumstance would.

Common sense also means that your communication lines with your inner voice are so clear that ideas flow out of you like a river. Whenever fate presents a situation to me positive or negative, I take a minute not only to think about it, but get in tuned with how I feel about it. It really doesn't matter if your current condition is good or bad.

Ask yourself, "How do I feel about it?" For example, when you were expecting an answer of "yes," and the answer you get is a definite "no" before you let your mind judge the outcome, quickly ask yourself, "How do you feel about the outcome?"

Let yourself feel for a few brief moments. The answer will come from deep within yourself. All of the times I was told "no" and all of the times I was told "yes," something deep within me guided me on what I was going to do next.

Common sense is a skill. The more you practice it, the more you can trust it. There's been many times when something good happened in the present moment. However, when I ask myself the magic question, "How do I feel about it?" sometimes my gut instinct told me not to trust it even though everything surrounding this current event seemed fine.

Listen to your heart. If your life has been a series of bad choices, you may be out of balance with common sense. Getting in tune with this extra ordinary inner compass will lead you in a new direction.

Again, remember, no matter what the choice you have to make present and future ask yourself the magic question which will ring the doorbell to the room inside your heart labeled common sense. Even though sometimes the outlook seems fine or other times it seems gloomy, ask yourself, "How do I feel about _____?" Wait patiently for a response. It always comes with a good answer.

8.

There are a few special moments in life that define who you are, but it's the small moments you cherish the most.

Life is a journey not a destination. The only way to beat death is not to live forever, but to live the present moment well and enjoy every morsel of life. It's easy to persevere when you have everything you wished for. It's hard to achieve your passions when life throws hardships at you and you move one step forward and two steps back.

However, if it was always easy we would all be the same. As human beings, we are all different, learning our life lessons at different levels. Have you ever tried to explain to someone your view on something and they simply don't get it? Even though to you it's as plain as the nose on your face? The reason they don't understand what you are trying to convey is because they have not mastered the lesson and you have.

Some people are basically happy no matter what happens in their daily events while other people cannot get happy no matter how abundant their lives have become. Happiness is a choice, a way of being, a state of mind, a habit. When you're thinking positive thoughts, your brain connects the neurons to make more happy thoughts. When your inner dialogue is negative, your brain connects the neurons to create more negative patterns of thinking. It takes weeks and months to retrain your brain away from the long strands of negative thinking. The best part is that your brain attaches itself just as easily to positive thoughts as it does to negative ones. It does not discriminate against either flavor.

Knowing to live in the moment and enjoying the small miracles that the universe performs in our lives a zillion times a day is a skill in brain training. Noticing nature as you're out for a walk, taking the time to have a positive conversation with a loved one, enjoying hard earned peace in our country, tasting good food, working hard to provide for your family, learning to live within your means, doing charity work for those less fortunate than you, sharing a kind word with a stranger, keeping the peace instead of fighting to win the argument, these are all examples of ways to revel in the moment and create peace in your daily life.

When you live a purposeful life on a regular basis, the road map you've created leads you to have great spiritual success. Therefore, the big moments in your life like choosing a career, getting married, having children, handling crisis and disappointment is not so stressful and overwhelming. When the little stuff is managed positively, the big stuff follows its lead and doesn't stumble and trip you.

In conclusion, when you make good small choices it is totally natural to be prepared to make big monumental good choices as well.

9.
The rules don't apply to me... rules are made to be rewritten.

The concept of 'the rules don't apply to me' is an age old personality trait in people who have defied the odds and the standards in their fields and have gone way beyond the call of duty to accomplish what they wanted in spite of what a normal person could do.

This concept has two sides to it. The first is a positive side, where a person still conducts themselves in an appropriate manner aligned with the universal truths of honor, duty, honesty and general well being. This person is not willing to compromise their own integrity to get their goals fulfilled. They are willing to work harder than expected, do the job that nobody else is willing to do, beg and plead, do it over, apologize first, keep the peace instead of winning the argument, and so on. This positive side of the fine line of 'the rules don't apply to me" is where I reside.

There is also a negative side. When a person is willing to lie, cheat, steal, betray trust, break promises, leave tasks unfinished and so on, they are working on the negative and dark side of this way of doing things. This is a train wreck leading to nowhere and should not be practiced by anyone who wants to be successful. The universal rules of life are never to be broken. You may always be sure that the way you handle your affairs, personal and professional, should be done with the positive points instead of the negative ones of 'the rules don't apply to me' concept.

So go ahead. Work harder than everyone else. Ask and bargain for a lower price or interest rate. Ask your management team to be innovative and give you their best. Shop around for the best price. Get your hands dirty to finish the job. Do the business proposal a sixth, tenth or twenty-seventh time until it is exactly the way you want it. However, don't ever steal the money or misuse funds, lie and take someone else's credit for their hard work, misrepresent someone to get what was rightfully theirs, don't make a promise you have no intention to keep, start a task and not finish it because something better, newer or more exciting comes along.

Inside every one of us, there is a moral compass. Some of us follow this compass all of our lives and it leads us in good places. However, there are people who forget that there are universal truths and they break this invisible code of ethics. Therefore, their inner moral compass breaks. They forget what the difference is between a good and a bad choice. They repeat their mistakes and end up in the same spot all over again.

Readjusting your compass becomes the first step to pulling yourself out of the bad habits you've formed and get yourself on the way to a better life through these choices. Start small and work upwards to the big ones in your character. It's never too late.

10.
Make a difference in people's lives by helping others and giving back to the community.

I've spent my life in automatic. Build, build, build. Achieve. Get to here. Get to there. Make new plans. Meet new goals. Reach those goals. Make new ones. Along the way, I've shared my story with so many people in an attempt to inspire them to want to achieve whatever they written on their own to do list. I've opened my home to many families who wanted to find their way in the United States.

I knew that coming to America would give me the opportunity to soar. Paying this country its due regard means that I have a responsibility to share my story in the hopes to inspire others. The saying 'paying it forward' comes to mind.

When I finally reached success in my life, I wanted to scream it from the rooftops. I wanted to tell everyone that when you work hard and you do your best, success is yours no matter how many times you've failed, success is yours.

As I've gotten older, I want to share my story with the world because it will make a difference in many people's lives. I feel that my story of inspiration is like all the others, but it is hard earned and heartfelt. Someone may find a common ground with me because I am every human being. I am a mother, daughter, wife, sister, and friend. The difference is that I have made it on my own, following my own rules and passions. And doing things Stella's Way.

THE END